HOW THEATRE EDUCATES
Convergences and Counterpoints with Artists, Scholars, and Advocates

Edited by Kathleen Gallagher and David Booth

Canada boasts a remarkable number of talented theatre artists, scholars, and educators. *How Theatre Educates* brings together essays and other contributions from members of these diverse communities to advocate for a broader and more inclusive understanding of theatre as an educative force.

Organized to reflect the variety of contexts in which professionals are making, researching, and teaching drama, this anthology presents a wide range of articles, essays, reminiscences, songs, poems, plays, and interviews to elucidate the relationship between theatre practice and pedagogy, and to highlight the overriding theme: namely, that keeping 'education' – with its curriculum components of dramatic literature and theatre studies in formal school settings – separate from 'theatre' outside of the classroom greatly diminishes both enterprises.

In this volume, award-winning playwrights, directors, actors, and scholars reflect on the many ways in which those working in theatre studios, school classrooms, and on stages throughout the country are engaged in teaching and learning processes that are particular to the arts and especially genres of theatre. Situating theatre practitioners as actors in a larger socio-cultural enterprise, *How Theatre Educates* is a fascinating and lively inquiry into pedagogy and practice that will be relevant to teachers and students of drama, educators, artists working in theatre, and the theatre-going public.

KATHLEEN GALLAGHER is an assistant professor in the Department of Curriculum, Teaching and Learning at the Ontario Institute for Studies in Education, University of Toronto.

DAVID BOOTH is professor emeritus in the Department of Curriculum, Teaching and Learning at the Ontario Institute for Studies in Education, University of Toronto.

EDITED BY KATHLEEN GALLAGHER
AND DAVID BOOTH

How Theatre Educates

*Convergences and Counterpoints with
Artists, Scholars, and Advocates*

UNIVERSITY OF TORONTO PRESS
Toronto Buffalo London

© University of Toronto Press Incorporated 2003
Toronto Buffalo London
Printed in Canada

ISBN 0-8020-8750-7 (cloth)
ISBN 0-8020-8556-3 (paper)

Printed on acid-free paper

National Library of Canada Cataloguing in Publication

How theatre educates : convergences and counterpoints with
    artists, scholars and advocates / edited by Kathleen Gallagher
    and David Booth.

    Includes bibliographical references
    ISBN 0-8020-8750-7 (bound).   ISBN 0-8020-8556-3 (pbk.)

    1. Theatre and society – Canada.   2. Drama in education – Canada.
    I. Gallagher, Kathleen, 1965–   II. Booth, David

    PS8039.D7H69 2003   792'.01'3   C2003-900020-6
    PR9182.2H69 2003

The royalties from the sale of this book will go to World Literacy of
Canada, a non-profit organization that has been promoting literacy in
Canada and around the world since 1955.

University of Toronto Press acknowledges the financial assistance to
its publishing program of the Canada Council for the Arts and the
Ontario Arts Council.

University of Toronto Press acknowledges the financial support for
its publishing activities of the Government of Canada through the
Book Publishing Industry Development Program (BPIDP).

For our students – past, present, future

Contents

Preface

As editors of this collection, we imagined a book where professional theatre artists would be found alongside educators and critics and students of drama, all of them concerned with theatre's power to teach in all of the different contexts in which we find this complex art form. With this book, we are arguing for a broader and more inclusive understanding and definition of theatre as an educative force, because we view theatre as a way of learning that continues throughout one's life. Keeping 'education,' with its curriculum components of dramatic literature and theatre studies in formal school settings, separate from 'theatre' occurring outside the frame of traditional contexts for learning diminishes both enterprises.

The carefully chosen eclecticism of this book – the essays, plays, reminiscences, conversations, observations, addresses, songs, and poetry – offers a cohesion of a different sort. Cohesion, conventionally understood, is not necessarily a value for such a collection as ours, which aims to play pieces against one another and create some unruly marriages between the fields of theatre and education. Such counterpoint suggests the liveliness and diversity, the real activity in the field of theatre/drama education in Canada at this historical juncture. The convergences between ideas and authors do emerge because of the different contexts and perspectives explored and not because of a prescriptive thematic mandate. We hoped that the varied chapters would begin to point to some of the unexpected ways that theatre educates and for that reason we did not constrain each contributor to remain closely tied thematically to fixed ideas of how theatre might educate. We have organized the chapters into smaller sub-groupings to feature the positive and critical differences and to create a dialogue between the richly different

fields of theatre and education. Since we view education and theatre as coexisting, life-long experiences, the selections in this book should be relevant to teachers and students of drama, educators in universities and colleges, those artists working in theatre, and the theatre-going community in general.

One reviewer wondered how to categorize this book, where to place it on one's shelf. It is its very interdisciplinarity that makes the collection so unique. To set up a dialectical relationship between theatre and education, to pull readers in several directions at once, is our hope for this book. In Canada, we have an astonishing number of brilliant theatre artists, many accomplished scholars writing and teaching about theatre, and a creative community of drama/theatre practitioners engaging young people's imaginations and animating their experiences of schooling. We are thrilled to have brought together such an impressive group in this collection, a group whose scholarship and artistry bring splendid scope and breadth to this project of *How Theatre Educates*.

Kathleen Gallagher and David Booth

I. INTRODUCTION

Emergent Conceptions in Theatre Pedagogy and Production

KATHLEEN GALLAGHER

In 1888 Johan August Strindberg wrote the play *Miss Julie*. In its preface he bemoaned the death of theatre, of playwriting, and of theatre's capacity to educate. Strindberg asserted:

> The theatre has always been a primary school for the young, the semi-educated, and women, all of whom retain the humble faculty of being able to deceive themselves and let themselves be deceived – in other words, to accept the illusion, and react to the suggestion, of the author. Nowadays the primitive process of intuition is giving way to reflection, investigation and analysis, and I feel that the theatre, like religion, is on the way to being discarded as a dying form, which we lack the necessary tools to enjoy. This hypothesis is evidenced by the theatrical crisis now dominating the whole of Europe; and, not least, by the fact that in those cultural strongholds which have nurtured the greatest thinkers of our age, namely England and Germany, the art of writing plays is, like most of the other fine arts, dead. (Trans. Meyers, 1964: 91)

I am grateful to the reflection, investigation, and analysis that Strindberg so despised because they attend to a different age, a more inclusive age and one in which the arts of the theatre have ruptured the scene, realizing their full potential to educate not only the middle classes, but all those who leave themselves open and have access to the story. The so-called 'primitive process of intuition' in its many new guises endures. I trust this book will disprove Strindberg's prophecy.

Insofar as I am able to introduce the chapters in this volume, I will, but in fact they need little introduction. Collected here is an exceptional group of theatre artists, educators, scholars, activists, and advocates whose contributions to the Canadian theatre scene and to education over the last many years is astonishing. Bringing just such a group together in one volume is long overdue.

Since this anthology is concerned with theatre and education, however, it is fitting to tell its story, each chapter made of its own small story, their sum amounting to a larger narrative. As an academic and a practitioner, it would be impossible for me to exclude the world of praxis when theorizing about work in theatre or education. It would be equally unworkable to ignore the larger theoretical implications of a tome such as this, so admirably grounded in the creative world of theatre practice, as well as in political and educational action. As far as I have been able to understand it, these disparate worlds of scholarship and praxis, presumed often to be incommensurable, enjoy an uncommon reciprocity in the 'field' of theatre and education, if such a domain can be so easily contained. What's more, it is difficult, I think, to tell any story of education without considerable appreciation of the stories of relationship contained therein. But to tell a story of theatre and education surely requires the essential details of character, setting, time, and action.

Spring 2001, the Canadian Congress of the Social Sciences and Humanities, Quebec City. I was scheduled to give a paper for the Canadian Association for Women's Studies and inadvertently found myself at an address given by Guillermo Verdecchia to the Association of Canadian Theatre: 'Seven Things about and 4 Readings from Cahoots Theatre Projects.' A title I couldn't resist. *Enter Guillermo.* This was not the first time I had seen Guillermo on stage. In 1993, when I was teaching drama in a girls' high school in Toronto, I had taken a crowd of drama students to his solo show *Fronteras Americanas* at Tarragon Theatre. I taught in an ethnically and racially diverse downtown school with many first-generation Canadian – and refugee – students. I didn't know Guillermo's work at the time, but thought the 'material,' the 'subjects addressed,' might speak to many of the students with whom I worked. I was, everyday I taught, acutely aware of the vastly different worlds in which my students and I lived. Guided by the imperative to seek out 'relevant curriculum' I often turned, instinctively, to the theatre – and good theatre, which we are spoiled for in Toronto – to connect with my students and challenge them to connect with each other through imagination and story. Guillermo shared a story of immigration, of language, of provocation and humour, which was not easily forgotten by my students. I was not surprised, some years later, to encounter again Guillermo's life projects based in equity and diversity, and giving voice to a theatre and education project that uses art to make visible the often excluded stories in our 'Canadian mosaic.' The art, the political action, the adversity, and the enormous possibility for education evidenced in Cahoots' projects will clearly bring our progressing understandings of 'cultural diversity' and artworks, as contested and emergent phenomena, to an important new level.

Flashback to graduate school, 1993. I am studying arts education at the Ontario Institute for Studies in Education and respond to a call for 'interested community members' who are concerned with the struggles for greater recognition and resources for the arts within the larger education curricula in Ontario. I attend the meeting. At the head of the table is a woman whose name I have known for many years, but whom I had not yet had the pleasure of meeting. The then artistic director of Toronto's celebrated Young People's Theatre was a key player in this movement to reclaim the role the arts would play in future education projects in Ontario. I was impressed by the political engagement of those present, and especially by the commitment to education evident in the thinking of a major Toronto theatre. Many years later, when I found myself again at Tarragon Theatre, taking in Maja Ardal's first play *Midnight Sun*, I was, a second time, struck by the wide embrace of her artistic vision. In her controversial chapter here, subtitled 'Two Solitudes,' we certainly get the sense of Maja's continued questioning about the place of theatre in the lives of adults and younger people, the wider political and pedagogical aims of education through theatre, and the broader questions of artistic integrity in creating theatre for any audience.

Return to high school classroom. Teacher stands before a large group of eager, self-conscious, angry, grinning, charming, rambunctious, quiet, splendid girls. In my first year of teaching, I am making a case to the school's administration and to the parents about why all drama students in the school must see eight plays a year, about how the students will fundraise in order to make this possible for everyone, about how the integrity of my drama program depended on it. The connections between the theatre world and high school drama were plain to me. The importance of seeing professionals work their craft was obvious. But anyone who understands school culture will know how difficult it is to persuade others – teachers who will have to 'cover' for you while you're away and whose classes will have to cope with absent students; principals who take a risk every time they allow students to leave school property; parents who cannot afford field trips or who believe that anything outside the classroom walls is a distraction from the real purpose of education; students who think plays are boring – of the incredible learning opportunities the theatre may provide. I made a persuasive case and some weeks later I was taking ninety drama students to Maria Irene Fornes's play *Abingdon Square* at Tarragon Theatre. It was a very interesting play that aroused lively discussions back at the school. A teenage girl with a man in his fifties? This is where I first saw Ann-Marie MacDonald on stage. Some months later, I called the Playwrights Union of Canada and asked whether they would forward a message to Ann-Marie, author of the award-winning *Goodnight Desdemona (Good Morning Juliet)* which my senior students had just finished studying. Would she like to come into a class of curious, noisy, intelligent, 'dramatic,' enthusiastic girls? She would and she did. Her work with my students has remained with me for over a decade now. She arrived with her chest of poetic sources, her Muse, and the girls created their own plays. We sat – until well after the school day had ended – in that musty basement drama room, riveted by each others' tales. And so began a long and fruitful relationship with an actor/writer/collaborator of remarkable talent who continues to reach out to young people and remain connected to the broader projects of education and of feminist politics through the theatre. The conversation you will read reflects the lively mind, the wit, the creativity, the profound generosity of Ann-Marie MacDonald.

Flashback to undergraduate Modern English at Victoria College, University of Toronto. Professor Knight, with his inexplicable medallions fastened around his neck, T.S. Eliot's Four Quartets *under his arm. Lori McDougall on my left.* We survived Gertrude Stein, Wole Soyinka, Alan Aykborne, and others through our on-going fascination with this lively professor who was so moved by literature. We survived because of our sophomoric notes to each other, with clever (or so we thought) commentary on Yeats's widening gyres and other far too difficult concepts. We giggled under our breath at some little nothing, our tear-streaked faces containing laughter. Years later, our mutual interest in (post)modern theatre and anti-racist education brought us together again. Lori's work with World Literacy of Canada and her development work in India has recently turned more directly to theatre education projects. 'As the World Turns' gives us extraordinary insight into theatre and television in the field of international development and leprosy education, the possible synergies between these two media, and the challenges facing popular theatre here and abroad.

Set: Boxing ring. Energetic women throwing jabs, uppercuts, hooks. Heavy bags and speed bags line the walls. This was not the first time I'd met Diane Flacks, but I was happy to discover that she shared my interest in boxing. In fact, I had seen Diane on stage many times in Toronto, performing in her own plays, in collaborative works, directing feminist theatre productions with Nightwood Theatre, appearing on the Comedy Network and the CBC. This is a woman who travels in many circles and creates at an awe-inspiring pace. And there she was in my boxing class. Our mutual support of feminist theatre would bring us together again, and it is wonderful to have Diane's contribution in this book. She is a tremendously inventive actor/playwright/director/screenwriter who works steadily in both live theatre and television, and easily considers the work she does as 'educational' for both herself and her audiences. Her chapter, 'Education through Empathy: Using Laughter as a Way In,' gives commanding insight into these worlds.

Karaoke night at Sudbury's gay bar. A warm July night, 2001. A vibrant crowd. Loud music. Much laughter. This is where I met Tomson Highway. Well, I'd once stood behind him in a line-up at a photo shop, but this was the first time I'd spoken to him. He was there to perform some of his music from *Rose* and a new musical for young audiences, *The Adventures of Mary Jane Mosquito.* I didn't know he was such an accomplished composer and pianist. Nor did I know of his great affection for Sudbury and for the North (he's originally from northern Manitoba). I did know that I had read his *Rez Sisters* years earlier and thought it was brilliant. Two weeks later I made my way to College Boreal in Sudbury for the opening night of Miss Mary Jane, a cabaret of music, trial, and triumph. The illustrious Patricia Cano, playing Mary Jane herself, enchanted audiences with this story of marginality, of exclusion, of personal power and voice. Tomson's writing gives us a small taste of his poetry and his enormous humanity. The song included here, 'Patty Cake' begins with the familiar melody, and as it picks up tempo we hear of the young Mosquito's terrifying first encounter with school, the insensitivities of a teacher, and the rejection she experiences. As she raps out this story, Patty's mellifluous voice and troubling staccatos indelibly mark my memory of Mary Jane's young life.

Daily Express on Bloor Street. Early morning, 1999. In my first year in my new faculty position at the Ontario Institute for Studies in Education of the University of Toronto, my colleague and friend Howard Russell suggested he knew someone I should meet. You're like-minded. You should meet, he said. So he arranged a breakfast meeting with Walter Pitman. A breakfast meeting was Walter's suggestion because he had several other appointments lined up that day. Of course I knew Walter's name, had read his important book *Learning the Arts in an Age of Uncertainty*, knew he'd been an academic director at OISE and Ryerson and certainly understood that he was a tireless advocate of the arts. Although I have known Walter only a short time, we have immediately connected on many issues and found ourselves increasingly in the same worlds. Since that breakfast, Walter and I have had some very interesting conversations and exchanged a few emails. His commitment to the arts and to education in Canada leaves me breathless. His sense of the country's history, his political and administrative work, his support of the arts and of schools, his magnanimity continue to inspire. And here, in a very personal chapter, 'Drama through the Eyes of Faith,' we have another of his adult education projects, which draws on the world of theatre to bring ideas and faith alive for a group of passionate theatre-goers.

A palpable sense of anxiety in the air. A long, intimidating boardroom table. Friendly chatter among faculty. Nervous pacing outside the room. Enter Janice Hladki. How fortuitous it was that my colleague Kari Dehli invited me to sit on Janice Hladki's doctoral defence committee in my first year on faculty at OISE/UT. Janice's dissertation research had looked at three feminist theatre artists negotiating across 'difference' through their cultural productions and personal relations. I was looking forward to the defence because I had enjoyed reading the dissertation, which explored the artistry of Kate Lushington, Monique Mojica, and Djanet Sears, all of whose work I admired. I found in Janice a person who was working diligently at respecting both her own theatre practice and her scholarly pursuits in theatre research. She was marrying two worlds in a way that I found engaging and provocative, working within a postmodern academic tradition that examined performances of gender, race, language, culture, and ethnicity in the everyday lives and theatre practices of three artists. Her chapter here, 'Negotiating Drama Practices,' gives us a sense of the tremendous complexity involved in realizing theatre research in a uniquely Canadian, contemporary context.

A puff of smoke. Blackout. Glistening brown, mischievous eyes. Linda Griffiths performing *Alien Creature: A Visitation from Gwendolyn MacEwen* left its mark. It wasn't the first time I'd seen Linda on stage, but it was, perhaps, the most memorable. Of *Maggie & Pierre* fame, she was again creating theatre around another significant Canadian figure. I am struck by

Linda's sense of place, her storytelling, her long and rich relationship with Theatre Passe Muraille, and her projects that continue to ask what 'Canadian' is. A late spring conversation with her over tea at a cluttered kitchen table seemed right. She worried that she wouldn't have enough to say; I turned the tape recorder off two hours (and many cups of tea) later. She was intrigued by my invitation to contribute to the book because positioning herself in the world of education was new. I could easily see the strong connections to education in her work and her ways of working: the improvising and leaving oneself open to stories, the risks and the stories of relationship, and her stunning sense of her own learning.

Flashback to graduate school. University of Victoria Conference. International Drama in Education Research Institute, 1997. I am accompanying my dissertation supervisor David Booth and responding to a master class he gives at the institute. It is on this lovely western campus that I meet Cornelia Hoogland. Later we would talk about our experiences in canoes, with nature. We shared our stories of deep appreciation of this Canada of many regions. She would share with me her book of poetry *Marrying the Animals*. It would not be the last time I would read Cornelia's poetry. Her chapter, here – 'The Land inside Coyote' – brings drama, children, and the natural world together as she carefully carves out the languages that strongly inform her scholarly and artistic work.

The present. A log cabin on the Spanish River, northern Ontario. A dry, hot summer day. Alex enters. Alex is a former student from my high school days, one of those remarkable young women who thought theatre was important enough to study in university. Before meeting me on the Spanish River this day, she had just spent three weeks in Calgary doing One Yellow Rabbit's theatre workshop. She came back brimming with excitement and told me about the speech John Murrell had presented to them – something he had given a month earlier at the National Arts Centre in Ottawa to a group of artists and educators concerned with arts education in Canada. Yes, Alex said, the John Murrell whose play *Waiting for the Parade* you had us read in high school. – Oh *that* John Murrell. Read the speech, she says. You'll see what I'm going on about. That speech, which so moved her, we have published here. Murrell's eloquent chapter speaks to a most natural and seamless connection between theatre and education, to the risks of making such a connection, and to the greater risks in not doing so.

A large computer screen projected on the scrim. Emails. Endless emails. Finally, lattes and freshly squeezed orange juice at Mercurio. 12:30 pm. Of course I'd seen everything she had written and directed. Of course, I'd used *Lion in the Streets* with my students. Of course I'd taken a monologue-writing workshop with her. And I now teach her former theatre students from Guelph University when they decide to become teachers of drama. Judith Thompson. An eminent voice in the theatre world, a practitioner and an educator. I knew her contribution would be important because she lives, every day, the alchemy about which this book is concerned. Were they separate enterprises for her? Did she teach through theatre and perform in her teaching? We had a lively dialogue that day about the thrills and fears of teaching, about the performances particular to classrooms. Her chapter, '"I Will Tear You to Pieces": The Classroom as Theatre,' shares her own, very personal story of the classroom as a stage.

Flashback to undergraduate years. Modern French theatre at New College, University of Toronto, 1986. Professor enters. I glance quickly at my Beckett text before the lecture begins. I probably owe my great affection for French theatre to him. Here was someone who acted in the Shaw and Stratford festival companies, who performed on stages in Canada in both official languages, who had worked with major Canadian film directors. But what was most remarkable to me was his brilliant pedagogy. He was an inspired teacher in addition to (because of?) his extraordinary experience in the theatre. For John Gilbert, the world of teaching and the world of theatre were inseparable creative projects. They required the same capacity to communicate clearly and 'let the text speak for itself.' I learned much about theatre from John, but I learned more about good teaching. Education, like theatre, is not meant to induce agreement, but to shake foundations. His chapter, 'Inside Out,' reflects his strong commitment to a politics of action, as well as his view of theatre and its responsibility to disturb, to disrupt, to displease, and to inspire. These years later, he remains an essential voice in my life.

As someone who continues to be influenced by the power of theatre in its many voices and contexts, I often ask myself what the projects of theatre will be in the coming years, decades, centuries in this diverse Canada. How will theatre connect with global education and citizenship in the twenty-first century? What choices will be made? Britzman asserts that culture is always a contentious space and that one of the places its contentions play out is in the arts. She asks: 'What do the arts want and what do we want from the arts?' (2001, 19). I think about the profound impact that school drama programs might have in young people's lives. I ponder the many possibilities of theatre for education, a subject explored carefully and artfully by the authors of this volume. And I am left with a simple reflection: pedagogically, theatre has much to offer. It is a question of both form and content. And it is a question of 'audience.'

Looking at urban classrooms, Fine, Weis, and Powell argue that democratic participation does not evolve spontaneously within multiracial groups of youth:

> If schools are to produce engaged, critical citizens who are willing to imagine and build multiracial and multiethnic communities, then we presume schools must take as their task the fostering of group life that ensures equal status, but within a context that takes community-building as its task. The process of sustaining a community must include a critical interrogation of difference as the rich substance of community life and an invitation for engagement that is relentlessly democratic, diverse, participatory, and always attentive to equity and parity. (1997, 252)

I would like to take this idea of 'relentlessly democratic' spaces into the theatre studio, where community-building is no stranger. While it is widely (and rightly) recognized that the construct of 'empathy' is central in drama education, how one pedagogically structures for empathy and what kind of empathy one elicits is another question entirely. Fisher, in exploring the ethic of 'care' in the classroom, decides that 'co-exploring' does not rule out disagreement and that caring can 'shore up our patience for dealing with the external and internal tensions that develop as we try to make sense of another's viewpoint in its relation to our own' (2001, 121). The trouble with a good deal of educational theatre is that we have often found ourselves consuming 'good stories' or the 'other's story' with an innocent reading that fails to reveal 'self' and 'other' as positioned and residing within social systems that shape human agency and even one's capacity to know/narrate one's own story. Boler (1997) strongly argues that passive empathy promoted as a bridge between differences is not a sufficient educational practice. She cites Aristotle's discussion of pity – a practice more about the projection of self than the understanding of another – in her persuasive analysis of the 'risks of empathy.' The distinctive educative force of theatre, however – its dialectics – invites us to take up points of intersection *and* confrontation, so that our dramatic explorations do not simply calcify cultural and ethnic boundaries and limit our own and our students' abilities to affiliate with multiple cultural identities, productively manoeuvre across borders, and develop capacities for functioning in diverse situations.

Maxine Greene speaks of the miseducation in much that is done in schools, thanks to the fixities and corruptions of our consumer-based and technicized culture. The hierarchical and bureaucratic nature of schools makes it extraordinarily difficult for openings to be explored and critical thinking to take place. But, she insists, all of us know that interstices can be found in the structures; communities can be created; desires can be released (1995, 56). And teaching, like acting, I would say, is ultimately about communicating, about the great desire to communicate.

What is clear is that there is no correct pedagogical model on offer for drama education. But education through drama does indeed have a particular role to play in the richly diverse Canadian classrooms where it is exploited. In these classrooms/studios, we might begin to observe differences differently, asking each time what we make of the story, where we sit in the audience, and how we might open up for discussion alternative aesthetic representations of 'self' and 'other.' It might be said, as well, that this kind of pedagogical imperative shares a great deal with the rather ephemeral event of live theatre itself. As Ellsworth observes, pedagogy is not a command performance with repeatable features; its only life is in relation to its context and moment:

> Perhaps one possibility of performing a pedagogical relationship lies in the active acceptance of the inevitability of a suspended performance, a performance that leaves no visible trace of its happening, a performance that paradoxically manipulates teacher/students into taking on responsibility for producing partial texts that reconfigure what counts as the world, and by doing so, what counts as valued and valuable bodies and lives in that world. (1997, 164)

What gets changed, Ellsworth argues, is our relationship to the meanings that circulate and vie for authority around us. Theatre for education, then, might demand that the borders on learning keep moving out, so that schools and theatres can be sites for both community-building and social change. Brecht's edict of 'theatre for pleasure or theatre for instruction' (1957, trans. Willett), a deeply rooted polarity in modernist conceptions of theatre practice, may need to be reconsidered in light of new modes of learning in/through theatre that both engage and disrupt creative impulses.

In theatre pedagogy, we not only endow experience with meaning, but we are – as players – invited to make manifest our own subjectivities in the world evoked through character and play, a world laden with metaphor and nuance, a world where relationship to other and self-spectatorship are in dynamic and unrelenting interaction. In this way, *How Theatre Educates* becomes a rallying call for the multiplicity of theatre expressions and their impressive potential to animate communities of people in all corners of education.

Peter Brook once asked some questions of the theatre event that might easily be asked of education today:

> What do we need from the event? What do we bring to the event? What in the theatre process needs to be prepared and what needs to be left free? What is narrative, what is character? Does the theatre event tell something, or does it work through a sort of intoxication? What belongs to physical energy, what belongs to emotion, what belongs to thought? What can be taken from an audience, and what must be given? What responsibilities must be taken for what we leave behind? What change can a performance bring about? What can be transformed? ([1973] 1995, 322)

Quite expressly, this collection brings together professional artists, scholars, educators, activists, and advocates to consider questions about Canadian cultural production and, especially, theatre and its capacities to teach us in ways different from most other things. I have the deepest esteem for all the contributors, who have carved out their lives in theatres and classrooms all around this country. It has been an immensely satisfying adventure to co-edit this collection with my dear friend and colleague David Booth. I am, as always, humbled by his many kindnesses.

Towards an Understanding of Theatre for Education

DAVID BOOTH

I grew up as a radio child and a television teenager, with CBC radio plays, and then American television dramas, filling the house every night. The Goodyear Playhouse, the Philco Playhouse, Playhouse 90, with original scripts, professional actors, famous directors. John Drainie, Bette Davis, the Barrymores, Rod Steiger, James Dean were every-evening entertainers. I was entrapped by the live exchange of ideas wrapped in home-delivered theatre. Those days are gone; theatre changes as culture does.

The first play I acted in was in eighth grade in St Thomas, Ontario. The centennial of this small town had resulted in a pageant that included our school's participation, along with dozens of citizens, all enacting the history of this place in an evening performance on the hill of the largest ravine within the town limits. I was a dancing skeleton with a glow-in-the-dark costume of bones, sewn by the women of the parent-teacher association. We were rehearsed by the school caretaker, who had emigrated from England, theatre-trained, to find no employment but in maintenance, and we children were fortunate indeed. He possessed those skills of the teacher of theatre that we dream of today – originality, compassion, commitment, and a British accent. No doubt many who read this book will harbour fond memories of this type of community theatre experience, where in an enactment ritual we witnessed the barber, the beautician, and the milkman creating the roles of those who came before, and perhaps for a moment or so, we left the present moment of our small-town existence and sensed another place, another time. The pageant was a significant experience for all of us, and the band of torches winding down the ravine continues to light up my memory.

In our wide expanse of country with so few citizens, schoolhouses offered families the only other theatrical experience around – the school play, the school concert, or the school festival. In scenes very similar to those described so acutely in Max Braithwaite's novel *Why Shoot the Teacher*, children, teachers, and parents came together to celebrate words and images that somehow connected through the gauze filter of childhood to the stages of Toronto and London and Moscow. And, of course, the Little Theatre Community, as it used to be called, appeared as a welcome venue in my world, and the circle that surrounded audience and actors sometimes wobbled and wiggled, but nonetheless remained connected.

Today, of course, we who watch or participate throughout this country are grateful for touring groups, repertory theatre, road shows (a little worse for wear), benefit performances, any troupe or group who represents the spirit of theatre in our arenas, cinemas, civic auditoriums, and renovated churches, and our once-in-a-while expeditions to faraway theatre centres.

My first experience with a touring group of actors involved the Crest Theatre Company, who brought *Hamlet* to Niagara Falls in 1957. Our senior high school class bused from Welland, courtesy of Mrs Brooks, a supply teacher who resembled Marilyn Monroe, and who knew what we adolescents required to extend our sense of script. The play was hilarious, one of Shakespeare's finest comedies, we thought. We laughed spontaneously, without malice, full of peer-generated revelry. We laughed at the make-believe world happening on the stage of that creaky auditorium, ignorant of any conventions, of audience/actor relationships, but responding as a town of adolescents to the machinations of men and women with strong voices dying all together, one on top of the other, in the last moments of the play. It was a visceral display – satisfying everyone. We didn't need the bus – we floated home.

As a teacher, the first play I directed was with my grade five elementary class. Fortunately, the memories of my older cousin's dance recitals that I had attended created a sudden mindstorm, and while untrained in theatre knowledge, I knew exactly what to do. For those annual concerts from my childhood included dances choreographed by the town's only dance-school owner, and she knew what pleased. From the tiny tots to the gay adolescents, her students moved across that stage to the recorded sounds of every hit performer of the time – Al Jolson, Judy Garland, Frank Sinatra, the Andrews Sisters – and insinuated into my psyche glimpses of the performance power of 'here and now' thrills that 'there and then' films seldom achieved. And for each year's finale, the instructor, garbed in satin with hair glistering, danced with the oldest of the boy dancers, and with the power of will and the grace of talent lifted him into her performance aura, and we knew magic. We stood and applauded and applauded in that hot and crowded auditorium.

And so, summoning forth those small town memories, I created with the children in my classroom a collage of small town numbers – a minstrel show – bereft of any theatre craft or wisdom, but with all my children in 'black' make-up that I applied myself. Those tambourines banged, those voices shouted, and the parents stared in shock. Thankfully, I have no pictures of that experience, just guilt and shame, but at my next school, life changed.

I was promoted to drama teacher in a junior high school, in charge of theatre arts and responsible for twenty school assemblies and a major annual play. I can't even imagine how I survived, fuelled by ignorance and inspired by what might happen when the house lights went down. By some stroke of theatrical fate, a group of well-off parents in the school took their children to Toronto to see Wednesday matinees of touring musicals. I noticed the student absences, and selfishly longed to accompany them, and so I organized school theatre trips under the aegis of the drama program, and off we went on a chartered bus to the O'Keefe Centre to see Ethel Merman heaved up by Harve Presnell in the last of her revivals of *Annie Get Your Gun*. Those same students came back from summer camp with their leftover scripts from the musicals they had performed, and we recruited them into our school auditorium. I was indeed mentored by my students, some of whom, like Ira and John, began writing scripts, sardonic parodies – the saving grace of adolescent boys – and we never looked back.

My school board sent me to London, England, on a scholarship, and I saw every single play on every single stage. My theatre world began to coalesce. As my knowledge and experience grew, my goals for drama altered. I began teaching drama in the early sixties, and the changes that affected society in those years and the decade that followed – the rise of social unrest, the growing awareness of diverse cultures, the issues of equity and gender – had an impact on education at every level, including the teaching of drama in schools and work in the professional theatre. 'In the avant-garde theatre of the 1960s, the work of experimental practitioners and theorists emphasized notions of presence and immediacy, process and transformation, and these ideas filtered into the work of drama teachers in schools and colleges' (O'Neill 1995, xvii). Teachers in elementary and secondary schools began exploring forms of drama that were inclusive, exploratory, concerned with contemporary themes, with personal development, and with ensemble work rather than focusing all the energy on the two gifted students. We were nervous about the area of performance with students who perhaps had no wish to become actors, and who were content to work with known participants in the classroom, but unwilling to share their work with strangers who stared at them. So we attempted to find strategies that would let youngsters feel the power of connecting with an audience without forcing them into public occasions with expectations that outstripped their needs and abilities. The complexities of balancing form and meaning grew over the years into our present-day dramatic arts, where improvisation, text exploration, movement, theatre craft, and presentation are significant parts of the whole experience of theatre in schools. Teachers began incorporating the conventions and structures of postmodern theatre techniques – 'the fragmentation and distribution of roles among the group, a nonlinear and discontinuous approach to plot, the reworking of classic themes and texts, a blurring of the distinction between actors and audience' (O'Neill 1995, xvii). While teachers new to the teaching of drama may be unaware of the fifty years of change and development, they will no doubt incorporate the hard-fought learning within their curriculum.

The power of the alternative theatre groups during those years has not diminished. George Luscombe, Ken Gass, and Ernie Schwartz twisted my head every way, and theatre possessed a diamond's facets. Canadian actors, playwrights, and directors emerged from the shadows, and gay artists presented audiences with other ways of knowing theatre.

One high school drama teacher told me that we should never take our students to alternative theatres, to off-Broadway-type exploratory productions, but only to the successful mega-productions, where 'they experience nothing but the best.' But we know the poverty of her failed judgment, for in those small and fragile spaces we seek out we also see the skeletons of theatre, the bare bones of those live performances, so close we can touch them and notice the spit and the sweat.

I needed to see in print here the bits and pieces of my theatre life to articulate the hopes I have for this collection of essays by such informed and passionate Canadian artists and educators. Of course theatre educates, but often not in the ways we think, and not always within the traditional confines of grand stages. We need to continually remind ourselves of the complex and different contexts that allow us to enter the 'as if, what if' world.

We build a theatre sense from all of our experiences with this live form as participants and observers – our own inspired dialogues in improvised drama classes, our recognition of the power of script writers, the awe of standing on a lighted stage, the wearing of a heavy mask we have constructed, the exercises with peers when we hold hands in a circle, the after-show chat with an actor, the sensation of the house lights dimming as an actor glides past. I want all of the above and I want it for my child and for the students I teach.

The field of theatre encompasses such variety – children playing in a sand box, students in the school musical, young people who have entered a university drama program, students exploring a script in the classroom, children in a gym watching a touring theatre group, adolescents busing to a performance at Stratford, students watching their teachers in an end-of-year send-up, older students putting a play on for the younger children, youngsters with their parents at the theatre on a Saturday night, teenagers watching street theatre at city hall, university students on a pageant wagon reinterpreting the Mystery plays. We explore make-up, lighting, sets, props, staging, costumes, music, and sound – the aspects of theatre that make it a collaborative art, a unique living collage.

Drama is an ubiquitous force in our present world, an everyday and everywhere occurrence, as evidenced by the dramatic performances we view and listen to on television shows, videos, DVDs, films, computer screens, radio, in school classrooms, and, of course, in live theatre. Drama has become our principal means of expressing and interpreting the world as we explore and communicate ideas and information, social behaviours, values, feelings, and attitudes, with mass audiences greater than anyone had ever contemplated. We are entertained, informed, angered, persuaded, manipulated, or touched, both consciously and subliminally, by the thousands of performances we experience, and sometimes we are changed because of their influence and their impact on our lives. Martin Esslin, in his book *The Field of Drama* (1987), supports this view when he defines the essential aspect of drama as acting, and says that 'drama simulates, enacts or re-enacts events that have, or may be imagined to have, happened in the real or imagined world' (24). In our present, media-filled world, drama surrounds us.

While recognizing the commonalties among the different modes of drama, *How Theatre Educates* explores, in the main, the world of live, staged performances, not as a judgment against other forms, but in order to reflect on the effect and value in contemporary Canadian society of the particular art endeavour we call theatre, both in formal educational settings (usually called schools) or in informal educational experiences (usually in theatres). Theatre involves an audience, even if it is only the actors themselves reflecting on their own and other players' performances, and the dramatic power lies in the social encounters between them. For me, theatre's unique strength lies in the fact that participants accept this event 'as though it were happening at that very moment before their own eyes' (Esslin 1987, 33). Space and time are imagined and real all at once, and each of us takes in a complex system of signs and symbols and attempts to make our own set of meanings. But we are influenced, and we may perceive, differently because we are engaged with others in interpreting the same event, whether audience or cast members; we are connected to those around us, sensing and experiencing their responses. And in the most deeply felt and artistically complex theatre events, we extend and stretch and multiply the scope of our world, perhaps transcending our lives in a concentrated emotional and intellectual experience that may be even more intense than life; the insights and meanings generated by a particular theatre experience may have a pivotal or lasting impact. Unlike film, where the performances are captured as an icon and may be viewed differently as cultural influences occur over time, a single theatre performance can never be replicated, for its effect is determined by such a list of variables that each occasion will hold a unique experience.

The imagined worlds of drama work in schools 'develop an internal coherence and are appreciated for the same insights and purposes that are valued in any piece of theatre ... [P]articipants in both contexts are engaging with a dramatic world, an imagined elsewhere, with its own characters, locations and concerns, developing in accordance with its own inner logic, manifesting tension and complexity' (O'Neill 1995, xi).

When my friend and colleague Kathleen Gallagher presented her idea for a book about theatre's power to educate, I was excited at the thought of seeing in print the puzzle pieces that make up theatre in my country, and recognized that such a book could help me to make sense of the hopes we have for theatre as a way of learning throughout life. Kathleen brings to our faculty of education a deep understanding of both theatre and teaching, and of the relationship between this particular art form and the world of schools. In our working together, she continually turns me toward theatre's significance in young people's lives. Through her perseverance and her commitment to theatre for education, we have developed this collection of articles, memoirs, essays, and speeches by informed artists and educators and critics who have attempted to articulate the educational force of theatre, but not always in the traditional confines of grand stages. Each of the writers helps remind us of the value of the different contexts that allow us to enter the 'as if' and 'what if' world of live drama events.

We need, within our theatre community, voices that will remind us of the variety of drama experiences that can fill our lives. Lynn Slotkin sees over two hundred plays a year in Canada, the United States, and England. For over twenty-five years, theatre has been her passion, and in her chapter 'Confessions of a Theatre Addict,' she talks about her beginnings as a theatre-goer and chronicles her experiences as a passionate advocate for theatre, from writing her own theatre letter for friends in the business to her work on CBC radio, where she comments on the Toronto theatre scene.

In his play 'The Poetics,' Jason Sherman causes us to consider the role of the critic, as he jabs away at the incompetence and triviality of some of those who share with us their views on theatre. And Jim Giles, a teacher-advocate who brings issues of equity into our schools, interviews Sky Gilbert, the controversial alternative-theatre personality, who challenges us to examine the nature of theatre's mandate in our contemporary world.

College and university students select their faculties and courses for the purposes of both preparing for careers in the arts and building a general knowledge and awareness of theatre's power and influence. Belarie Zatzman, in her article 'The Monologue Project: Drama as a Form of Witnessing,' describes a unit of work she carried out with her students at York University that is based on Holocaust education and designed to use theatre forms in order to blend students' personal stories with history, to connect their lives with the historical evidence. She reveals some of the students' memories for us, and her work reminds us of theatre's unique potential for helping participants to find their voices and listen to the resonances that develop among them, inside sacred and safe spaces for sharing.

Domenico Pietropaolo was director of the Drama Centre at the University of Toronto, where students have an opportunity to explore the different aspects of theatre by working inside and outside the art form, blending studio work and academic study, historical and contemporary theatre, acting and directing, researching and performing. Still, he recognizes the need for building partnerships with theatre companies that are operating in the professional milieu, and it is gratifying to see an academic in a university setting call for strengthening the relationship between the professional and the academic worlds in developing the strongest possible models for the growth of theatre students.

Throughout these last few decades, professional theatre for young audiences has exploded into a variety of performances and workshops, both in formal theatre spaces and in school cafeterias and auditoriums. I remember sitting in Susan Rubes's living room with a group of educators and artists brainstorming the possibilities for a professional theatre space devoted to productions for young people accompanied by connected workshops, only to see it realized a few years later as Young People's Theatre. Larry Swartz, the principal of our faculty's additional qualifications courses for teachers, includes theatre performances as an integral component of the curriculum for the teachers who are exploring drama as a learning medium with their students. I have come to recognize over the years that those teachers who are most effective with their theatre arts students support professional theatre experiences; they recognize the symbiotic relationship of the artist and the teacher, of the art form and the learning process. Larry has a heightened historical awareness of the different companies that create productions and workshops for young people, and in his contribution here he advocates finding ways for bringing youngsters and theatre presentations together. Children develop theatre muscles from being there with live performances, over time, and by participating in the theatre-building activities in their school programs. Both types of experiences help form their understanding of how this art form works, and what it can mean in their lives. As in all true art, theatre for young people encompasses the play for the youngsters and the play for the adults, both at once.

Ten years ago at an international theatre and education conference in Toronto, the guest speaker, a professor of theatre studies from Florida, boldly announced that the only goal of theatre for education in North America was to provide knowledgeable audiences for the New York theatres. I knew that she had missed the boat, that it had sailed without her. At that moment, I knew what I believed in, what I would continue to work towards in my school/theatre connections. I want so much more for the young people I meet. I need for students of all ages to be shocked and surprised by ideas that can only be shared in the safety of the theatre frame; I need the sounds of powerful language filling their impoverished word world; I need for them to sense how they and those on stage breathe simultaneously as one; I need to witness the struggle of students of every age participating in drama work, listening to each other as they interact, so that they begin to see that everyone matters if the fiction is to become real; I need to know that my students can read the conventions of theatre as proficiently as they can a Friday night film. I know that theatre can help them to enter their worlds more fully, to see more clearly, and feel and think all at once. I need theatre that will continue to teach them for all their days. Richard Rose, in his address given at Thorneloe College on the occasion of being honoured with a doctorate for his contributions to the theatre world, urges us to remember that theatre's significance lies in 'the personal thought the play provoked – the moment of recognition.' This is what I hope for – theatre experience, whether as audience or participants or both, that feeds the education imperative, the need to make felt-meaning. I need theatre in all its forms and guises and formats to enter my world more fully, to help me see more clearly, to feel and think at once. I want to behold the world somehow differently. I want to be educated by theatre.

II. THEATRE, THE ARTS, PEDAGOGY, AND PERFORMANCE

'I Will Tear You to Pieces': The Classroom as Theatre

JUDITH THOMPSON

When I was eleven years old, I became Helen Keller. As I rehearsed the role for the amateur production, I felt I was, for the first time, vivid; the caul that seemed to always surround me slipped away while I explored this desperate, mythic character. I had been largely an invisible child with no opinions or even thoughts of my own; I lived by sensation. From that time I remember the purple of violets, the yellow of buttercups, and the cherry of Popsicles, suffocating. New England summer afternoons, dirty feet, and dark chocolate cake against deep green grass, these sensations were like hands in soft clay; I had, as a child, the constant and overwhelming sensation of being excluded from the world, of living in somebody's dream; the child who met the outside world was faceless and voiceless, and so I was typecast, in a way, as a girl who was blind, deaf, and dumb. I felt pure, dizzying joy and freedom being on stage, screaming and throwing the forks and knives to the floor; snorting like a pig, writhing and moaning, clutching the sweaty hand of the faculty wife who played Annie, the teacher. Her hand became my whole world during that time, the hand was language, my door to the outside world and my protection from it; the hand that smelled so strongly of sweat and metals; I was not surprised to find out many years later that the actress had died of liver cancer. In some ways, this role was the template for my role as a dramatist, and as a teacher.

My next big theatrical role/moment was *The Grand Mal Seizure*. I was graduating from grade six at Stillman School in Middletown, Connecticut – 'We wish we could stay at Stillman School for E-E-E ver' – and I was wearing my carefully ironed pink linen dress, sitting in assembly with every student in the school from kindergarten through grade six. I suddenly felt a sharp evil pain in my stomach, whispered to a friend that the worms in the film about fishing were going to make me faint, and then fell to the floor convulsing in a tonic-clonic seizure for the whole school to see. In this seizure, there was, again, a horrible kind of freedom; not only was I free to scream, I had to scream to save my life, to breathe; my face turned purple and I became incontinent; my dress was soaked in front of every student in the school. They watched, and of course snickered as I grunted and convulsed and struggled for life.

The seizure had the force of a great volcano erupting, the bubbling, white hot lava trammelling over the fragile, spindly structures that make up a conscious self.

My next role, at the Domino Theatre in Kingston, Ontario, was Betty, in Arthur Miller's *The Crucible*. I remember auditions well – the possibility that there was a way out of day-to-day existence in a Loyalist university town with nine federal prisons within the city limits. Of course I did not know this at the time; all I knew was my new street, which still smelled of sawdust and oil paint. And my school, St Thomas More, was full of tough-talking Catholic kids whose southern Ontario drawl I had learned immediately, as a matter of survival, to deftly imitate. As soon as I stepped into the musty dark theatre and sat and read a script, there was that rush again. The rush that I would live for. I was given the role and my life in the theatre truly began. These were seasoned amateur actors, the best in the city; many of them could have been professional, some of them are now. The production went to the Sears Drama festival, and won awards. It was the most thrilling time in my young life; in fact, it was the first time I knew what thrill was.

As Betty Parris, I was allowed to scream the scream to end all screams. Years of rage, and of feeling invisible came out in that scream. I was told that pregnant women had to leave the theatre. I would lie on the stage bed in the first act, and listen to all that exquisite, musical language and then try to fly – 'Mama, Mama, I want to fly to MAMA' – and scream until I passed out.

Every time I sit down to write, to create a drama, I feel that I am again playing Helen Keller and Betty Parris; I am in the assembly, surrendering to the nuclear power of a seizure. I am deaf, dumb, and blind and I am screaming: free to have tantrums, to groan and grunt and foam at the mouth and bite and be an animal, and to fly. I am screaming to save my life.

I have no sense of decorum or structure. I have no control, no idea of what I am going to write, only faith in my fingers, for the play lies in them, just as Helen met the world through her fingers. Touch is all. Betty Parris is in a trance just as I am, she believes she can fly, she believes she is the devil just as I believe I am in the play I am writing, and I am all the characters. To write, I have to become, basically, a child who is a wild animal.

The rest of the time, I am an ordinary, rather slow-witted but good-humoured woman, the kind of mother who falls asleep in front of CBC documentaries at ten fifteen every night, and does two loads of laundry before waking the kids at eight in the morning.

It's when I enter the sphere of drama that I become Helen and Betty again. And teaching drama, of course, means entering that sphere.

Since my first professional production, of *The Crackwalker*, in 1979 at Theatre Passe Muraille, I had taught here and there: a few night classes, a few workshops, and many readings followed by animated discussions with students, but I had never thought of myself as a Teacher. I was a playwright who, I had naively thought, could just continue to live on small grants and smaller royalties, the occasional job with the CBC, making about twelve thousand dollars a year. And as a childless artist I could have, but as I began to have children, a choice that was a spiritual imperative for me, it became apparent that we would need a reliable source of income.

When I was first offered a tenure-track teaching job at Guelph, I was nonplussed. I somehow did not see clearly what a tremendous coup this was, and how it would save my life as a playwright and as a mother. For this is one of the only institutions that values artistic work enough to actually pay us to do it.

Sadly, I shared the bias against teaching that many of my colleagues in the theatre have, believing teaching to be something one does for finan-cial reasons only. It was, I thought, something of an admission of failure. Many of my colleagues actually said, 'Oh you won't stay there long,' and when I was finding it stressful, advised me to quit. Every day I thought about quitting.

I am so thankful that I didn't.

Not only because working at the university allows me to continue to write for the stage, which I would not be able to do if I were frantically pursuing film and television gigs to support my family, but because every class is the creation of a new drama. And aside from my children, and the occasional blissful walk through a park, or bite of fresh hot bread, that is where I find pure joy.

When I first started to teach, I had stage fright. I was floundering and improvising; I am shy in a profoundly visceral way, and found the scrutiny of the students excruciating. Because of self-esteem problems rooted in childhood, I found it impossible to think of myself as any kind of expert, even though my success and experience in the field of theatre should have persuaded me that I knew something. Politically, I found the idea of The Teacher as Regent to be abhorrent. I had a few vague ideas about thwarting the pedagogical model of expertise and paternalism, but I wasn't sure what I would replace it with. I had hoped the students would just have faith, as the theatre practitioners who worked with me did. I had hoped we would discover together. What I hadn't realized is that many of the students, schooled in our tired, bureaucratic system, wanted me to perform the role of 'teacher'; they wanted a strong hand, an expert who would firmly guide them, give them a little book of rules, so that they wouldn't have to think for themselves. But I refused to play along. I blithely told them that I knew nothing. There were no rules. The only rule was to leap, and to trust what came out. A few of them were excited by this, but most of them were perplexed. I tried to teach them about leaping, and trusting one's deeper, rawer instincts and one's life stories. But it was like one of those wrenching roller-coaster love affairs; one day would be wonderful, the next terrible.

At the end of the first semester, I received a couple of evaluations so filled with hate it shocked me. One said that I was completely unapproachable, while the next in the pile said I was very approachable. And although there were already quite a few who were very positive, it seemed to me that the majority found me 'disorganized.' A couple of students complained to my chair that they were not learning anything. He told them to listen harder, and accept that my teaching style was unique. What they called disorganization, I called flexibility, immediacy, and fluidity. Much of our learning culture is a stale leftover of the British military model, and Canadians traditionally have always preferred the precise, hierarchical rule-centred approach to learning.

I began to hate and fear teaching. I started to arrive a little later every day, and feel huge relief when the class was over. When I was away from the university I tried to forget the existence of the students. A few of them, whom I found threatening because they were resisting my approach and aggressively arguing with all my choices, began to take over my psychic landscape. Their faces would invade my pre-sleep cinema, filling the screen, moving closer, suffocating me. I never slept the night before a teaching day, and therefore found myself so exhausted I would have to fight sleep even while I taught. I wanted to quit, but I was not in a financial position to do so. So I was forced to find a way to make the classroom work.

It was like the moment in my worst seizure, when I was fifteen, when I felt I was at the middle of the earth; I knew that I was about to die, and if I didn't want to die I would have to somehow find a way to breathe, and to scream, to scream myself out of the earth and into the air, and life, and a future. Through sheer will I breathed, deeply, and I screamed so loud that the principal came running out of the school, scolding me for disturbing people.

My transformation into a good teacher began with a deep breath, which enabled me to see clearly what I needed to do. The first step, of course, was what I, as an artist who valued immediacy so highly, had ignored: basic organization – a watch and a day book – clearly symbolic outward signs of commitment to the art of teaching. Next, I convinced myself that teaching and artistic practice are not mutually exclusive, but that one could in fact be a necessity for the other.

Second, I accepted that yes, of course, I was qualified to teach about the theatre; that I had in fact a great deal of experience in the theatre, and a mine of knowledge about the art and craft of theatre that could be of tremendous value to the students. I did not stumble into my success through sheer dumb luck. I actually did know something about my discipline that I could pass on. If that mantra sounds only half-convincing, it is because I am still working on convincing myself of it. Some days I walk in believing it all, and some days, well, I am just not so sure.

Perhaps that uncertainty exists because I do believe that when a play is successful, as a piece of writing, it is because I have allowed the underbelly of the culture I live in to reveal itself through the play. I have shaped the play, using my craft, so that certain hidden truths, about who we are, are illuminated. And 'rules of dramatic writing' are the last thing on my mind when I am creating a new play. This is why I do not teach them rules, but rather sensibility.

The most important epiphany for me may sound like something out of a dime-store self-help book: I realized that if I truly valued the students, they would value me. For somehow, mixed in with my low self-esteem, there was a certain arrogance – which came from the general attitude in the theatre towards teaching. I liked working with my peers, artists who would take chances and question all traditional methods of discovery and hierarchy, not with some cocky high school kid from

Whitby whose sole exposure to the theatre was the school musical, and who might be sniggering about me behind my back or talking all the way through class. I finally accepted that I had something to learn from that ordinary girl in the back row from Brampton. Instead of looking at teaching her as an eye-rollingly tedious task, I came to understand that the idea of talent is a Hollywood invention, and a form of elitism; in fact, every person in the world has talent, because there is pure genius in each person, a universe in every soul, and now I always approach my first class with this idea. Indeed, I do witness a moment of genius from every student. And even if it is only a moment, the knowledge that they have this genius changes students forever.

My standards are high, and I treat the classroom as a rehearsal hall. Punctuality, respect, and concentration are all important. And now my evaluations are overwhelmingly positive. I am still frightened to read them, always fearing the bad review – but I have been pleasantly surprised since the second or third semester.

Thus, teaching is like writing a play. If I write from an idea about writing, or structure; if I write something I am assigned to write that I am not very excited about; if I write with a view to getting it over with, getting the paycheck; and if I do not have blood on every page, I do slovenly work. But if I write from my deepest self, with strength and raw passion, with respect for my characters and the structure they dictate, I have a play, and I have a classroom. Teaching drama is, in fact, writing drama. A class can only succeed if the dramatist, or teacher, makes the right choices. Are the most dramatic choices always the right choices? And is it possible that a dramatist of my sensibility can make dangerous choices as a teacher? choices that, like high diving, can produce either spectacular results or, possibly, tragic accidents?

Some theorists, such as Keith Johnstone, claim that all theatre is about power. Within the classroom the power dynamic is inherently theatrical; it seems to be set in steel – Teacher as Regent and Students as Peasants – but in actuality it shifts and changes. Sometimes I can feel certain individuals resisting my efforts to communicate in an egalitarian way, trying to force me into a mythical teacher role, or objectifying me. I try to communicate with them until they are forced to see me as a human being, and not as 'teacher mask.' We are discovering together, and everything that happens in the class is a collective creation. But in the end, however deeply we communicate, and however much I respect them, I will be giving them a grade. This makes me a threat. This makes me the enemy.

Because I encourage students to use the classes and the exercises to find themselves and reveal themselves, because I believe that the writing of a play is the writing of the self, and the acting of the role is the acting of a deeper and invisible part of the self, there may be a few students who find and reveal a self that makes for great drama, but in the real world is frightening and dangerous.

This unavoidable reality makes the classroom deeply Shakespearean. I am the Queen who never wanted to be queen, and, like Hermione in *A Winter's Tale*, sometimes standing accused of crimes (too strict, unapproachable, plays favourites) of which I know I am innocent.

The reality is, no matter how nice the boss is, everyone resents their boss, and most people, at one time or another, hate their boss. Because we hate it that people can be more powerful than we are; we hate for our future to be in their hands. In students who are somewhat emotionally unstable, a psychological transference occurs. And although this usually is revealed in the form of a positive focus, sometimes it is extremely negative. I think the power dynamic will always disturb me. I live in fear of being corrupted by it, in the sense of believing too much in my own power and expertise, of becoming complacent, like so many teachers before me.

Sometimes, out of this theatre of power in the classroom arises a harrowing drama.

He was from a small northern Ontario town, and apparently he was king of the bar crowd there. He had a big voice with a strong northern Ontario accent and his language was full of hilarious and vulgar regional idioms. He was elfish-looking, prematurely bald, and chubby with small hands, with a fire in his eyes that was sometimes mistaken for a twinkle. He was an incandescent presence in the classroom and on the stage. He was compelling in the manner of a hypnotic union leader, with an authority and a charm that could persuade the listener that what they thought was right was wrong, what they thought was red was blue. When he cracked a joke, everyone laughed, no matter how lewd or violent. Once he told a story from his childhood about the brutal beating of another boy for the sole reason that he and his buddies didn't like the boy's pants, and he had the whole class chuckling. I confess even I had to resist the urge to chuckle: this urge came from his charm alone, not from the words I was hearing, because the words he was uttering were the words of a violent bully. He was proud of what he had done. There was not a hint of any kind of regret. He had broken the victim's jaw and nose. He was excited by the blood. And all the other students, who for the most part were progressive, deeply emotional, and giving individuals, were grinning like fools. He looked at me when he finished the story, expecting to be scolded. All I said was 'That was an excellent story; it tells us a lot about our culture.' Yet inwardly I marvelled at the power of theatre, of propaganda. From the very first class I noticed that, in contrast to the openness of the rest of the students, his eyes were veiled when he addressed me. For some reason, he had decided that I was the enemy.

Perhaps he did not like my gay-positive, feminist sensibility; perhaps he just did not like me. He was the kind of person who could find someone's weakness immediately, and it was almost as if he could see through my success and authority to the shy girl who had pennies thrown at her in grade eleven because her acne was so bad, the incompetent waitress who was fired several times, the girl who had always felt ugly, an outsider. I hadn't felt hatred from anybody for a long time, and he hated me. He continually tried to shock me, but I was professionally impressed by his efforts. For a class presentation in which I ask the students to prepare a theatrical collage about their own lives, he came unprepared, as usual. He simply related every moment of a weekend in his northern town. I knew he hadn't prepared this 'solo' piece, as others had spent a great deal of time preparing, and he thought he was putting something over on me. But what he did was theatre at its best. It was simply brilliant and ready for any professional stage. I just wish he had had a bigger audience.

He resisted Shakespeare, at first, as being part of my world, I suppose, and nothing to do with holding court at bars and backyard swimming pools or drag-racing drunk through the main street of town. One day in class I was helping him with a monologue in which the character declares his hatred for another character; he recited without any affect. I asked him if he had ever hated anybody. Something flared in his eyes and when he did it again he was brilliant. I told him so. A few minutes later I was in the washroom and I heard him walking by with friends: 'And when she asked me if I had ever hated anyone I wanted to say, Yeah you, you fucking bitch.'

It was hard to believe, but I had an enemy. I suddenly felt that I was in a Shakespearean drama. I felt threatened, but also challenged, in the mode of a Shakespearean character. What I ask myself now is, How did I make my choices in this scenario: as a detached and calm and wise teacher, or as a scared girl, or as a dramatist? Did I know on some level that to ask him, 'Have you ever hated anybody' was possibly offensive to him, and therefore dangerous to me?

One day the students were presenting their scenes for 25 per cent of the final grade. This young man and his scene partner were next. I saw him putting on his coat, and asked him where he was going. He said he was going to meet a buddy. I told him that he was obliged to stay and perform his scene, that his partner was prepared, and that out of respect for her he should stay. He stayed, performed well, and then left. I was offended at his leaving so quickly, and gave the class a short lecture on professionalism. From that moment on he was openly hostile. His hostility was so great that I approached him privately one day, and apologized for having offended him. I told him I thought very highly of his work and I hoped we could communicate. He murmured the right things, without any eye contact, and went his way. But the hostility became worse. Apparently I had 'centred him out.' Oddly, he enrolled in my 300-level acting course the next semester. I was careful around him, and slightly fearful. He had changed the power dynamic. I was a woman, and I was intimidated. One day I was coaching him and another male in a scene from *Othello* in which Iago enrages Othello and we see the full force of Othello's jealous rage – this student's anger was like nothing I had ever seen. He scared the student playing Iago, and he scared me. It was as if there was lightning coursing through his body; his eyes were those of an attacking animal; his voice was like an exploding building. At one point in the scene, he, who had never broken the 'fourth wall,' looked out at me, the only other person in the room, and said his line: 'I will tear her to pieces, I will *tear her to pieces.*' Long pause. And then he resumed the scene with his partner.

He had become the wild animal, just as I had while playing Helen Keller. His scream, like my screams, had transformed him, and sickened the audience. He had done the unthinkable: he had threatened a teacher, exerted power over the oppressor, and made me cower. He had risen from the rank of student and, for a moment, had become king.

A moment of theatre. Did I stop the scene? Did I confront him there and then? I wish I had. No. I did the cowardly thing he knew I would do, because he had a diabolical ability to perceive weakness. I was trying to give him the benefit of the doubt, although in my gut I knew there was something very wrong. And I was probably afraid of him at that point. So I did nothing. But I was up all that night.

The next class, I quietly approached him at the break and said that I wanted to point out that he had broken the fourth wall during the coaching session, and he looked at me boldly and said, 'I know exactly what I did.' At this moment he had all the power. I was a scared little girl and he was one of the guys who had thrown pennies at me. I think I gave him a nervous smile and said, 'Oh good, well at least you know ...' and moved on. I did not confront him.

Had he threatened me because he feared a low mark over poor attendance? I didn't even consider that for the longest time, because his work was so strong. He finished the course and he got a good mark, because his acting was brilliant. I still wonder what would have happened if I had given him a poor grade. Or if I had had the courage (or recklessness) to give him a poor grade, if he deserved it. Wouldn't just giving him an 'A' be much easier than enduring further threats or even violence? Luckily, I never had to struggle with that question. Even so, as long as I knew he was on campus, I was frightened.

I walked a mile out of my way at lunch every day to avoid him on campus. One day he saw me, and walked with me. 'Would you like some help, Judith? You look real discombobulated.' His manner was extremely menacing, so I ignored him. I was shaking from my toes to my scalp. Even though I was trying to persuade myself that he intended me no harm, I knew kinetically that he was a danger. My animal instinct to flee overwhelmed me.

Of course, I reported the incidents to the department chair and others, but when I was at the university I lived in fear. I am still fearful – and yet, I will confess that there is an element of drama in the danger that I find professionally compelling. I ask myself hard questions: Did I make the choices I made in my interaction with this student as a teacher in order to keep everything calm, or as a dramatist looking for the most dramatic outcome? Should I modify my teaching style so that these moments of animal rage remain contained, and restrained? Or was he just a wild card, the enemy we all have waiting for us somewhere?

I am afraid that if I teach in a more conventional way, the genius in each student will no longer be revealed in my class. Instead, the students will remain inside the caul that we all must wear to survive in this world. I think there is peril in all art. In fact, there is no art without peril.

As a teacher, I have finally become the student I should have been in school: I am greedy to learn from each experience, because I know I will be stronger and more able when the next rough and dangerous moment happens. But just as I feel that, I return to a state of innocence, of deafness and blindness and trance each time I write. I must approach every new semester in a state of readiness and child-like innocence, unarmed, but with seeing eyes and enduring respect for the sometimes dangerous power of theatre.

The Monologue Project: Drama as a Form of Witnessing

BELARIE ZATZMAN

We must learn to use the tools of the theatre to help our students create not just their own drama, but produce their own culture; a culture where their experiences matter; where their questions matter; where their voices matter.

(Booth 1994)

In my work, I am carried by this powerful sense of drama and of education into the backcloth that is the Holocaust and beyond, to immigration stories and to the construction of identity, as we place ourselves, with deliberation, in relation to the other. Young people need to know that they themselves are the intersection of histories, memory space, and art-making. Teachers need to understand that they have the opportunity to construct a pedagogical architecture that leaves spaces for our students' narratives.

The shape of the memory-work I produce together with my students is designed to locate our own narratives and memory – personal, political, and historical – specifically within the territory of Holocaust education and, at once, to acknowledge the lacuna that is the Shoah. To speak more broadly, drama educates by pressing against historical consciousness, connecting the personal with the public, form with content. We cross boundaries in drama work, both in and out of role, carrying memories from the other: witnessing. With respect to the study of the Holocaust, witnessing is defined as receiving the obligation to retell, to re-perform testimony. Through drama and theatre, our students' memory-work is meant to inhabit those spaces between the Holocaust and their own lives, like filling the spaces between dialogue in a theatrical text, where the breath of the performative lives. It is drama that allows for the possibility of creating a landscape of intersection, where remembered/ forgotten/unknown/invented histories can live. Of course, the danger is that historical evidences can be displaced, even blurred; yet they can be underscored by the present too. When students gather and reassemble their own retelling, the obligation to witnessing and the performing of identity is made vivid. Ours are shadow narratives, as it were, built in the liminal spaces of subtext, between histories, and in spaces mediated by imagination. Students must have the opportunity to make meaning, to write themselves into their and others' generational stories; to discover how fine-arts research and performance might be constructed and to explore the possibility of *creating* memory. James Young, writing extensively about memory and memorial, acknowledges principally artists who recognize the significance of Holocaust history that is 'passed down to them in particular times and places': artists who know that 'the facts of history never "stand" on their own – but are always supported by the reasons for recalling such facts in the first place' (2000, 2). Theatre practices likewise can teach even by the recognition that what we choose to tell and to whom we choose to tell it, and indeed *how* we choose to tell it, all matter. As the students' particular and individual reflections spill into these shadow narratives, layers of art-making and knowing are revealed, as if one of artist Charlotte Salomon's vellum sheets have been laid over the shape of our stories. Salomon left a legacy of paintings after being murdered in Auschwitz. Her work *Life or Theater?* was exhibited at the Art Gallery of Ontario in Toronto in 2001. Salomon's process was to produce a painting and then affix to it a vellum sheet, by hinging it to the original piece. The vellum's opaque transparency was itself illustrated with both drawings *and* text, laid overtop and in direct relationship to the painting beneath. This vellum layer served either as an extension of or a commentary upon the moment Salomon had been recording in the painting. In this way she reframed the piece, creating layers of meaning over time, and moving back into a work to reinscribe it. We do that, too, in drama. It is, in essence, how we both deepen and open meaning. Shadow narratives create a new image-text, layered evidence of both a temporal and imaginative journey. Here drama educates by filling spaces in the struggle to 'trace [history] both remembered and not remembered, transmitted and not transmitted' (Horowitz 1998, 278). Drama educates through reflection, helping young people to re-tell, reshape, reinscribe, as they figure out who they are in the world. And our narratives, these acts of retrieval, can find theatrical form in the writing of monologues, which translate as central acts of memorial and reciprocity.

Degrees of Separation

The Monologue Project was developed as a series of dramatic structures from which to represent the experience of memory-work itself. Each version of the Monologue Project was designed to support our students' displacement with respect to events they themselves had never experienced, and to which they could find no immediate connection. One variation of the Project was designed to mark a link to the Holocaust, or its absence, from the specificity of the students' particularly Canadian and contemporary context. The simplicity of the instructions belies the complexity of the task: 'Write about your relationship to the Holocaust. Whatever it may be.' For those who did not know, who could not begin to imagine their connection, or their response, to a piece of history seemingly closed to them, even the search to place themselves in relation to the Shoah, to frame their memory-work, became significant. Students from very different backgrounds, with diverse ethnic, religious, political, and racial identities; theatre students and students of history, education, and religious studies; psychology and social-work students; 'second generation' children of survivors born in DP camps; first-generation Canadian children of immigrants, so characteristic of our York University population; Jews and non-Jews: all focused on transforming the spaces between the Shoah and their own lives into the dense 'poetry' of a monologue:

Hello, my name is Shane and I am a shiksa – that is shik, with a definite sa [*moving her hips*]. Goy from the tip of my head to the bottom of my feet. Now, this isn't a declaration of pride – it's moreso a fact of truth. Raised mostly in a small prairie city, the concept of the 'holocaust' was foreign and alien to what I knew and who I was. The only contact with anything or one to be related to the holocaust was reading the 'Diary of Anne Frank' in junior high, several gay friends, my politically communist grandfather; my Jewish counselor in University and the specials on A & E. These were my links, fragile though they might be. I lived in the land of the WASP – white Anglo-Saxon Protestants. Where hardships were dictated by the weather, as were the deaths. Racism existed, of course, but this was directed to mainly the 'lazy Indians' – whether this was due to the fact that they were the most recognizable minority or possibly because they were the only minority – I don't know, perhaps there would have been equal opportunity racism given a chance. We had Remembrance Days, but this was to remember what 'we' had lost – the boys in the war; the use of ration cards; the lack of silk stockings. On questioning my grandmother on this time period, all she could recall was that it was difficult to get a date. This reality, in which I was brought up and that my family enjoyed, is so far removed from the actual atrocities and horrors of what human beings suffered, it makes me wonder how such ignorance could exist. But this ignorance surrounds all of us on a daily basis – if not, how could we continue on in our daily life. The horrors of East Timor, Rwanda, Myanmar, Yugoslavia, Germany – all inhuman, all horrible, all holocausts. As long as the dichotomy of 'us and them' exists, we can set the horrors aside and continue on in our mundane lives – people become an impersonal other. For me the realization of the personal came over a year ago when riding the trusty TTC. As I sat, blankly looking out the window of the bus, I glanced over and saw a woman well-aged by time. She had an interesting face, and being a painter, I studied it. But as I looked down, I noticed something on her arm. At first I thought it was varicose veins, but then I realized it was a tattoo – numbers engraved on her arm. I sat there stunned – how did this woman, who had been demoted to an animal, a thing, a NUMBER survive? What kind of things had she seen? What kind of things had she experienced? What kind of strength did she have to survive these things and continue on? After everything, why did this human being have to take a bus and be stared at by a shiksa like me? I wanted to reach out – touch her arm, give her a hug, say thank you, I'm sorry – but instead I sat there in silence with tears in my eyes. The impersonal war/holocaust had become, slight though it was, personal. So what have I learned from this? Hello, my name is Shane, and I'm a human being.

[*Shane*]

I am scared.
For the past three months, I have been terrified.
Not for my life or anyone else's, but because of what I've learned.

I remember one day when I was thirteen, I was walking home with my bestest friend in the entire world. We were so close ... Well, this one day, a boy ran up behind us and pushed my friend down and started punching and yelling at her and all I could do was freeze in my tracks and stare. When I came to, I jumped on him and pushed him off of her, but the damage had been done. She had been targeted for being Korean.
What did I do?
Nothing.
I watched.

That day my friend was beaten up, I froze.

About sixty years ago, when Jewish people were being beaten up, the world froze.
What did they do?
Nothing.
They watched.

And I am scared because I can't understand how anything like this could have happened ... in front of so many people's eyes.
It has made me question everything about myself and the world around me.
And now, I wonder what role I play in all of this?

I can't stop thinking about what it would be like to lose my family, *my mother,* or not to be able to go to school with my friends. (slowly) I can't stop thinking about the pain in the eyes of the survivors ... There are so many questions in my head:
What would it be like to sleep on ground covered in shit knee-deep?
Would I, or even could I, walk away from my child in order to survive?
What would happen to me if my father were murdered right before my eyes?
How much torture would I have to endure to stop crying for over forty years?
Could I help someone else knowing that I was sacrificing my very life?
How would I cope knowing that I am hated simply because of who I am?

And today, even with the horrific knowledge that we have about the Holocaust, people are being faced with these very questions.
Rwanda, Cambodia, Kosovo ... every day, in so many shapes and forms, people are targeted for who they are. What do I do? What do we do? Nothing?
It's frightening how our newspapers and media become filled with reports of worldwide atrocities and suffering,
yet *our* daily lives move on.
Is that what happened to the lives of many around the world during World War Two?
Was the Holocaust an event that they listened to on the radio and after it was turned off, *their* daily lives moved on?
I don't know, I just wonder.

How have we helped, how have we donated, how have we tried to make a difference?
I can honestly sit here and tell you that I have done hardly anything.
THAT is what scares me.

I don't want my life to simply move on. I want to be different.

Three months ago, my conscious journey to make a difference began and
slowly, my role in learning about the Holocaust begins to develop.
I must challenge my fears.
I have to stop being scared.
I can't freeze and watch ...
[*Vale*]

Impossible, it seems, yet for so many Jews the impossible became routine.
Routine – brush teeth, wash face, eat, sleep. Routine – strip naked, run
across a field, RIGHT/LEFT, saying good bye. Forever. Kinda sends a shiver
down your spine when you realize how much we take for granted. I mean
how often do you pick on your brother just to pass the time? Now every
sibling battle becomes a comfort. Wake up, love, be loved, kiss your uncle,
sing with your Bubbie.
[*Shoshana*]

While these examples relate specifically to the Holocaust, the Monologue Project can be opened up to hold reflections of other histories and
memory as well. From the Japanese internment to the spectre of 'None
is too many' (Abella and Troper 1982), we can confront our inconsistent
Canadian history of tolerance, and meet the challenges of our Canadian
diversity, by teaching drama with an acute awareness of how 'theatrical
techniques in the theatre and in the classroom conspire with the social
and cultural backgrounds, education, and expectations of audiences
and students to produce meaning' (Knowles 1995, 88).

Narrative Research

In another variation of the Monologue Project, writing and performance work were proposed as a three-part assignment:

1 First, students were asked to do research about their family's immigration to Canada, examining documents as necessary. (Documents
   themselves can become the stuff of art-making; see, for example, the
   work of Canadian artist Susanne Caines 'where she slept' [Pier 21,
   Spring 2000] and Monica Bohm-Duchen's *After Auschwitz: Responses to
   the Holocaust in Contemporary Art* [1995].) The young people were
   asked to move 'beyond the fourth wall' of the classroom to engage
   their parents and grandparents about their immigration stories,
   about the family's arrival in Canada, whenever that event took place.

Documenting these interviews served as a counterpoint to the Canadian immigration history that they had or had not learned about in
school, specifically with respect to unpacking the story of Chinese
immigration to Canada, and examining life in 'Salt Water City'
(Vancouver, City of Tears) and the building of the Canadian railroad.
Similarly, standing in counterpoint to stories of loss and survival
during the Holocaust were the narratives students gathered when
they went home to ask their families where they had been during the
Second World War. In each variation of this project, interviews were
documented and the students were asked to write up these emergent
family immigration stories, opening up possibilities of what being an
immigrant might mean, particularly in the face of the very diverse
backgrounds of their classmates.

2 The second stage of the project used students' written research as the
ground on which to create a storytelling assignment. They were to
reconstruct their narrative as oral tradition, and to share the telling
of these immigration stories in small groups. 'It is storytelling above
all that shapes collective and personal memory in that transmission,
and the way the story is told, the issue of narrativity itself, therefore
must be central to any discussion' (Sicher 1998, 13).

3 Subsequently, students were asked to layer the storytelling assignment by reconceptualizing and building their research into a monologue for performance. In this final component of the Monologue
Project, all of the student pieces are performed in class as part of a
set of theatre presentations.

The development of this project through the stages of research and
writing, to storytelling, to the performance of the monologue itself
allowed students the possibility of shifting into role, moving from an
external third-person telling to a reframing of the piece to take on the
voice of the immigrant. How? 'In particular times and places' means that
our drama work must encourage students to take into account their
audience, to be aware of the specific context of the telling, and, specifically, to place themselves in relation to that telling. These issues are
integral to understanding how drama educates. The participants may
choose to tell the story entirely from *their* contemporary context or they
may take on the role of the immigrant. They may shift the telling of the
monologue in terms of character, or they may navigate time, moving
either from the present or from inside the past, shifting both place and
point of view. But even when the immigrant voice is apparently reflected

directly, students are reminded that their monologues will nevertheless be mediated by time and imagination and the specificity of their context.

Angela writes: 'I am a Roman Catholic of Italian extraction and my monologue begins there. It asks questions about God, faith, and loyalty. The character Rosa is here alone and afraid. She is speaking to God. It's a prayer.'

Rosa: There was nothing! I could do nothing! I couldn't save them. It wasn't my fault. It was a time of war. The Nazis were all over Rome and I was told that they were searching, hunting for the Jews. They were going door to door. I couldn't hide them anymore, it was too dangerous. The Nazis would kill me. They would have killed all of us. That's what we were told. I did all that I could. I really did! I hid them for as long as I could. (pause) (lowered weak voice) They were my friends, my neighbours. Anne was my friend ... she was the one who gave me this rosary (clutches the rosary tighter in her hand and stares at it for a long while). I kicked them out, in the middle of the night. I forced them to leave, in the middle of the night. I could no longer protect them. I did my duty. I'm a good Christian woman. I go to mass every day, I say the rosary, I pray every day, I take communion, I go to confession. What more do you want from me! (looks up to heaven) I obey the church, I listen to my priest, I do what I'm told, I trust my church, I have faith in my church. They can't ask anymore of me (looks out into the audience), you can't blame me. I did what I had to do, what was asked of me ...

It is the voice of the character to be sure, but what our students represent in theatrical terms is a *translation* of received narratives, whose meaning continues to shift as they figure out what and how their histories shape their present selves. In the Monologue Project, sometimes the telling – a kind of witnessing – becomes an opportunity to re-present acknowledged family history. Sometimes, these 'official' stories are juxtaposed against often-untold stories, revealed unexpectedly by a parent or grandparent. These are stories sometimes buried or perhaps long hidden by the family, and Naomi Norquay asks us to be vigilant about what is left out and what is kept hidden in considering family immigration hi(stories) and the construction of identity. Each of the students' families 'would have had reasons for not including events in previously told versions of the family's immigration story. What's left out is not devious, but rather, strategic. The gaps suggest that stories are shaped by the pedagogical intents of the people who tell them' (Norquay 2001, 10). These gaps are strategic in our drama work, too.

For some, there is no access to family histories, either because all those who might have shared with them the story of their family's arrival in Canada have died without being asked or wanting to share, or because the immigrants who first came to Canada arrived too many hundreds of years ago, or because, for a variety of reasons, no contact remains with members who might hold the collective memory of the family. Two cousins: one smothered the newborn infant, the other, the mother, gave birth to it. That night it was an unspeakable act taken to protect fellow hidden partisans from being revealed; they never spoke about which one was which. This information remained absent from the telling; it made no difference, the cousins said, even years later (Tova 1998). One student shared her mother's recollection of the 'greener' who had come to live with her family in the midst of the war. She had escaped the Nazis and was alone in Canada. Her mother recounts feeling very jealous of the girl, an interloper, and reveals that she hated her. The girl stayed with her family for a couple of years – and then disappeared from their lives. The mother does not know what happened to her, where she went, where she ended up. Never before had the mother spoken of this episode in their family's history. In another untold story, which a student translates from her grandmother's Italian into English for us, we learn that during the war, in Italy, her grandmother, her 'Nona' was thirteen years old, when she was pulled, grabbed fiercely from her bed by soldiers. Only her mother prevented her from being raped, while her father was held at gunpoint outside the front door of their home in the village. Her Nona tells her that she was never the same again.

This was a project designed to be inclusive, to honour lived experience, theatrical forms, and historical knowing; to open up possibilities of what immigrant stories might be. And yet, some students found that they walked directly into difficult knowledge in facing this exercise. One young woman explained that she had no knowledge of a family history beyond that of her immediate family (her brother and her parents), and that even those stories were, at best, meagre. Her parents were reluctant to speak in any detail about their early experiences before their arrival in Canada from the Philippines, and wished 'only to look forward.' My own grandfather was part of the immigrant community of garment workers, and so I entered the discussion with her small group, and we focused on our immigrant narratives made from the cloth of 'I do not want to re-live the past. Here, in Canada, there is a second chance to

make something different.' Facing these strategic gaps, however, ultimately helped her shape the very content of her monologue. I asked her
to weave into her monologue the belief that she has no history, as well as
her search for an unspoken history. Here, her need to create her own
memories, her own history became paramount. [A month after the class
was over, this lovely young woman sent me a poignant email, writing to
say that her father had died suddenly, and that for her the significance of
creating her own memories had been set in relief, and given yet another
layer.]

   This is drama and how it educates: for each of the students, their very
acts of discovery and questioning are inherent parts of the theatre they
produce when responding to a wide range of historical and personal
narratives. When Roger Simon at the Ontario Institute for Studies in
Education articulates a pedagogic ground for the creation of public
memory, his response mirrors educational drama practices in which we
help students learn to interpret and construct meaning by asking them
to include questioning as an integral part of their process of developing
drama work. 'Transactive public memory,' Simon explains, 'should be in
a position to raise the questions: Who counts as our ancestors? Whose
and what memories matter – not abstractly – but to me, to you? What
practices of memory am I obligated to, what memories require my
attention and vigilance, viscerally implicating me – touching me – so that
I must respond, re-thinking my present?' (2000, 6). Cate described her
struggle to 'fulfil the criteria of the assignment because I didn't feel that
I had enough details about a family history to share.' Hers is a history
unaccompanied by anecdotes of survival, one within which she felt her
privileged immigration experience keenly. 'I really don't identify myself
through my heritage but rather through my family as people and not as
nationalities.' She needed 'permission' to follow her process of discovery: 'I finally decided to write about the importance of my family,' and
deconstructing her narrative, she solves the monologue 'without attach-
ing the element of immigration to Canada. In the end, I think that the
project totally achieved its purpose of research and connection nonetheless.' Indeed, the project was designed to hold this variety of individual
responses, deliberately opening the form to make room for these varia-
tions of what it means to be Canadian, of history, of family, of otherness.
Consequently, Cate moved through three drafts of writing until she
found those fugitive pieces of her own history that resonated for her.
Rethinking her present, she took ownership of the telling, and was able
to shape those fragments into meaning and performance:

Version 1

There are many gaps within the story of my family's arrival in Canada. I cannot tell you the whole story. As far back in lineage as my grandparents on both sides, we collectively cannot tell you the whole story. My grandfather on my mother's side came to Canada from England with his parents when he was 4 years old in April of 1923. On the boat ride over from England, a tidal wave came over the side of the ship and almost washed my grandfather and his parents overboard. But they survived and arrived in Canada.

Cate's first draft goes on to trace her specific genealogy, in as much detail as she can provide. In its second version, the monologue moves toward analysing Cate's fears and the notion of survival:

Version 2

I just think sometimes things happen that make you take a look at your own life and question it. Like why I turned out exactly the way I did, and what will happen from here. If things were supposed to happen this way, and how much control I had over that. My good friend Tara's grandpa just got diagnosed with like his fourth type of cancer really recently. And as I'm talking to her about it, I can't help but think about my own grandfather, and about myself in the same situation. And I just come up empty about what I would do – how I would deal with that. And then it's all downhill from there, cuz I get thinking about the rest of my family and the fatality of it all and ... it's scary.

The final version of her monologue was performed for the class. Here, Cate's immigration narrative was driven by the telling of *her* and her grandmother's story, shaped by her own developing conception of the construction of love. These discoveries signal the significance of historical memory in which the intervention of history is one 'which constitutes identity as "a matter of *becoming* as well as being"' (Stuart Hall in Simon 2000, 136).

Final Draft

I sometimes think back and wonder what would have happened if he hadn't made it here. If that tidal wave really had killed all the passengers who were making the trip to Canada on that particular boat ... I try not to, but it's hard not to wonder that right now. As she lies there, and he acts like she's doing this just to put him out, it's really hard not to wonder. Might she have found someone else ... And might the love have lasted with him? But would we have been so blessed as we are with the rest of the family that he has given her? And which sacrifice is worth the other? He always provided for her, that's true. Our family never went without food and clothes and shelter. But I can't help but think that he could have done that more out of obligation. I don't know, maybe that was love to him. Maybe that was his understanding of love, and all that he was capable of. He probably thought that was enough. I imagine there was even a time when she thought it was enough. And there was a time when I didn't realize that it wasn't. I imagine that was because it was all she and I had ever known. And I think that was fairly common at the time. That was just what people did. That was the way marriage worked. She took care of him for more than 50 years. She cooked, she cleaned, she cared for the children, and she didn't question it. She didn't once question him. But it came back to haunt her later, didn't it? Now that she desperately needs him to turn the tables, he says he can't. I find it hard to believe that he can't. It seems a whole lot more like he won't. For as long as I can remember, I have always wanted to leave this world in love. I have to think that my gram wanted the same thing. But she won't. It's too late for that. At least she'll be leaving surrounded by love.

In her written journal, where she documented the process of writing and performing her monologue, Cate reflected on the significance of connecting with her family history and her Gram, in particular:

The threat of her not being able to share the rest of my accomplishments, successes, and failures with me is scary. It is a lesson in the frailty of humanity. It is a lesson in making the most of every second. It is a lesson in not putting off till tomorrow what you can do today. It is a lesson in love. And in this, it is a source for me. What it is to love this much, to be loved this much, to prove your love, to lose this much love, to love from afar, to love from beyond the grave, to be worthy, to show love, to live on in memory, to follow in footsteps, to make proud ...

Another quietly determined student arrived at the doorstep of our classroom to announce that he had chosen not to take on his received history, all the while feeling he had not really completed the assignment as it was intended. In the rehearsal space, he finds that we are engaged in practices that make room for his process of discovery, resistance, and questioning in order to allow him and the other students to find themselves in their histories. He expressed his great reluctance to lay claim to any history wrought from difficult family relationships. Indeed, rather than wanting to find points of intersection with his family history, he wished to distance himself entirely. In crafting his monologue, and in mixing fact and fiction, he has, with deliberation, found other ways to shape and name his identity. He re-presents his story, challenging his given history with a history of his own making: 'in particular times and places'! I explained that his translation of history is precisely what the content of his monologue could be about! Once again, his dilemma is not outside the process of the making of the monologue, whatsoever; rather, it *is* the monologue, beautifully spoken.

> Hmm ... I don't know how my ancestors came to Canada. I really don't. I don't think I have any way of knowing either. See, my mom was adopted and my grandmother is evil. She won't give my mom the name of her true parents.
>
> When my mother and grandmother are fighting, in rage, my grandmother tries to stab my mother with the words 'Your parents are Jewish.' She is evil. Just last week, my grandmother got angry and said two things. First, that all my friends are Jew-Boys. That made me laugh. I told my friends that they are a bunch of Jew Boys and we all laughed. Ah ... the second thing. She told my mom that I am eccentric and can't she do anything about my hair. Eccentric, I like that. Thanks Grandma. My mom took her insult as a compliment. She taught me to be my own person. She's a crazy woman.
>
> But anyway, my mom's health is failing and for health reasons, she needs to know her true genes. My grandmother won't tell her. Hmm ... she is evil.
>
> When I'm asked, 'Where do you come from?' I can only say 'My mother.' I like that though. I like it a lot. She is a crazy woman. Just this week my parents were in a fight. I was facing the computer up against the wall and my parents were behind me. My step-dad lay on the couch watching the TV and my mom stood in front of it, demanding his attention. When she turned it off my heart stopped. My step-dad threatened to beat her up. I couldn't see her but I could feel her passion. She is too strong to let that go. She challenged him, voice quivering with disgust, she said, 'You just try.' Nothing. She challenged him again. He didn't move. She made a sound like 'hmmph' and walked away. She is a crazy woman. So that's why when you ask where I come from, I say her.
>
> So I won't ever know from her side where my ancestors came from and their trip to this country.
>
> My biological father, now that's a short story. He is an emergency doctor

and he thinks he saves everyone from hurt ... but he doesn't. We talk about every six months. I would never ask him when his family came to Canada and how and why because I am not it.

So there it is. A crazy woman. That's where I come from. She came to Canada through the womb of a woman. I hope it was a Jewish woman.

The struggle to find a story, to create meaning in our received narratives, is also part of the 'difficult return' to witnessing the immigration stories. Acknowledging this difficulty is an important part of learning and performance. Even our inability to imagine links, or to glimpse only difference; to bridge the rupture between how we see our world and what we know we can never know of another's experience finds a place in this work and is underlined by it. Salverson writes about other forms of resistance to locating oneself in historical or traumatic contexts when working theatrically. In articulating students' resistance to her land-mines script, *Boom*, she suggests that 'some of these student teachers were exercising a form of refusal, an unwillingness to approach until they could do so without *disappearing themselves* in the encounter; refusing to approach until they at least registered their own relationship with another's pain. They may also be resisting not only the enormity of the task they suspect is before them but the impossibility of that task, the inevitability of their complicit failure before it' (2000, 65). And as in this deeply thoughtful monologue above, students discover that it is also possible to learn from the gaps in their stories. The struggle to find one's story, and the offering up of a pedagogical architecture within which to locate and re-present oneself, is the challenge and adventure of drama and its function as education.

Formations of identity and inter-generational points of view were significant for yet other students. Again, an immigration history was tied to a grandmother, one whom the student had interviewed before Christmas for the project, but who passed away suddenly during the course of the class. With her grandmother's death, the sense of loss was too great, the stories too close, too intimate now to be shared without carrying the student to weeping; the stories caught in her throat with each effort to tell, to speak. The young woman was encouraged to discover safety in fiction, rather than in the immediacy of her loss, so she created her monologue, instead, around the bones of the original narrative she had developed for the storytelling portion of the exercise. As a response to her own history and identity, she opted to build a monologue about her great-grandmother, completing the gaps with imagined experience. Laura chose to fill the spaces with moments from inside of her grandmother's memory of *her* mother. These were the stories retold to the granddaughter by her beloved grandmother. Thus, the theatrical centre of the monologue was the story of the great-grandmother, retold and reinvented as the granddaughter needed to imagine it. It was a fictional monologue built on the doubleness of Laura's memory of her grandmother and, at once, *her* grandmother's translation of the great-grandmother. In this layering, the loss was distanced and the stories could be shared.

Clearly, students' monologues can become translations, reinvented histories. Sometimes, the Monologue Project was witness to histories of ordinary women whose stories, too often, we do not hear. Lena narrates what she imagines her great great-aunt might have seen from her kitchen window, as her man works the land. In fact, it is *his* story she has heard about all her life – her great great-uncle's story of coming to Canada, of building a farming life, of working the dry earth. But it is her great great-aunt's story she chooses to perform. She moves in-role. The performance is marked by her slow, methodical movements and deliberate speech; you can feel the wall of heat around her, almost palpably, on this particular day she has pulled out of time. We have moved into the landscape of the domestic. Through her immigrant eyes, we see the sheer curtain fluttering almost imperceptibly in the breath of wind. The aunt narrates as she watches, watches the men in the field through the open kitchen window. Her niece sits some distance behind her washing and peeling potatoes, but never responds to the aunt, perhaps lost in her own reverie. The aunt is kneading bread dough. She wipes her hands on her apron. She wipes the sweat from her brow and from her eyes. Repeated again and again, the series of gestures seem almost unconscious. Clearly her hands know what to do without being told. As she fills the space, watching and narrating, we come to understand she is surviving. We never learn her name, but the internal monologue feels remarkably intimate. The monologue is a particular moment out of time and, at once, a forging of memory-work that fills the space between Lena's present and a past 'not remembered,' as she reinscribes her history with a chronicle of women in her family who must have survived prairie life (Sicher 1998, 7). Lena herself is in a difficult time she understands she must survive, and so, she later reflects, this invented story resonates for her contemporary context.

Scene Study

Stories often untold, historical narratives that too often live only on the periphery of our consciousness, that fall headlong into the gap between history and memory, this is the territory of my remembering with my students. It is also the territory of many playwrights, artists, and choreographers, whose work we also examined in the process of developing their performance work for the Monologue Project. My students were asked to consider many contemporary Holocaust productions mounted in Canada over the last few years. For example, between 1993 and 2002, *Kaeja d'Dance* produced two trilogies examining after-images of the Shoah, as well as three films. The company has just completed production on a fourth dance film, a version of their most recent dance theatre piece, *Resistance* (2000) – one of numerous theatrical events we attended as a class – which has just been released (2001). In addition to exploring Jason Sherman's adaptation of *None Is Too Many*, which was commissioned by the Winnipeg Jewish Theatre and mounted as a co-production with the Manitoba Theatre Centre in 1997, we studied other critical responses to this rupture on Canadian stages, including Theresa Tova's *Still the Night* (1997–9), which toured Canada from east to west; George Tabori's *My Mother's Courage*, at Toronto's Theatre Passe Muraille (1997); Brecht's *The Jewish Wife* and Cynthia Ozick's *The Shawl*, produced as dance theatre pieces at the 1999 Ashkenaz Festival; and producer Krystena Henke's *Through Roses*, at the 1997 Ashkenaz. Other acclaimed Canadian productions included Janese Kane's 1996 production of Barbara Lebow's *Shayna Maidel* and, of course, the *Diary of Anne Frank*, in a new adaptation by Wendy Kesselman (one reflecting the 30 per cent new material of the definitive edition), produced at the Stratford Festival for their 2000 season. Each play, respectively, was directed by Al Waxman. On smaller stages were found the extraordinary Judith Thompson's *Barely Breathing* piece and new playwright Marlene Charny's *Fathers and Daughters*, both produced as part of the annual 1999 Toronto Holocaust Education Week; Toronto also saw performances of Diane Samuels's *Kindertransport* (1998) and Lisa Rothman's movement/image production of *Replika* (1998) by Jozef Szajna.

One group of students who were beginning a scene study in class, chose to work on Jason Sherman's adaptation of Troper and Abella's *None Is Too Many*. Initially, they felt the lacuna between themselves and the events of the script. Canada had a terrible record for providing sanctuary to European Jews between 1933 and 1948. When asked how many Jews would be allowed into Canada, the senior ministry official replied, 'None is too many.' Despite this compelling and disturbing history, they could not seem to find their way through the first rehearsals. Conscientious students, they had brought thoughtful research to the rehearsal space. Their dramaturgical work ranged from an examination of the specific Canadian historical and political context of the play to identifying issues in their role as teacher-candidates. With intent, they endeavoured to link their learning about history to the framing of theatrical strategies (pedagogical needs identified by the range of teacher-candidates in the group, including history teachers, a social worker, and theatre/English majors). Nevertheless, the work was fixed as a historical piece for them primarily. Their initial run-throughs gave us no real sense of the lives of the people Sherman had sketched, with his characteristically powerful and vibrant sense of dialogue, voice, and place. Consequently, I asked them to look at the process of their own making. In fact, this was a group composed of participants who were all children of immigrants. They had yet to acknowledge this shared experience and were surprised by this recognition. Each student was a first-generation Canadian; each was pulled between the traditions of very traditional Greek or Italian families, for example, and the particular contemporary Canadian context of their growing up. They had come to this class having grown up in the spaces between cultures, between the home left and the home their family was trying to create. Thus began the process of both distinguishing that which they shared in common – or not – with one another and with the immigrant stories of *None Is Too Many*. In this context, the Monologue Project also offered an opportunity to interrogate Canadian immigration policies and practices and to reflect on their own family immigration histories in relation to their own identities. Theatrical forms allowed them to unpack ideas about immigration and displacement, about finding a home. To help extend their engagement, these students also set in motion research for their own Monologue Project; in this case, one that asked where their families had been during the war, on the one hand, and their relationship to the Holocaust, on the other. These interviews were recorded, and again strategic gaps in their histories were often revealed during the writing/rehearsal process. Students' narratives were full of evidence of these kinds of strategic rememberings and forgettings. 'Strategic remembering and forgetting suggest that the audience is carefully taken into consideration when family stories are told – or not told' (Norquay 1998, 11). Here, too, the intensity of the project – of writing themselves into history – was shaped by biography and place, certainly, but also by in-role (fictional) or out-of-role (their own lived experience) contexts, as they chose. Once again, for some, drama's capacity to teach was located in the safety of the fiction; for others, in the complex combining of fact and fiction. Students' questions, their doubts, their impatience, their uncertainties, their fears all became part of the text of their individual monologues. As such, the monologue became a kind of vellum sheet, too, laid over the geography of our individual histories.

For the *None Is Too Many* group, the actual process of researching and rehearsing in preparation for their monologue work was later reconfigured in order to become a specific part of their scene study work that followed. By design, their research was transformed into product on stage. The vellum sheet was now laid over other works of art. Given the juxtaposition of their lives as children of immigrants, this scene study group eventually chose to use the photographs of their parents and grandparents to actually line their rehearsal space. Those photographs came to define the set itself when they moved to performance. In rehearsal, we ventured from the photographs to an exploration of suitcases as metaphor. I brought in images to show them – based on Fabio Mauri's *Western or Wailing Wall* installation (1993), one in which the collection of baggage deliberately evoked Auschwitz and those heaps of suitcases that were the traces of human life (see also Zatzman, *The Suitcase Project* in 'Drama Activities and the Study of the Holocaust,' 2001). As fragments of our past and present, these suitcases immediately became suggestive of displacement, dislocation, and annihilation. Indeed, for many of these students, luggage still carries meaning as a marker of uprooted and imprisoned identities, and remains a testament to the struggle for survival.

Acknowledgment of their own histories and identities as children of immigrants in relation to the stories told in *None Is Too Many*, meant that they decided to bring in their own family suitcases – the old pieces that their families had used on their respective journeys to Canada. Each member of the group brought in this luggage, replete with labels marking the different countries through which the suitcases and their owners had passed. Handwritten marks, so clearly European, on identification tags; worn suitcases; leather, smaller or larger, brown and black, all sitting there on the studio floor. These traces of history became the setting from which the group built all their subsequent scenes. The suitcases were used as suitcases, to be sure, but they also functioned as chairs, tables, desks, bars, and pillows. The suitcases were reshaped and transformed with each scene and even the transitions between scenes became highly choreographed moments. It was their shifting from one configuration to the next that helped us to see the actors' transformations from immigrant to government worker, for example, as they moved in time and space. It was a reflection of both the fictional and real lives documented in Sherman's play, images at once layered with their own familial histories, their own stories of arrival and departure; continuity, survival, longing, and completion.

Other Artists

It was just as we were completing the Monologue Project that I discovered Canadian playwright Judith Thompson's *Barely Breathing* text. Thompson's monologue was my students' first exposure to current theatrical performance that focused on the Shoah. Her brilliant monologue carried the impulse of our drama and education work into the realm of the professional theatre. It provided the segue into contemporary Canadian practices, a particularly important representation given our challenge to balance, to negotiate differing agendas in exploring the Holocaust through a fine arts course. In the persona of Albert, Judith Thompson asks us to enter a shocking moment of confrontation. The character has been overwhelmed by the force of hatred, when he is mistakenly identified as a Jew. Thompson's incredibly evocative piece thrusts the audience into moments of choice, into the struggle – in which, of course, we each recognize ourselves. In this courageous and beautifully crafted monologue, Thompson/Albert leaves us with fists clenched, with a powerful and deeply visceral response to the tension of action and memory in the piece. 'I cannot say with certainty ...' gives voice to possibilities we do not comfortably admit. It not only allows us to consider our relationship to the Holocaust, but also questions further how it shapes our lives in the present.

Canadian performance pieces have provided my students with portraits of art-making and artists who have claimed ownership over retelling. Whether in the quiet fierceness of Thompson's Albert, whose seemingly distant connection to the Holocaust suddenly stands in direct juxtaposition to the immediacy of his struggle; or in the struggle to live with the weight of memory, ambiguity, uncertainty, questioning, and survival in Theresa Tova's award-winning *Still the Night*; these texts stand as manifestations of mapping this landscape of intersection. *Still the Night* began its theatrical life as a retelling of Tova's mother's stories, and moved inexorably toward the now published version, which allows the daughter's relationship to her mother's story to emerge as central. In the linked images of Allen Kaeja's *Kaeja d'Dance* theatre, we witness Kaeja's attempts to grapple with the impact of the Shoah on his own life by using dance to mediate the loss of his father's first family in the Holocaust. He chooses to choreograph a sensual experience or reveal an idea – for example, 'Resistance' – rather than provide literal retellings of Holocaust events. We discover examples of contemporary theatre practices in which the Holocaust becomes inscribed not only on the bodies of those who survived, but also on their children and, beyond, onto a post-Holocaust generation who will witness and retell (see Rokem 1998).

In Tabori's *My Mother's Courage* (1979), my students found compelling the carrying in of the figure of his mother, Elsa Tabori, swung over his shoulder. In the 1997 Canadian production of *My Mother's Courage*, the opening scene was blocked so that the son sits her down, and begins dressing her in the coat, hat, and shoes she wore on her extraordinary journey that day, all the while telling his mother's story. Occasionally she interrupts him, 'correcting' the narrative. Whose story is it? It is his script, but her history. Both mother and son comment on the events; both points of view live in performance, as if they are passing the telling back and forth through time, from mouth to mouth; resuscitation, of history, of memory, of fiction. In their own scene study of *My Mother's Courage*, my students chose to face issues of representation in the script by making use of video and live performance simultaneously, in order to rehearse and re-present their different narratives and the post-memory dynamic of past/present, parent/child, and art/artist (reminiscent of Spiegelman's *Maus*, 1997). The scene worked as a specific response to their study of Holocaust survivors and their children, and as reflections of their own lives, positioned as they are between history and memory, as young Canadians.

These are theatre practices that claim ownership over retelling by providing opportunities for our young people to construct spaces for shared remembering; spaces that respond to the immediacy of our lived experience, in light of our remembering. As artists and teachers, we can '[c]ite and re-site what one is learning – not only about what happened to others at/in a different space/time, but also ... what one is learning of and within the disturbances and disruptions inherent in comprehending these events' (Simon, Rosenberg, and Eppert 2000, 3). In citing and re-siting, we can share narratives, become communities. In the recovery of the past and in restaging our histories and narratives, we can name and re-present the experience of the memory-act itself. As artists and teachers we can 'return the burden of memory to those who came looking for it' (Young 2000, 7) by inviting students' participation in remembering as an active and collective force.

With special thanks to Gordon Jocelyn, and to my students at York University who have developed this work with me between 1999 and 2001, in particular: Helen Vlahogiannakos, Stephanie Parolari, Dave Farro, Shannon Hayter, Antonia D'Aguanno, Cecily Restivo, Mike Crossland, and Kathleen Garrett.

The Professional Theatre and the Teaching of Drama in Ontario Universities

DOMENICO PIETROPAOLO

Fifty-three years ago, in an essay on 'Drama and the University,' Wilson Knight warned the Faculty of the University of Leeds, which he had joined two years earlier as reader of English literature, of the serious risks involved in establishing a university drama department, remarking that, unless its programs were correctly structured, such a department was likely to do more harm than good to the development of the art of drama. Its courses were bound to overwhelm with abstract knowledge the creative imagination of potential artists and would tacitly mislead students into thinking that, upon graduation, they could find a place for themselves in the commercial theatre outside academia. Unless it proceeded with great caution, the university would at best, as Knight put it, take 'the strong wine of dramatic art' and reduce it down to 'a dead level of mediocrity' (1949, 220).

An accomplished actor and director as well as a respected scholar – having been, among other things, Chancellors' Professor of English at the University of Toronto and having achieved considerable distinction as a Shakespearean actor on the stage of Hart House Theatre – Wilson Knight was concerned for the university, which might be blindly walking into confusion, but even more so for the professional theatre, which was bound to suffer the consequences of that error, now that it seemed possible for the *art of drama* to be transformed into the *discipline of drama* by way of the new administrative concept of a *drama department.* Thus, he argued with passion that drama departments are at best products of an age of poor dramatic understanding, and great dramatic interest (Knight 1949), an age that demands courses and degree programs in drama that go beyond the literary analysis of texts – a service that was already provided by literature departments – in order to focus on performance as the unique essence of the art. As an actor, and as a theorist persuaded that the essence of drama derives from the performer rather than the director or the playwright, Knight voiced the anxiety he felt at the prospect of incorporating drama into the academic curriculum as an independent discipline. When he wrote this essay, the only drama department in England, founded in 1947, was at the University of Bristol, though many other institutions, including Leeds, were already planning to follow suit (a fact that encouraged Knight to issue his warning and to express his scepticism). In that same year, the first drama department in Ontario was founded at Queen's University.

In the half-century that followed, we, both products and agents of the institutionalization of drama in the university, have come a very long way. While we fall into different administrative structures (from the drama program to the drama department to the drama centre; and from the theatre program to the theatre department), with labels that stand for the degree of administrative autonomy with which our programs are endowed, for the range of fields that they cover, for the vocational or academic nature of their mandates, and for the types of degrees to which they lead, there can be no doubt that drama has made institutional gains of a magnitude and at a speed that can be matched by few other humanistic disciplines in the English-speaking world. We would do well to remind ourselves of the fact that drama, as a freestanding field of study within the humanities, has advanced its institutional frontier greatly in a short period of time.

On the positive side, contrary to Wilson Knight's prognostications, the essence of drama, in so far as drama is conceived as a freestanding discipline and not as part of a literary curriculum, is increasingly appreciated by students and faculty alike. On the negative side, it helps to explain why, in times of economic uncertainty, drama is charged, more frequently than the older and slow-moving disciplines with which it is usually grouped, with having reached the limit of development that current university policies can sustain. Indeed, the possibility of institutional diminishment looms large on the horizon. Our anxiety is quite different from Wilson Knight's, in that we fear drama may lose the very space that he feared it should enter.

In the province of Ontario, the reasons for such anxiety are not at the present easy to dismiss. In the business of corporate donations and endowment funds, which has become so central to the self-understanding of academia, the humanities – and drama no less than its older sister disciplines – are all paid lip-service, but no self-respecting paladin of the new funding culture could seriously regard them as the primary foundation of our civilization. (Though one could argue that by teaching them we can better protect ourselves from the dark forces of history.) In this context, it is easier to think of the humanities, especially those that involve research in the form of artistic production alongside conventional scholarship, as an intellectual luxury that we can allow ourselves in times of abundance, when market value is not the first item on the agenda, but which we must keep within limits or even sacrifice in times of need, real or fictional though the crisis may be. In this unhappy perspective, the disciplines are automatically arranged in a market-driven hierarchy that places at the top fields of endeavour generally perceived as immediately relevant to the economic well-being of society, and at the bottom fields regarded as being merely decorative. The devaluation or valorization of a given discipline in response to external factors becomes a fairly easy matter of reclassification, achieved by means of its forced institutional grouping with other fields, until, in the general awareness, a characterization of the discipline that before appeared so natural can be taken for granted.

In the past six years or so, the discipline of drama has been undergoing significant changes in Ontario. It is not unreasonable to expect that a few years from now, typical entry-level graduate students may come to master's and doctoral programs with a perception of the discipline as part and parcel of other areas of the curriculum. Until a few years ago, Ontario Graduate Scholarship applications in drama were placed in a category that, in addition to drama, included only music, since both fields have stage performance at their core. Within this category, however, the two disciplines were treated independently, with the consequence that drama students competed for funding only with students in the same field, while their applications were adjudicated by a three-member panel that included at least one professor of spoken drama and one of musical drama. At a certain point, the ministry made music a category by itself and started assigning drama applications to the category of 'modern languages.'

Students of drama therefore began to compete for funding with students of modern languages, and their files were adjudicated by a committee that may or may not have included someone familiar with drama curricula. It appears that, for the ministry, the discipline of drama did not have conceptual autonomy because its essence was located in the same area as the study of modern languages (i.e., in dramatic literature). The system, in other words, was designed to reward candidates with a literary background, and to create a cohort in which advanced students of drama were difficult to distinguish from students of literature, all in the name of budgetary effectiveness. Small drama departments, especially those shrinking due to faculty attrition, were to be rolled into the drama programs of language and literature departments, which would encourage the alienation of production work from the discipline and the reconfiguration of research priorities in drama along the lines of literary scholarship. These changes would reverse the course of drama's fifty years or so of evolution as an autonomous field of study. If we add to this picture the fact that significant budget cuts – which in drama departments normally concern production work – occurred around the same time, we can appreciate how the temptation to abandon optimism might appear difficult to resist.

In times of crisis, market-conscious university policies threaten progressive reductions of all programs that have made themselves vulnerable to the charge of isolation from the related disciplines outside academia. Knowledge that does not have an immediate professional outlet can be easily presented as irrelevant or even superfluous. Budgetary anxiety marking the last few years of the millennium continues to make evident a concern for the survival of disciplines like drama. This situation calls for more reflection on the nature of our discipline in the larger context of the world outside academia and on the curricular structure best suited to its teaching. The key expression here is 'the larger context,' since too frequently, in examining the objective nature and academic configuration of our discipline, we have paid attention to narrow contexts and, in the process, become out of focus with the outside world. Still, questions of relevance are always foremost in the minds of those charged with the task of what is dispassionately called rationalization.

Now, if I can sketch anything positive in our precarious situation, it is the urgency with which we feel called upon to examine what we do in comparison to what is being done elsewhere. Serge Eisenstein once suggested that in the analysis of film one could practise long-shot criticism, which takes into account the larger context of production; medium-shot criticism, which is concerned with proportional analogy between the film and the observer's experience of reality; and close-up criticism, which focuses our attention on what we might call the molecular configuration of a film's form and message (1945, 297). If we generalize this suggestion and apply it to the manner in which academic policy has preferred to view the discipline of theatre in the past fifty years or so, we are forced to conclude that the frames of long-shot analysis have been regarded, more frequently than not, as somehow foreign to the nature of theatre education. Where, then, are our larger contexts? From everywhere, it seems, we are being summoned to curriculum reform. We are asked to examine the principles on which we structure our programs, the goals that we pursue, and the pedagogy that we employ in pursuing them. The rest of this paper is a response to that call in so far as it concerns the relationship of our programs, chiefly those at the level of graduate teaching, to the professional theatre, and my purpose here will be to offer an argument for orienting curriculum reform in the direction of collaboration with extra-academic partners.

I should like to begin constructing that argument by suggesting that, in a long-shot of the institutional structures of university disciplines and of their links to the outside world, drama appears to have more in common with the sciences than it does with other humanities. This, of course, is not the case in medium-shot and close-up views of the field, where the quantitative methods and exact measurements of the sciences could hardly mirror a field that is concerned with imaginative constructs and that stands at the very heart of the humanistic tradition. But in the long-shot frame of institutional configuration and extra-institutional relations, the teaching of drama is unlike the teaching of cognate subjects such as history or literature, and very much like, say, the teaching of chemistry. For in addition to a library and a classroom, the teaching of drama, unlike the teaching of literature and like that of chemistry, also requires a laboratory, where interpretative hypotheses can be tested and research of a non-library nature can be carried out. Moreover, this would have great relevance to large professional and commercial interests in the economic base of the community. The laboratory of drama, of course, is the stage, or, in the case of radio drama, the recording studio. However, it is not with this aspect of the scientific analogy, important though it is, that I am here concerned, but with the other aspect, in which the professional and commercial theatre figures as the dramatic counterpart of the large industries to which the sciences are related. In Ontario, CBC Radio and the Shaw and Stratford festivals are related to the discipline of drama in the way that companies like Union Carbide are related to the discipline of chemistry. In the long-shot view of the discipline, the philistine charge of irrelevance, economic as well as intellectual, is refutable, at least in principle, to the extent that this relationship can be incorporated in the curriculum.

In practice, however, it is another matter, since the relationship between the university and the professional theatre cannot be one of subservience in either direction, but must be critical and objective in both directions – a rather difficult balance to achieve in the best circumstances. There are enormous obstacles – ideological, aesthetic, and financial – to overcome on both sides of the relationship, but the most formidable are surely those that concern, on the one hand, the preparedness of the university to enter into partnerships with the professional theatre community and, on the other, the perception that collaboration would not be useful to the academic institution and to the professional theatre. For while the sciences, always ready to take a long-shot view of themselves, have formalized and institutionalized their relationship with those sectors of industry that have material interests in the foundations of their field of research and teaching, drama has not done so to any significant degree. Drama instead has grounded its institutional self-understanding as a university discipline in medium-range and close-up views of itself, on a scale that seems to guarantee the objectivity of its methods and to protect researchers and students from the perils of tendentiousness.

Thus, more frequently than not, drama curriculum includes programs in theatre history, and promotes the production and use of textbooks that are designed to focus attention on the changing character and chronology of the commercial theatre of the past, available to students only through the proxy of written documents or, more rarely, video recordings, while politely ignoring the chance to use the commercial theatre of the present, which is instead available to all in its full material existence, as an artistic point of access to the past. Yet the fallacy on which this approach is based could hardly be clearer. For it is neither possible for the historian to move into the past, which is materially no more, and which, as memory, is only an aspect of the present, nor logical to assume that, in looking at the theatre of the past through written testimonies we can somehow avoid using the here and now of our present as the source and shaping principle of our perspective.

The expression 'theatre history' has different implications for us if we stress the first rather than the second term. By emphasizing 'theatre' we make theatre history a branch of theatre studies and by stressing 'history' we make it a special category of the study of history. We thereby automatically locate it in the domain, theoretical as well as budgetary, of history. Similarly, the history of philosophy, the history of chemistry, and the history of literature has a lower degree of significance for the study of philosophy, chemistry, and literature unless the meaning of the expressions and the self-understanding of the disciplines that they represent are derived from due emphasis on the terms 'philosophy,' 'chemistry,' and 'literature.' In so far as it can be conceived as a view of the past, the history that one writes, it must be conceded, is always a view from the present, and the present is not only where one stands, with biases and personal knowledge, when one turns towards what survives of the past as scripted or iconographic memory in our libraries and museums, but also the legitimating agent of the semantic field covered by the words 'theatre,' 'drama,' 'literature,' 'chemistry,' and 'astronomy,' used as the names of the living arts and sciences whose story one wishes to tell. In the here and now of the present, when we assign to the terms 'theatre' and 'drama' meanings that are not informed by current practice in our part of the world, we run the risk of turning these words into abstract labels devoid of relevance to material reality and we consign them, at best, to the protective dust of theatre archaeology. Clearly, the task of the historian is to stand firmly in the here and now, fully cognizant of the fact that he cannot and should not stand anywhere else, and to turn towards the past, looking at it and into it, as if through a window. The frame of that window, if we can take the metaphor a little further, is determined by the state of theatre art in the present and will always be visible in our view of the past, though the rhetoric of our historiography may do the utmost to conceal it. The living meaning of these terms is represented by current practice, and current practice is, for better or worse, not what we find in our archives and museums but what we find in our theatres, from the least to the most expensive, and from the least to the most sophisticated. Hence the theoretical relevance of the contemporary commercial stage to the theatre history curriculum.

Similar arguments can be built for those other parts of the curriculum we generally regard as the core of our programs, and, with little effort on our part, as theatre educators, we would have enough support to overcome the bias of traditional text-based philology. Even courses on the drama of specific periods of history can be approached through living theatre events, provided that representative plays are still being produced. The area where I see the greatest need for a self-reflection in this manner is perhaps dramatic theory, a field in which academic discourse has, at times, fallen prey to the lure of pure concepts, relegating dramatic form to the level of a pretext for theorizing, and one which, with the odd exception, is perceived as too abstract and academic to be of interest to professional theatre practice. If the long-shot perspective is accepted, then the theory of drama, whose task it is to contemplate only one question – namely, 'What is drama?' – must likewise include the field it encompasses, both synchronically and diachronically, starting with the notion of drama shared by the practising playwrights and theorists of our time.

Dramaturgy is an obvious area of the discipline in which fruitful partnerships can be established with relative ease. One way of conceiving dramaturgy is that it is an area of analysis in which theatre history and dramatic theory come together to identify issues outside of the domain of both but central to the commercial practice of drama, from script development to final production and interpretation. The dramaturgical core of a drama program can be reformulated in the direction made plain by a long-shot consideration of the discipline. Accordingly, both in the area of developmental dramaturgy, as the practice has institutionally evolved in Canada, and in the area of production-support dramaturgy, it is possible to form a series of partnerships in which students of dramaturgy are given a field placement, not unlike the internships common in the sciences, in the theatre community, where they can work on a dramaturgical project – such as script development, dramatic adaptation of narrative, script preparation for production, contextual research, or production history – under the supervision of an experienced professional, and, in their final essays, analyse their field experience against the background of the theoretical and methodological material covered in class, in the general context of the practice of dramaturgy in theatres of the same type elsewhere in North America.

The benefits to the student and the program of such an approach are obvious and require no further comment. But what the theatre has to gain from this type of partnership is perhaps worth spelling out: the services of intelligent, well-trained researchers, capable of asking difficult questions and of making available to the theatre personnel a wealth of relevant information. It is well known that the vast majority of theatres in Ontario do not, at present, employ dramaturges. Those that do tend to derive the dramaturge's salary from the most vulnerable part of the budget. But that does not mean that there is no dramaturgy to speak of. It means rather that dramaturgical work is project-specific and is assigned, chiefly in response to funding practices, to other members of the team, from the artistic director to the archivist. The task is to link the research interests of a given student with an appropriate project. The Graduate Centre for Study of Drama at the University of Toronto has had considerable success in this area, with regular field placements in several companies operating in the city or within commuting distance.

Once the idea of a teaching partnership has been factored into the research programs of individual students, it is an easy matter to extend collaboration to other areas of the curriculum. A good advanced academic program in drama, like analogous programs in the areas of science and technology, presupposes a lively form of collaboration between, on the one hand, the university and, on the other hand, the professional institutions in our arts and entertainment community. The latest artistic products of interest to scholars and students alike are being presented in the most accomplished form that the community is currently able to sustain. This type of dynamic makes it possible for the university to study and teach theatre as a living and a socially and economically relevant art form. At the same time, it enables distinguished theatre professionals to participate in the teaching mandate of the university, to which they can bring the freshness of their own work, and encourages the arts and entertainment community to contribute in a meaningful way to the education of young professionals who may well play leading roles in its own future development.

The key theoretical implication of an academic policy that validates professional partnerships of this nature concerns the traditional concept of academic work. Though challenged by colleagues of vision and integrity as well as by committed students, the received wisdom on this point is still that, in a respectable program, academic work, which is based on reading lists and essays, is to be carefully correlated but never confused with production work, which has to do not only with the written text, but also with artistic reinterpretation and with the mechanics of performance. This line of reasoning presupposes that production work has no academic status, that its only purpose is to illustrate and reinforce what is properly academic, and that is, regrettably, the case in many well-known programs.

The thrust of the argument here has been to suggest that we must go one step higher to a concept of academic work that includes production as one of its parts, recognizing it as a component that is no less academic than the others, though it is materially distinct from them. Unfortunately, there is still too much resistance in the discipline to the reclassification of production work as academic, and so reform in this area is likely to be slow in coming. Yet our universities have never been as well disposed towards the academic validation of performance and production as they are at the moment, and we would be foolish to ignore the signs. The honorary doctorates that in recent years have been issued in this area, whatever other factors may have motivated our universities to offer such degrees, are for us institutional gestures that publicly assert that the work of directors like Giorgio Strehler and Robert Lepage, to name two distinguished recipients of honorary degrees from the University of Toronto, is worthy of the highest academic recognition. The category of academic work in drama is in urgent need of a new definition, to be formally introduced into our degree programs (MFA, MA, and PhD) and approved by the appropriate committees on academic policy. And the most propitious time in which to contemplate meeting that need is the present.

This is not an easy task, of course, not only because of the scepticism of colleagues unconvinced of its validity, or because of the at times complicated mechanisms of approval that the new approach may have to go through, but also and primarily because of the practical issue of the credentials necessary to impart academic teaching of the more practical kind. The problem is difficult indeed, but as Croce once remarked with incisive elegance, the difficulty of the task at hand has nothing to do with the obligations of intelligence: if we are convinced that this is the course to follow because it reflects a logical consequence of a dominant trend in the discipline, then our question should be how to overcome the obstacles, whether they are of an administrative or an intellectual nature.

But what if we are not all convinced that our discipline needs to undergo such reorientation? Now, there's the rub. The chairs and directors of the drama programs in Ontario colleges and universities can play a significant role in the collection of the precise data we need in order to assess the situation. Recommendation 20 of the Committee of Inquiry into Theatre Training in Canada, prepared under the aegis of the Canada Council in 1977, should be our logical starting point. The committee, chaired by Malcolm Black, a graduate of the Old Vic School in London and a professor of fine arts at York University, recommended that universities involve experienced theatre personnel in their programs, extending to them the academic role and teaching authority to which they are entitled by their professional credentials (Black et al. 1978, 90–1). Senior theatre artists could become what, in the language of our more experienced neighbours to the south, we may call master teachers of theatre.

The roles of such mentor teachers would not replicate those of teachers of studio courses who do not meet the admission requirements of graduate academic programs – as happens in most undergraduate departments, or as instructors of workshop courses that require the validation of an academic – as they still do, for example, in the program structures of the Graduate Centre for the Study of Drama. Rather, their professional credentials would confirm them as colleagues whose teaching comes with internal and autonomous guarantees of academic validity. Academic programs on the art of drama have only benefits to derive from partnerships with the community, and these will give drama concrete existence in society and history.

National Symposium on Arts Education: Opening Address, 1–2 July 2001

JOHN MURRELL

Part One

Teachers, Learners, Artists, Scientists, Enablers, Facilitators, Honoured Guests:

I am so happy and I feel so fortunate to be able to share some thoughts and feelings with you for an hour or so over the next two days. Although I customarily require a lot of persuading to do anything at all nowadays – other than to listen to music, to daydream, and to write down some of those daydreams – I am sure that those who invited me to present this opening address would confirm that I leapt at the opportunity to speak to this important gathering of movers and shakers. Yes, I literally *leapt*, if you can imagine such a spectacle. For I believe that we have all come together here because we *can* still use our imaginations, even the rapid-moving and risky parts of our imaginations – and because we believe that it is essential to go on doing so, taking all the big, necessary risks involved in imagining a better future, until the day they put the lid on the box.

This evening, instead of delivering an opening address as such, I am going to initiate a little conversation with myself – something which I often do and, if my family is to be believed, at virtually the same volume that I will use with you tonight and tomorrow morning. I am going to talk with myself about the thrilling and complex uses of arts in education, and education in the arts, about the risks of infusing arts into education, and about the risks of not doing so.

Some thoughts from this internal monologue of mine may possibly spark further conversations over the next few days during which I can learn from the rest of you. Perhaps these thoughts will lead to conversations that you will have with others among the engaged and engaging group gathered here – and to conversations that you will continue to have within your professional and personal circles for years to come. I am speaking about learning in partnership, learning through partnerships of all kinds, and at all levels.

For a long time, I have believed that the most vital conversations we can have with others begin with the conversations we are obliged to have with ourselves. At this point, my soliloquy begins:

Restlessness.
Dissatisfaction.
Secretiveness.
Stubbornness.
I remember how much I dreaded discovering any of these qualities in my students, way back when I taught junior high school on the prairies, more than thirty years ago. (Of course I was very young then, and a novice schoolteacher: I dreaded discovering almost everything which I was about to discover.)
Restlessness.
Dissatisfaction.
Secretiveness.
Stubbornness.
Today I believe that every genuinely creative person possesses these 'unpleasant' qualities. I might as well admit that such qualities are disruptive and aggravating, whether encountered in the old or in the young, in a student or in a teacher, in artist or scientist. And yet, these are qualities that every great creative thinker, every friend of the progress of humankind, seems to have possessed, often in disruptive abundance, ever since there were teachers or students or artists or scientists among us.

But don't these qualities contradict creativity and progress, more than they contribute to them? Perhaps even contradict one another? The poet Walt Whitman (in Cowley 1959), probably the greatest guide we have had so far to the true spirit of North American democracy, with characteristic restlessness and stubbornness said:

Do I contradict myself?
Very well then I contradict myself
(I am large, I contain multitudes).   (1959, 85)

And even his punctuation, in an excerpt like that, is disruptive and aggravating to me. But I believe that it is part of my job, as a caring and creative human being, to read past and around the disruption and aggravation on the surface, to the ever-fresh, ever-startling thought inside, simmering underneath.

As a matter of fact, whenever I could manage to go on tolerating and encouraging them for long enough, those same junior-high students of mine who were restless, dissatisfied, secretive, or stubborn, or all of the above, were the very ones who most frequently demonstrated unbridled creativity – if I could refrain from putting on the bridle of classroom discipline too harshly or hastily.

Restlessness.

How can a *restless* student, or a restless teacher, a restless artist or scientist, a restless enabler or facilitator, be a good thing? Wouldn't we rather have tranquillity in our own lives, and especially in the personalities of those with whom we work and learn and teach, tranquillity in the atmosphere around us, as often and as constantly as possible?

Maybe. But many times, I think, the price of tranquillity is just too high. Tranquillity is too often the name we give to social timidity; worse yet, to moral cowardice. We crave tranquillity instead of effort, tranquillity instead of struggle, tranquillity instead of the twisting, restless thought, spun out for ourselves and for others. Would we really rather make do without the challenging new thought, in order to create an artificial tranquillity – in the classroom, in the home, in the halls of government? Maybe. But it is a very high price to pay.

Socrates, one of the first, one of the greatest, and one of the most disruptive and aggravating teachers in the history of Western civilization, espoused two highly volatile tactics that I think should interest any teacher or learner, any facilitator of teachers and learners. First, he believed that the search for truth and the search for beauty are one and the same. Second, he believed that his students should be stirred up, should be made restless and dissatisfied, and should stubbornly hold to their own opinions and points-of-view, until truer things could be put in their place. Socrates relished disagreement and difference of opinion, and with his genius he channelled these disruptive and often aggravating human preoccupations into the restless search for beauty and truth. He would not simplify, he would not streamline, he would not cheat, he would not take shortcuts. He did not insist on hasty, artificial tranquillity.

Socrates opened up the wide and deep and turbulent stream of human differences, and confidently believed that, out of that murky stream, a clear unified current could eventually be identified – a powerful and genuine current that can lift and carry humankind into the harbour of enlightenment. He believed that unity, struggled and fought for, would always be more beautiful, more truthful, and more useful than any artificially engineered majority opinion.

I know that, in my own life and work, I have not yet fully absorbed this lesson from Socrates. When I am teaching or learning, even now, I often try to select a prefabricated, unified and tranquil, non-disruptive approach to truth and beauty, a single simple path, which we can all use, at little or no risk to ourselves or others. But I also know, when I am beautifully truthful with myself, that, on the road to better human thought and feeling, those freeways without speed bumps and inconvenient detours always lead to boring and sterile destinations.

Socrates and his first few followers – his students, who were also his teachers – understood that the way to beauty and truth is arduous, but that, for all its hairpin curves and its bridges that must be built overnight, it is the only human journey worth taking.

Just as importantly, Socrates understood that the path to beauty (creativity, imagination, art, dreaming, emotion) is exactly the same route as the path to truth (discipline, reason, science, precision, thought). You cannot reach toward the one without reaching toward the other. He taught his students aesthetics in order to teach them logic. He taught them to use the mind as a means of knowing the heart, and vice versa. Socrates' heated and contradictory and fearfully lively debates with his students dealt with how to put more beautiful things into the world, *and* about how to use the mind more effectively – and this was a single curriculum, not parallel curricula, and certainly not competing or conflicting curricula. He was a pioneer in arts-infused education.

I wish I could have sat there and shared food and thought and feeling with Socrates, and could have put forward my own arguments. Whenever I wander through those dialogues again, I think, 'If only I could have been there – at that moment! – I might have been able to disagree with him so powerfully, so eloquently, that he would instantly have been a better teacher, and I would instantly have been a better student! I only missed out by twenty-four hundred years of time and ninety-three hundred kilometres of geography!'

Socrates was repeatedly accused by prominent politicians of corrupting the youth of Athens – through encouraging them to have new ideas. Eventually, he was sentenced to die for this offence. His accusers knew that he would never settle down and stop questioning the status quo – that he would never stop insisting that beauty and truth, art and science, are one and the same thing – so they had to find a way to silence him.

In his defence to the court of inquiry, Socrates related his own personal journey, that most essential journey, in search of wisdom. First, he went to a politician. He discovered that this man, because he knew so much about politics, assumed that the whole world was like the world of politics, and so his wisdom stopped abruptly at the borders of that dynamic but limited world.

Next, Socrates went to a poet. He found that the poet was not only unable to describe beauty and truth with any accuracy; he could not even explain or account for his own poems. And yet this man of words assumed that words were the only truly important things in the world. The poet had highly developed instincts and a sensitivity to verbal music, but wisdom was far beyond him.

Finally, Socrates went to a carpenter – who seemed both more serene and more pragmatic than either politician or poet. But even the carpenter assumed that knowledge ended where his measuring tools, where his lumber and saws and hinges, ended. He was not interested in a world that extended beyond his immediate personal experience – and it was perfectly clear to Socrates that no one man's or woman's personal experience could include all the realms of wisdom.

At the conclusion of his 'pilgrimage,' Socrates told the court, 'I understood, at last, that the only truly wise human being is someone like me – because, unlike the others, I realize that I possess absolutely no wisdom.' Of course, they condemned him to die. He had not only questioned the wisdom of the state – he had pointed out how difficult a commodity wisdom is to acquire, for anybody, no matter how highly placed or how successful you may appear to be.

Restless – and recklessly proud of his restlessness to the very end of his life – a creature of exploration, of adventure and risk, rather than of intellectual knowledge and wisdom: that is how Socrates saw himself. And he probably taught the world more than anybody else, before or since, about teaching.

Restlessness ...
Dissatisfaction.
Michelangelo Buonarroti was not just a scientist (though he was certainly that too), not just a master of lofty thought, a master of painting and sculpture and architecture, which he wrestled out of inert materials

for the glory and edification of popes and potentates. Michelangelo restlessly and recklessly investigated poetry and music as well. He had to find out what makes poetry and music tick, because he felt that poetry and music were the foundations for each towering edifice he built – music and poetry were at the heart of every statue and every flawless perspective he created. Has there ever been a bolder or more splendid opera than the one presented on the ceiling of the Sistine Chapel?

But for all his accomplishments and all the knowledge he passed along to the rest of us, Michelangelo, as a human being, was disruptively, aggravatingly, one might almost say terminally, dissatisfied.

I recommend his poems to you, if you don't know them already. In a sonnet written near the end of his life, Michelangelo says to a fellow artist:

Already now my life has run its course,
And, like a fragile boat on a rough sea,
I reach the place, which everyone must cross
And give account of life's activity.
Now I know well it was a fantasy
That made me think art could be made into
An idol or a king. Though all men do
This, they do it half-unwillingly.
The loving thoughts, so happy and so vain,
Are finished now ...
Painting and sculpture cannot any more
Quieten the soul ...   (Jennings 1970, 102)

I remind myself: this is Michelangelo speaking – Michelangelo, creator of sublime, indelible shapes and sights. Still, in his poetry he does not talk about the wonder and achievement of his own art, or anyone else's, but about the dissatisfying limitations of art forms to which he had devoted nearly eighty years of his life.

In his poetry, as well as in many of his canvases and sculptures, I can feel, so powerfully, how Michelangelo's adolescent restlessness and recklessness – and he was a hellion even in his early teens! – ripened beautifully into the fierce dissatisfaction that would fuel all his later work, in whatever medium. Dissatisfaction with form, dissatisfaction with media, with marble and tempera and sonnets, dissatisfaction with philosophy and religion, dissatisfaction with love and with the absence of love – these were such provocative blocks of resistant stone for him, out of which he persistently, heroically tried to chisel beauty and truth, to the end of his life, to the benefit of us all.

I feel that dissatisfaction can be such a powerful tool for all of us – for teachers and students, artists and scientists, and enablers of the same – unless we shame dissatisfaction into silence.

There has never been a healthy inquiring infant who wasn't frequently dissatisfied with his parents, dissatisfied with her fullness or emptiness, with his wetness or dryness, with her general lot in the world.

There has never been a healthy, restless, ambitious teenager who did not develop his or her infantile dissatisfaction into a strong rebellious stance, a song of protest, in defiance of the adult world that offered either too much or too little at any given time.

There has never been a healthy, thoughtful, engaged and engaging grown-up artist or scientist, teacher or learner, who did not hang on persistently to his or her adolescent anguish – in order to forge a deep, constantly renewable dissatisfaction that would drive her or him onward, drive him or her to tear down old structures of thought and to build up new ones – to paint over what seemed beautiful enough a few months ago, in order to create something infinitely more beautiful, which will also have to be painted over in due course. Dissatisfaction is that essential impulse which drives us on to *re*think, *re*dream, *re*birth, *re*create, *re*new.

One of my most heartfelt wishes for any creative person, or any person who facilitates creativity, is that he or she will hang on to childhood and teenage dissatisfaction, and will nourish them so that they ripen into a mature, considered, and perennial distrust and impatience with the status quo, and with the clichés, even the most beautiful, soothing, and seductive clichés, of those who came before.

Those who came before have left us treasures, but they have also left us their debris, no matter how well meaning they were. On this layer of past debris we build the treasures (and the further debris) of the future. I think we must go on doing so, with heroic dissatisfaction as our guide. Heraclitus was right: the world is a vast fire that constantly consumes itself, while producing the heat and energy needed to inspire tomorrow's work.

Restlessness.
Dissatisfaction.
These are noisy and public, disruptive and aggravating, and yet potentially productive tools with which to fashion a new world. But now I am

thinking of two quieter and much more private qualities which we all possess in some measure – and which every creative person must nourish, although they, too, are often dismissed as disruptive and aggravating:

Secretiveness.

And Stubbornness.

In the small secret corners of her New England home, or hidden among the hedges in her family's garden, or crouching among the universe of snakes and insects in a field of grain, or walking defiantly solo beside the sea, the poet Emily Dickinson (in Johnson 1960) pursued her restless, dissatisfied search for beauty and truth in the world – a world that characterized her as a harmless eccentric, at best – and, more frequently, as a selfish and opinionated recluse. She addressed her book, or the birds and insects, or the very stones, in preference to human beings – with whom she was either too shy or too proud, or just too aggravatingly secretive, to hold conversation. The world accused her of secretiveness, and she wore it like a badge of honour:

> I'm Nobody! Who are you?
> Are you – Nobody – Too?
> Then there's a pair of us!
> Don't tell! they'd advertise – you know!
> How dreary – to be – Somebody!
> How public – like a Frog –
> To tell one's name – the livelong June –
> To an admiring Bog!   (1960, 133)

Emily Dickinson kept her jewels of knowledge and wisdom about the world secreted away in her mind and spirit, brewing and steeping them like the rarest, most aromatic tea, until she was satisfied that it was full-strength. In fact, she never felt ready, in her lifetime, to share completely with the rest of us. At the time of her death, in 1886, a mere handful of her poems had been published, and even those she parted with reluctantly. Years earlier, some scholarly men had come from Boston to investigate her – 'They asked me for my mind,' she said – but she felt that her mind, her vision, her perception were still too limited, and told them the world would have to wait until she was ready to speak. She was not perfectly ready, I guess, until quite recently.

Fifty years or so after her death, Emily Dickinson began to be discovered. She began to become a touchstone and a guide for all of us who wish to search deeply, quietly, patiently for what really matters, rather than broadcasting our shiny, boisterous new discoveries the moment after we have made them – and only a few moments before they will begin to tarnish and fade. She was one of the most obstinately and courageously secretive geniuses that time has yet produced:

> To fight aloud, is very brave –
> But *gallanter*, I know
> Who charge within the bosom
> The Cavalry of Woe –
> Who win, and nations do not see –
> Who fall – and none observe –
> Whose dying eyes, no Country
> Regards with patriot love –
> We trust, in plumed procession
> For such, the Angels go –
> Rank after rank, with even feet –
> And Uniforms of Snow.   (1960, 59)

I admire and love her for that image of silent suffering infused with heroic thought – a proud and difficult search lived out in secrecy, as it was by the snow-clad angels of her imagination.

Hidden away, drably dressed, whispering to herself, Emily Dickinson eventually, long after her own lifetime, helps to fill the world with thoughts that, for all their brevity, are enormous, richly clothed – ideas and images that sing much louder than the cavalries and choruses of official, conventional patriotism – or religion – or education. And she achieved her big courageous miracles of discovery by keeping to herself, shutting herself away, remaining secretive and selfish until she was ready to share her great gifts with all of us – one hundred and sixteen years later. And ever after.

It seems to me that secretiveness can and must be developed as an art in itself, an art for us to cultivate in an era as garrulous and hasty, and as relentlessly overexposed, as the one we inhabit.

How strange, that two of the people who have moved me and taught me most should both be named Emily: Emily Dickinson and Emily Carr. But I suppose it's not strange at all that my two icons for Secretiveness and Stubbornness are both women – because women, in most times and in most places, have had to possess these two qualities, whether they came naturally to them or not. Women have had to keep their beliefs and passions and strengths stubbornly secret, much of the time – or risk having them stumbled over and then stolen by men.

I am holding Emily the Second strongly in my mind right now – Emily Carr, a visionary in both paint and prose, living out a life of remarkable insight, while those around her categorized her as secretive and stubborn, as a selfish and opinionated recluse. God knows, she had to be stubborn, or she would have been annihilated – first by her stiff-upper-lip colonial family, then by her prudent and prudish schooling – and, when she had survived those, she still had to deal with Canadian society in the 1910s, '20s, and '30s, which had no convenient or comfortable pigeon-hole for the serious female artist, and, most assuredly, not for one who was more interested in flagrant gouache than in polite watercolour, more interested in totems than in tea-houses, more interested in the breadth and height and depth of life's experience than in the various beautifully tailored straightjackets then used to bind all that splendour.

Emily Carr's stubbornness was her best feature, and her constant necessary armour. Even as she moved into her sixth decade, and at long last began to achieve a tiny modicum of recognition – 'I am famous *in Victoria!*' she sneered! – she remained as restless, as dissatisfied and *stubborn*, as ever. These qualities emerge powerfully in her remarks to the Victoria Branch of the Women's Canadian Club in spring of 1930 – a flagrantly beautiful and stubborn song, in which we also hear her secret hope, her cautious optimism that the world – and Canada, in particular – will one day wake up to the risks and to the usefulness of its own arts scene:

Canada wants something strong, big, dignified, and spiritual that shall make her artists better for doing it and her people better for seeing it. And we artists need the people at our back, not to throw cold water over us or to starve us with their cold, clammy silence, but to give us their sympathy and support!

I tell you it is better to be a street-sweeper or a char or a boarding-house keeper than to lower your standard. These may spoil your temper, but they need not dwarf your soul.

Oh, just let them open their eyes and look! [The West] isn't pretty. It's only just magnificent, tremendous. The oldest art of our West, the art of the Indians, is in spirit very modern, full of liveliness and vitality. They went far, and got so many of the very things that we modern artists are striving for today. (Cited in Tippet 1994, 193–4)

Frighteningly, refulgently stubborn. And accurate.

Restlessness.
Dissatisfaction.
Secretiveness.
Stubbornness.
Socrates.
Michelangelo.
Emily Dickinson.
Emily Carr.

These four disruptive, aggravating, and magnificent human icons remind us that we must indeed invite challenge, discomfort, and a healthy
amount of confusion – that we must indeed take risks in allowing the arts
and artists into our lives, and into that most important facet of our lives,
education.

I hope that I will always be willing to take these risks, more often than
not, and that those with whom I work and live will be interested in taking
them too.

Will this society, will Canada, take the risk of sometimes living and
working without tranquillity, so that new ideas can burst into the world
with all the restless and reckless vitality that is their birthright? It is not
only bad new ideas that are aggravating and that explode with disruptive
energy. All new ideas are like that. Are we willing to risk it?

Will we take the risk of sometimes living and working without satisfaction, writhing and striking out in frustration with the status quo, and
allowing those around us their own full measure of writhing and striking
– so that dissatisfaction can sometimes boil over into a new and higher
level of consciousness – which then sets up a more exalted status quo
than ever before, a new high-water-mark of status quo, with which the
teachers and learners and artists and scientists of the future will become
terminally dissatisfied, and out of which they will restlessly fashion the
future?

Will we take the risk of sometimes living and working without the
generosity and transparency of our helpmates, so that they can nourish
in secrecy their seeds and seedling ideas for improvement? Are we
willing not to insist always on instantaneous revelation, in order to
permit richer, stronger revelation to creep slowly along through the
green-shoot and blossom in its appropriate season? Or are we too insist-
ently curious and anxious and fearful to permit slow, rich, deep, private
growth?

Will we take the risk of sometimes living and working without being
able at the end of every day to reach consensus? Can we tolerate inflex-
ibility and downright pig-headedness – which are constant characteris-

tics of both the young and innocent and the old and experienced – characteristics of the non-thinker, yes, but also of the very best thinkers we have ever had among us?

Will we put up with the stubborn recklessness and dissatisfaction and secretiveness of others – and with our own – because, ultimately, we believe that beauty and truth are discoverable, at least in small-to-medium-sized packages – and why in God's name shouldn't somebody be stubborn about the validity of such a discovery – and go on and on and on being stubborn about it – until the world opens its mind and its heart wide enough, so that new beauty and truth can be presented to it as a gift?

Will we risk looking at and dealing with the less glamorous, less pleasant facets – the disruptive and aggravating facets – of creativity, of human learning, in order to reap the true deep-rooted and high-reaching harvest?

I say to myself, 'Yes, I think we will. I hope we will.' And I wait for us to take a big unanimous breath, to welcome in the fresh air, the entire fresh air of arts in education, and education in the arts-infused education, this very ancient and still very new concept, which is fuelled by restlessness, dissatisfaction, secretiveness, and stubbornness, even as it leads to discovery, fulfilment, sharing, and community.

Tomorrow morning – Part Two of my soliloquy (spoken out into the world, as all good soliloquies are) – I will try to say a few intelligent and/ or provocative words about how important it is for all of us to work together, in all our various jobs and responsibilities, among all our various assignments and dimensions, in order to take these big risks knowingly and courageously, with wide-open eyes, hearts, and minds – with the ever-renewable courage needed to respond to this old and tremendously significant new question: How can we work together, in order to permit creativity to remain as uncivilized as it sometimes needs to be, so that it can persist in its work of civilizing us?

I wish you much happiness this Canada Day. And I thank you for this opportunity.

Part Two

Late yesterday afternoon I stood here and had a somewhat disruptive, sometimes aggravating, but rather stimulating, conversation with myself – about the risks of allowing rampant creative vitality to flourish in the classroom, in the boardroom, in the corridors of learning and the corridors of power, among teachers, learners, artists, scientists, enablers, facilitators. I must say, though, that the conversations which I had with others here, following my little chat with myself, were infinitely more stimulating – which is just as it should be, and just as I hoped it would be.

This morning I would like to continue my internal monologue for a few minutes longer, and this time I would like to harangue myself about the risks involved whenever we are unwilling to take the risks involved in allowing human creativity to be its restless, dissatisfied, secretive, and stubborn self.

I would also like to soliloquize briefly about how essential it is for all of us to work together, at all levels, in all dimensions of our private and public lives – and through as many different means and methods as are appropriate or necessary – in order to take what seem to me to be indisputably necessary risks – risking the explosions associated with human creativity, with arts in education, and education in the arts, risking the intense heat and light, in order to harness deep and wide and high energies – rather than eliminating risk and thereby harnessing only the inertia and stagnation that inevitably come from keeping the bottle-cap screwed down too tightly.

The bottle-cap on creative thought and creative action, on creative teaching and creative learning, may be screwed down for financial, theoretical, or moralistic reasons. Each of us could provide plenty of scary examples.

The bottle-cap on the risks of creativity can be screwed down – air-tight, not an ounce of life-giving oxygen available! – in order to stream-line our administrations, in order to write tidy theoretical papers for our superiors (or our bosses), or in order to kowtow to the latest transitory indications in socio-economic statistics. Yet the outcome is always the same: we clean up and streamline and perfect the system, and some-where in the process we destroy the purpose for which the system was created – the forward movement of humankind in both knowledge and wisdom. This forward movement requires, has always required, and always will require, some disruption and aggravation – some restlessness, dissatisfaction, secretiveness, and stubbornness.

It is the artist's job, and it is the job of the arts in any human society, to 'stir things up' – to express and to cause a healthy degree of dissatisfac-tion – to search in risky secret places for beauty and for truth – and to be stubborn about insisting upon their revelation and their relevance, once they have been found. Society is not always happy to have this stimulation and this insistence, but society always needs them – requires them, along with other nutrients, as a staple of its diet. In the wonderful, old-fashioned play *Inherit the Wind*, a lawyer who is more thinker than lawyer, and more artist than thinker in many ways, says: 'What is my job here? I am here to comfort the afflicted, and to afflict the comfortable.' I like that, and that is what I have always felt my job to be, as an artist, as a teacher, and as a learner – as a component of this society, which I love, and with which I continue to wrestle.

What is the quick, painless, and thoughtless way to quiet the creative soul? What is the antidote, so often – much too often – prescribed for Restlessness? Tranquillity. Rest.

But too much rest can indicate a lack of vitality, a timid or cowardly avoidance of renewal, an 'arresting' of forward movement, an inert barrier to progress in human thought and feeling. Tranquillity can become a tranquillizer, which poisons us, if we take it too often, or if it is manufactured from artificial, unstable, unnatural ingredients. We should want our young and our old, our teachers and our learners, our artists and our scientists to have as much tranquillity as they can honestly grab on their restless journey toward a better world. We should not, however, wish synthetic rest on them, just so that society as a whole can withdraw from stimulation, while fabricating a tranquillity that it has not yet earned.

What is the antidote for Dissatisfaction? Contentment, placidity. But contentment, like tranquillity, must be earned. Otherwise, contentment is mere smugness, deadly self-satisfaction – a status symbol, artificially manufactured, which we use to set ourselves above those who are still struggling toward the improvement and enlargement of life, long after we have yawned and given up on humankind.

Contentment is a first cousin of cynicism in the family tree of many people's emotions. We accept contentment because we fear that fulfilment is beyond our reach. Socrates and Michelangelo went to their graves without contentment, but which of us would care to step up and measure our fulfilment against theirs – or, more importantly, against the fulfilment for which they planted the seeds in millions of others?

What is the antidote for Secretiveness? 'Come on, blurt it out, spill your guts, share it around, right now, right here!' But it seems to me that all this indiscriminate contemporary blurting and spilling and so-called sharing are more frequently signs of selfishness than of generosity. If I don't care enough about my audience, about my fellow human beings, to ripen and distil my thoughts, to let my feelings ferment until they are as potent as possible, then how much concern for the future, or for my friends, can I really be said to demonstrate?

Instantaneous, quasi-ecstatic vocalizing and yowling on any and every subject is the stuff of each day's 'latest news-breaking story' – and of the majority of political speeches nowadays – and of a great many best-selling works of would-be literature.

Honestly, I think I would rather wait until the brew is ready to be served, and I don't need to be given every detail of the brewing process along the way. I can wait. Art and life require quiet darkness, stillness – secrecy – just as much as, or more than, they require noise and spotlights and frantic public activity.

What is the antidote for Stubbornness? Collaboration. Compromise. In the classroom or the boardroom, in our houses, and in our House of Commons, we rely upon the communal spirit of teamwork, cooperation. We are suspicious and resentful of those who cling to their own insights too assiduously, who will not give in to the group. But what if those stubborn individual insights are profoundly correct?

Not dozens, but literally hundreds of times – in directing a play with student actors, or conducting a choir of young singers, or editing the script of some aspiring writer – I have insisted upon my superior knowledge of the art, or upon my greater experience of life in the real world, or upon my more sophisticated instincts – I have insisted that *they* make changes, that *they* do things *my* way – only to discover, days or years later, that their superior freshness in the art, their purer experience of life, their more primal instincts were right on the money. And then I thought, 'If only I had honoured their stubbornness – which is sometimes a truly God-given gift – if only I could have learned from their innocence, rather than making them bow to my experience!' I must always try to remember that teaching which does not include an equal measure of learning is tyranny, not to mention a waste of precious time.

And, yes, I think we all have to risk bold, outwardly visible stubbornness, rather than caving in to polite hypocrisy. A real tragedy of our hyperactive contemporary society is that we are often more interested in changing someone else's public or published point of view than we are in changing his or her mind. Too often I say to myself, 'I don't mind if the others, especially the young others, cling stubbornly to their instincts and their ideas – as long as they don't feel compelled to voice them.'

But the genuine stubbornness of old and young, artist and scientist – the true creative stubbornness in you or me – is such a beautiful thing, in spite of all the disruption and aggravation it may cause, when it is actively injected into life's recipe. It only turns to poison when it is sealed off in an airless pore of the personality or the community, and allowed to fester into resentment, or shame, or cowardice.

The two Emilys – Dickinson and Carr – were gloriously, consistently stubborn, *publicly* stubborn, as often as it was required of them. Their stubbornness protected and intensified their 'letters to the world,' and infused those lucky enough to converse or study with them with a similarly righteous (though not self-righteous) stubbornness, when facing down the forces of mediocrity, compromise, excessive spontaneity, unearned contentment, and phony tranquillity.

Carr, Dickinson, Michelangelo, Socrates –
These four artists, these giant creative spirits, about whom I have been thinking out loud, yesterday and this morning – and, indeed, all genuine artists and lovers of art, and, in fact, all truly creative people and enablers of creative people – collectively present a problem, we present problems, for society. That is a big part of the job we are here to do.

Young or old, urban or rural, influential or invisible –

I would like for us to let the student be restless.

I would like for us to let the teacher be dissatisfied.

I would like for us to let the artist be secretive.

I would like for us to let the scientist be stubborn. I would like for us to let the enabler, the facilitator of learning and teaching, to be as disruptive and aggravating as the specific occasion requires, to take whatever risks are necessary, in order to put human creativity on the front burner, whatever the subject being learned or taught. Arts-infused learning requires that we take the risks of restlessness, dissatisfaction, secretiveness, and stubbornness. *But how much greater, the risk of not taking these risks!* And what a beautifully unsettled, constantly evolving, perennially renewable society the taking of these risks can engender!

Arts-infused education will naturally create a certain amount of healthy disruption and aggravation in any society. It always has. It did in Socrates' and Michelangelo's times, in Emily Dickinson's and Emily Carr's times and places, and it will today, right here. Let us face those risks squarely, and go on facing them.

Surely we are prepared, even anxious, to risk some disruption and aggravation – to pay that relatively modest everyday price – so that Canadian society can partake in the banquet of inspiration, thought, discovery, challenge, emotion, insight, reflection, agony and ecstasy which is forever set before us when we dine in a home where art is the host.

There is not yet a perfect, or even an adequate, model for infusing arts in education. But I sense that there is a strong desire, brewing within every person in this room, for Canada, her provinces and territories, her cities and towns and villages, her schools and her homes, to lead the way; to establish such a model. The arts in particular – and human imagination, human creativity in general – add strange and beautiful and useful new pieces to the Canadian and the universal mosaic. Profound, enfranchised creativity also provides a safeguard, a steam valve, a steam vent, a productive outlet for deep, restless, selfish, and stubborn impulses of dissatisfaction and disassociation, that seize each of us from earliest childhood – impulses that can be turned by courageous nurturing into channels of delight and instruction – impulses that, without an outlet or channel or vent, become genuinely inflamed and anti-social, and that produce a lingering bitterness and smallness, rather than the abundant blessings of the beautiful, the true, and the new.

Truly, the arts can heal and make us whole, can give us sight, as long as we are willing to bear with their minor side-effects. If those slightly unpleasant side-effects – the frustration and the impatience that we all feel with the world at times – are not permitted their share of oxygen, however – are not allowed their share of time and attention – then they can become the very diseases of apathy and anger that art is there to cure, when properly and patiently administered.

A wonderful amount of work lies ahead of us: to climb this majestic and challenging height – arts-infused learning – to climb it, as the overworked and heterogeneous team that we are – this is daunting activity, even after we have agreed on why we want to do it. And I believe we do agree on the why.

It is still difficult to know how to work together on this intricate but supremely important task – how to orchestrate all spheres and agendas – how to integrate governments at all levels, with teachers and learners at all levels, with art of all kinds and at all levels.

And it is still difficult to know when. When should we cling to our restlessness, our dissatisfaction, our secretiveness and our stubbornness? When should we unleash them, in spite of the risks, in order to fuel the engines of change? And when, by contrast, should we insist on sufficient calm, within ourselves, on sufficient contentment and collaboration and cooperation, in order to forge genuine consensus, sharing in unified forward movement, upward movement?

There is one gauge, one simple measuring system, that has always worked for me. *Paradox*. Or what a good friend of mine calls 'cutting on the bias' – going against the grain of your own inclination, confronting your own discomfort – in fact, using your feelings of discomfort and disinclination as signs that you should be doing further investigation in the very area of your greatest discomfort.

In our overpopulated age of overly aggressive, underinformed over-achievers, I know that inertia can be such a rosy-tinged, such a seductive temptation. *Inertia* – the music of the word itself sounds so sweet to me, at times! But it is so dangerous – far beyond the dangers of restlessness, dissatisfaction, secretiveness, or stubbornness.

The trick that works for me is to combat the attraction of inertia with blatant paradox, with an irrational insistence, not just on confronting my demons, but on actively embracing them. I say to myself, 'This topic makes me restless. So I will not avoid it, I will major in it.' I say to myself, 'I am dissatisfied with all my efforts in this direction. I will not shift focus therefore. I will continue to batter away at this same wall, because any barrier this high and formidable must guard secrets that are worth knowing.' I say to myself, 'The people I am forced to work with seem both secretive and stubborn. So I will not demand to know all their secrets immediately, I will respect their stubbornness, I will wait for the moment of ripeness, while I go on listening. I will allow these difficult, disruptive and sometimes aggravating people sufficient space and time, and I will allow sufficient space and time within myself, for both patient discovery and sudden change.' I will embrace *paradox*.

I will 'cut on the bias' – as Socrates did, when he stood up to his accusers, even though he knew they were more powerful than he was; he also knew his message was the one that would endure. I will challenge myself with those very tasks that seem to me insurmountable – as Michelangelo did, when he insisted on sculpting verse, long after he was a recognized and revered master of stone. I will 'possess myself in patience' as my grandmother used to say – as Emily Dickinson did, waiting for each precious word of her next poem to drop like manna from heaven; she knew it would be worth the wait. I will embrace my demons – as Emily Carr did: the more parochial and stifling Victoria seemed to her, the louder she sang, the louder she painted, the louder she lived.

In my own endless struggle to infuse education with life-giving creativity, with life-changing art, whenever and wherever genuine deep collaboration and shared forward movement seem least likely, I will insist on discovering them, then and there. Whenever and wherever those with whom I must work seem most disruptive and aggravating – most prone to restlessness, dissatisfaction, secretiveness, and stubbornness – I will take this as a good sign – as a sign of kinship – as a sign that they are headed for the same difficult but indispensable destination to which I have pledged myself. I will trust that the 'why,' on which we have consensus, unites our seemingly disparate 'wheres' and 'whos' and 'whens,' not to mention the ever-puzzling 'hows.'

Well, my soliloquy is starting to sound a bit like the cast list for a Dr Seuss epic, with all those 'Whos' and 'Hows.' On that wry but sobering note, I should really bring my internal monologue to an end.

Of course, there are, and there should be, many alternative points of view – different from these I have been sifting through, last night and this morning – and all equally valid in their potential. There are divergent opinions on life and art and learning, less boisterous, less romantic, less effusive, and more systematic than my own.

Good. If my sharply inflected and disruptive thoughts provoke others to more solid, pragmatic, and systematized methods and maps – while leading to the same freedom of expression, the same inventiveness and respect for freshness that are precious to me – so much the better.

We do not need to agree on the kind of vehicle that is best for the journey. I go on believing that all of us, all of us, essentially agree on the final destination. That is the chief thing. If I dog-paddle to get there, while somebody else performs his or her apparently effortless 'butterfly' – good. If someone else works in brick and mortar, while I construct castles only possible in the imagination – excellent! If some of us are struggling to put it into poetry, while others strive to put it into law – we are all equally courageous, all equally necessary.

Restlessness.

Dissatisfaction.

Secretiveness.

Stubbornness.

These are not everything that you require to be an artist or a scientist, a creative person, or a person who facilitates creativity in others. You also need some of those less controversial, less 'unpleasant,' more highly regarded qualities:

Vision.

Faith.

Generosity.

Open-mindedness.

But those are the ones on which we most readily agree – so, quite naturally, those are not the ones I love to preach. I believe I am on the earth 'to comfort the afflicted,' but, just as importantly, 'to afflict the comfortable.' The world can always use 'a little more mustard with its meat,' as Virginia Woolf was fond of saying.

The chief thing is to infuse the search for truth and beauty, which we call 'Art,' into the world. And there is no better machinery for this infusion than the marvelously intricate and precise, and yet flexibly human, machinery of education.

Surely we all agree on these basics – from which we hope to build not just better institutions, but better human beings – the teachers, learners, artists, scientists, enablers, and facilitators of the future – who will be sufficiently tolerated and liberated, sufficiently tolerating and liberating – and, therefore, astonishingly creative enough to invent whole new kinds of institutions, the likes of which we have not yet dreamed.

I believe that we will accomplish this thing together. Am I ever disheartened? Of course. I am not completely out of touch with this difficult world. When I am a little down – or a lot down – I remind myself of what Emily Dickinson (in Linscott 1959) wrote to a dear friend, who was feeling spiritless and defeated:

> You speak of 'disillusion' ... Not what the stars have done, but what they are to do, is what detains the sky ... That is one of the few subjects on which I am an infidel ... To have been made alive is so chief a thing, all else inevitably adds. (1959, 324)

Bless you, and thank you so much.

III. CRITICAL VOICES

The Poetics: A Play

JASON SHERMAN

Big city newspaper. Office of the editor-in-chief. With him, the arts editor. The arts reporter, outside the office, addresses the audience.

Arts Reporter. There I was, stringer in the arts section of a Very Important Newspaper. We had a Dance Critic, a Book Critic, a Movie Critic, and a Drama Critic. And when these men were sick, I was called to fill in, to 'string.' It was a Tuesday morning in late fall. A handful of leaves threw themselves against my window. I looked up just in time to see the sun race behind a cloud, and this snowy owl sittin' on my windowsill, turning his head like they do. You don't see owls in the city real regular, and though I'm not a religious man, I took it for like an omen. I had a two p.m. deadline, 500 words on this experimental piece of – theatre. Phil, the drama critic, he'd asked me to cover for him. The piece had something to do with a pig. What did I know about it? A buncha skinny kids in black boots kicking this dead pig around the stage. I think it was real. The pig I mean. I didn't know what to say, what to write, so I was glad when the editor-in-chief called, asked me to take a meeting with him, him and the arts editor. I hit the save key and walked the length of the newsroom to the ed's office.
Editor-in-Chief. Come in.
Arts Editor. Come in.
Editor-in-Chief. Have a seat.
Arts Reporter. Sit down. We're all sitting down, see.
Editor-in-Chief. How's it going?
Arts Reporter. How's what going?
Editor-in-Chief. The work, dummy, how's the work going? What are you, getting cute?

Arts Reporter. Nah.

Editor-in-Chief. I think you are. I think you're gettin' cute with me.

Arts Reporter. Honest, I ain't being cute.

Editor-in-Chief. Then answer the question, Cutie.

Arts Editor. Yeah, answer the question.

Arts Reporter. What question?

Editor-in-Chief. There you go again. What is it you're doing, Cutie, the work, today, what is it that occupies your precious time today?

Arts Reporter. Oh. I'm doing a theatre piece.

Editor-in-Chief. Theatre piece.

Arts Reporter. That's right.

Editor-in-Chief. Like Les Miz like?

Arts Reporter. Nope.

Editor-in-Chief. What then?

Arts Reporter. It's this experimental theatre piece, see.

Editor-in-Chief. 'Experimental.'

Arts Reporter. That's right.

Arts Editor. They do this thing with a pig, ain't that it?

Editor-in-Chief. A pig.

Arts Reporter. That's right. They do this thing with a pig.

Arts Editor. The carcass of a pig.

Arts Reporter. They do this thing.

Editor-in-Chief. With the *carcass* of a —.

Arts Reporter. I don't pretend to get it myself. Phil asked me to do it.

Editor-in-Chief. Phil did.

Arts Reporter. That's right.

Arts Editor. That explains it. That explains a lot.

Editor-in-Chief. Here we are, supposed to be running a Very Important Newspaper, and we're running stories about the carcass of a pig which is implicated in an experiment. I find that amusing. Don't you find that amusing, Cutie?

Arts Reporter. Sure, sure, real amusing.

Editor-in-Chief. You like writing about such things, Cutie?

Arts Reporter. Sure I do. It's okay, you know what I mean?

Editor-in-Chief. Sure, Cutie, I know what you mean. All right. Let's get down to it. Make with the door, Cutie.

Arts Reporter. Sure.

Arts Editor. Shut it tight.

Editor-in-Chief. Now listen. We got some news to share with you.

Arts Editor. Some news about Phil.

Arts Reporter. Phil?
Editor-in-Chief. Phil's leaving.
Arts Reporter. Phil –?
Editor-in-Chief. Phil is leaving.
Arts Editor. Phil's going to Kweebek.
Editor-in-Chief. Been brushing up on his French, see.
Arts Reporter. Phil is leaving?
Arts Editor. Phil's burnt out.
Editor-in-Chief. Been here what – ten – ?
Arts Editor. Almost eleven.
Editor-in-Chief. Almost eleven, been reviewing theatre almost eleven years.
Arts Editor. Can you imagine?
Editor-in-Chief. I'd be tired, too.
Arts Editor. I'd be dead.
Arts Reporter. Phil's leaving?
Editor-in-Chief. He's going to cover Kweebek. All of it. Theatre, film – the arts.
Arts Editor. He's going to do all of it.
Editor-in-Chief. This leaves an opening.
Arts Editor. A vacancy.
Editor-in-Chief. A void, which we must fill, in the area of drama critic.
Arts Editor. It's an exciting time.
Editor-in-Chief. In the theatre.
Arts Editor. Things are looking up. In the theatre.
Editor-in-Chief. Big things are happening. You know who just called me, Cutie?
Arts Editor. You know who we just spoke to?
Editor-in-Chief. Johnny K just called me.
Arts Reporter. Johnny K?
Editor-in-Chief. That's right. Called me right here on my private line.
Arts Editor. Things are happening. Listen to this.
Editor-in-Chief. Johnny's bringing in a Big Show. Big, Big Show.
Arts Editor. The Biggest.
Editor-in-Chief. A Musical, yet.
Arts Editor. Lotsa singin' and dancin'.
Editor-in-Chief. Lotsa coloured folks.
Arts Editor. With this like boat on the stage.
Editor-in-Chief. But here's the best part. Go on, tell him.
Arts Editor. Two-page ads.
Editor-in-Chief. Four Colour.

Arts Editor. Front-page banner.

Editor-in-Chief. Inserts even.

Arts Editor. It's very exciting.

Editor-in-Chief. Then there's Shep.

Arts Editor. Shep called.

Arts Reporter. Big Shep?

Arts Editor. Big Shep *and* Little Shep.

Editor-in-Chief. It was like a conference call.

Arts Editor. Listen to this.

Editor-in-Chief. Big Shep's building a theatre.

Arts Editor. A new theater.

Editor-in-Chief. For a big new show.

Arts Editor. A musical.

Editor-in-Chief. With lots of parking.

Arts Editor. You know what this is?

Editor-in-Chief. Eh, Cutie, you know what this is?

Arts Reporter. This is Big.

Arts Editor. Very Big.

Editor-in-Chief. How big, Cutie?

Arts Reporter. Two-page ads?

Editor-in-Chief. That's right. Cutie's gettin' smart. Too bad for Phil he's leaving. Just when things are looking up.

Arts Editor. Bad for Phil.

Editor-in-Chief. Good for you.

Arts Editor. If you want it.

Editor-in-Chief. If you want to be part of it.

Arts Editor. The explosion.

Editor-in-Chief. The beginning of something Big.

Arts Editor. Real theatre.

Editor-in-Chief. World-class theatre. No more self-indulgent crap in one-hundred-seat closets, with no cushions on the lousy seats and no back rests, and half the time you don't know what the hell you're listening to, and the other half the time you know exactly what you're listening to, and it makes ya sick, cause it's all whining and therapy, all the crummy little artists spouting off bout things they don't know nothing about, see?

Arts Editor. Come on, come on, we're not here to –

Editor-in-Chief. Burns me up is all.

Arts Editor. We don't want to influence the way you think.

Editor-in-Chief. Can't a guy get something off his chest? You know what I mean, don't you, Cutie? Theatre for the people. Lots of people.

Arts Editor. You could be part of it. You could be at the forefront. Helping to light the explosion.

Editor-in-Chief. Your reviews will be quoted.

Arts Editor. Right across the top of them two-page ads.

Editor-in-Chief. Your words.

Arts Editor. Helping to make things Big.

Editor-in-Chief. Your words.

Arts Editor. If you want it.

Editor-in-Chief. No more things with pigs.

Arts Editor. Think about it.

Editor-in-Chief. Don't give us an answer.

Arts Editor. Think it through.

Arts Reporter. ... Boy ...

Arts Editor. So you're interested?

Arts Reporter. ... Sure ...

Arts Editor. It's just that you hesitated is all.

Arts Reporter. Well ... I was thinking about Phil.

Editor-in-Chief. To hell with Phil. Forget about it, he's nowhere, get me? You remember what he said last time Johnny K tried to bring in a Big Show? Said he didn't like it, got all uppity, all lippy, said the show was lousy, said it wasn't good art. Johnny K got all mad, started pullin' out ads. It was a no good time for the buncha us, all on account of that lousy Phil with his lousy ideas bout art. Well let me tell you something, that lousy no-good show is still going, and Phil is packing a laptop for Kweebek.

Arts Editor. And he ain't coming back.

Editor-in-Chief. Ain't never coming back.

Arts Editor. Johnny K'll make sure of that.

Arts Reporter. What's that s'posed to mean?

Arts Editor. Never mind, you.

Arts Reporter. I mean that stuff about Johnny K makin' sure of ...

Arts Editor. Shut your lip why don't ya? You want the job or doncha?

Arts Reporter. Sure I do, sure.

Arts Editor. All right then, shut your trap before you fall right through it.

Editor-in-Chief. The point is, we need someone to step in.

Arts Editor. Someone what wants it.

Editor-in-Chief. Do you like it? Theatre, I mean.

Arts Reporter. It's okay, I guess. I mean, yeah, yeah, I like it fine.

Arts Editor. This, for example, musical. You like it?

Arts Reporter. The Shep thing?

Arts Editor. For example.

Arts Reporter. Sure. With the parking, you mean?

Editor-in-Chief. That's it.

Arts Reporter. Yeah!

Arts Editor. Good.

Editor-in-Chief. What about the other one?

Arts Reporter. Uh ...

Arts Editor. With the coloured folks singin' and dancin'.

Arts Reporter. Right. Sure. I like that old-time stuff.

Editor-in-Chief. Exactly. Only it never goes outta fashion, see, cause its rich with like plots, and characters.

Arts Editor. Tell us something.

Editor-in-Chief. We need to know something.

Arts Editor. What do you like?

Editor-in-Chief. In theatre.

Arts Editor. In general.

Editor-in-Chief. In theatre.

Arts Editor. What kind of theatre do you like?

Arts Reporter. You mean ...

Editor-in-Chief. What grabs you?

Arts Reporter. Well.

Arts Editor. Take your time.

Editor-in-Chief. Off the top of your head.

Arts Editor. First thing pops into your mind.

Arts Reporter. Gee. I like a good story. Like that you mean?

Arts Editor. Exactly.

Arts Reporter. I like a good story with ... a good beginning, a good middle and ... uh ... a good ending point.

Editor-in-Chief. Yes.

Arts Reporter. And I like good direction.

Arts Editor. Good direction?

Arts Reporter. Yeah.

Editor-in-Chief. What does a director do, you figure?

Arts Reporter. What does he do? Well. I guess he ... he tells a guy where to stand, is he sayin' the words right, that kinda thing. If he's good, he makes a play what flows ... he makes it flow, see, and that's what I like, flowing direction.

Editor-in-Chief. Flowing direction, okay.

Arts Reporter. And strong acting. That's *very* important. The acting has to be strong. And there has to be plum roles. And, and, and oh! I like a hoot.

Editor-in-Chief. A 'hoot.'

Arts Reporter. Yeah I like a play that's a hoot. You know – lots of laughs.

Editor-in-Chief. 'Lots of laughs.'

Arts Reporter. Lots of laughs.

Editor-in-Chief. Good.

Arts Editor. And sets?

Arts Reporter. Sets?

Arts Editor. And costumes. Do you like sets and costumes?

Arts Reporter. Oh yeah. Didn't I mention –?

Editor-in-Chief. No.

Arts Editor. No, you didn't.

Editor-in-Chief. You left that bit out.

Arts Editor. Ignoramus.

Editor-in-Chief. Fucking idiot.

Arts Editor. What do you know about theatre?

Editor-in-Chief. Dick.

Arts Editor. Nothing.

Editor-in-Chief. You're stupid.

Arts Editor. You've got no *business.*

Editor-in-Chief. No *business.*

Arts Editor. You're a joke.

Editor-in-Chief. A sham.

Arts Reporter. I ... I ...

Arts Editor. Come on.

Editor-in-Chief. Give it *back.* You're gonna get it.

Arts Editor. You're gonna be hurt.

Editor-in-Chief. They're gonna tear you apart.

Arts Editor. Fucking artists.

Editor-in-Chief. They'll hate you. Every time you write a review, it won't be good enough. They always want more. You'll say it's good, they'll say what about great? You'll say it's great, they'll say what about brilliant? You give em two stars; they say what about three? Give em three, they want ... See what I'm getting at? Then there's the shows you won't like, and there's gonna be a lot of those, get me, and you'll say so, and they'll call you names, they'll make fun of you, maybe they'll put on plays about you for some two-bit theatre company who wants to produce art, it don't matter, the point is they'll come after you.

Arts Editor. We think you owe them a living. They're all a buncha welfare bums, anyway. They ain't artists, they don't even get paid most the time they're workin', and when they do, it ain't hardly enough to pay the rent, let alone the drugs and booze what keeps them goin'. So they're gonna let you have it, brother. So come on. Fight back.

Editor-in-Chief. Faggot.

Arts Editor. Turd burglar.

Editor-in-Chief. Mama's boy.

Arts Editor. Scaredy-cat.

Arts Reporter. Am not! Am not! Am not! Shut up! I like good sets and costumes. Big, Big sets that let the actors move around a lot and costumes that, that, go with the set like.

Editor-in-Chief. Good.

Arts Editor. Good.

Editor-in-Chief. Very good.

Arts Editor. Okay.

Editor-in-Chief. I like it.

Arts Editor. That's good.

Arts Reporter. That's good?

Arts Editor. Very good.

Editor-in-Chief. Okay.

Arts Editor. Okay.

Arts Reporter. Okay?

Editor-in-Chief. Now: what doncha like?

Arts Reporter. What don't I like?

Editor-in-Chief. Exactly. What in a play which when you see it causes you not to like it?

Arts Reporter. Well ... okay here's a biggee ... I don't like *talky* plays ...

Editor-in-Chief. Talky.

Arts Reporter. You know, lotsa words.

Arts Editor. I understand exactly.

Arts Reporter. I especially don't like it when the words are like supposed to be real. Like when they do them plays which when people speak it's supposed to be like real speech which who cares which it is or not? Like they do these plays where people uh ... they ... like they ... lose their train of ... uh ... thought ... or –

Arts Editor. Uh huh.

Editor-in-Chief. We under—

Arts Reporter. Hold on –

Arts Editor. No, no, we understand exac—

Arts Reporter. Like when they –

Editor-in-Chief. We said we heard you, so why doncha –

Arts Reporter. Like when they keep gettin' interrupted. I hate that. Or when a character takes a long drag off a cigarette, I hate that, too.

Arts Editor. Good.

Editor-in-Chief. Well, that pretty much covers it.

Arts Editor. That's good. A beginning, middle, and ending point, flowing direction, plum roles, a hoot, sets and costumes, no smoking, and no funny talking.

Editor-in-Chief. What else do you need?

Arts Editor. That's all you need.

Editor-in-Chief. Not like Phil.

Arts Editor. No.

Editor-in-Chief. Phil was so ...

Arts Editor. So ... What was Phil?

Arts Reporter. ... Critical?

Arts Editor. So critical.

Editor-in-Chief. *Very* critical.

Arts Editor. Very unfair. *His standards* ...

Editor-in-Chief. Very high.

Arts Reporter. He was so unfair.

Editor-in-Chief. Didn't like the chandelier thing.

Arts Editor. You're not going to be unfair, are you?

Editor-in-Chief. Uh uh.

Arts Editor. To the musicals?

Arts Reporter. Not me, boy.

Arts Editor. And the rest? The self-indulgent, theatre-as-therapy crap? What about that?

Arts Reporter. ... Well ... Gee ...

Arts Editor. Don't worry about it.

Editor-in-Chief. Trick question. We're cutting back.

Arts Editor. Cutting way back.

Editor-in-Chief. Nobody goes to these crummy little shows in crummy hundred-seat church basements, and even if they do, who cares, it's only a hundred people a night, which multiplied by a typical run of maybe sixteen performances is, what, not even two thousand individuals who would be seeing this particular piece of therapy crap, which is not even what you would find in Big Shep's new theatre on any given weekend evening.

Arts Editor. See what we're getting at?

Editor-in-Chief. Waste of space.

Arts Editor. Hardly worth the effort.

Editor-in-Chief. Fuck em. We'll give em a paragraph once in a while, keep the dogs at bay.

Arts Editor. Rename the section.

Editor-in-Chief. Arts for the People. Television, film, a couple books now and again, and, of course, big four-star reviews for the big shows.

Arts Reporter. Eh?

Editor-in-Chief. Which part didn't you hear, Cutie?

Arts Reporter. About the four stars ... you mean all the musicals get four stars no matter what?

Editor-in-Chief. Listen, Cutie ... you know they got a very exciting arts scene in the Yukon ... you know about this? Oh yeah, it's big ... We're lookin' to send someone to be our reporter in the Yukon, cover all of it, theatre, movies, the whole thing.

Arts Reporter. I could do four-star reviews.

Editor-in-Chief. And every once in a while, you can go see one of these pukey little nothing shows, say some nice things, or not so nice things, I won't lose sleep neither way, and we'll run em when we can. Okay?

Arts Editor. Don't you worry about it.

Editor-in-Chief. Just think Big.

Arts Editor. Think Big.

Editor-in-Chief. Are you thinking?

Arts Reporter. Oh yes.

Arts Editor. Good.

Editor-in-Chief. Good.

Arts Editor. Okay.

Editor-in-Chief. Okay, Cutie. Get out.

Editor-in-Chief. Go on.

Arts Editor. Back to work. Go finish the pig story.

Arts Reporter. Thank you. Yeah, I could get to like it. Thank you.

He addresses the audience.

Well. That was it. My big break. Sure, I felt bad for Phil. He deserved a better ending point. Oh well. I finished the pig story. Got a real good hook into it. I wrote, 'What do pigs really want? This is going to sound strange. I say, a piece of absurdist theatre in the rich vein of Louis Pirandello, which had as its main attraction a pig. But hold on. It was a hoot. The direction flowed, and the costumes went really good with the set. Also, there was no funny talkin'. I would highly recommend this

evening of experimental theatre to anyone what likes experimental art.'
I don't know. I felt inspired. I wrote and wrote and wrote, and as my
hands glided over the keyboard, the wind picked up outside, and more
leaves hurled themselves at my window, and that snowy owl what I saw
before, sittin' there, turnin' his head, like he had a kink what he couldn't
work out. The sun played hide-and-go-seek, so the office was like lighting
up, and getting dark, lighting up, and getting dark, and I thought,
'That's exactly what life is like, a little light, and a little dark.' And right
now, I'm standing in the light. The day my first theatre review went in, I
saw my name there, my by-line, and right underneath it, the words:
Drama Critic. My name. Drama Critic. What a hoot. What an absolute
hoot.

Confessions of a Theatre Addict

LYNN SLOTKIN

My mother took my sister and me to the theatre one Saturday afternoon in November to see *Oliver*, which was playing the O'Keefe Centre, before it went to New York. It was 1962 and I was fourteen. It was cold and we wore galoshes, even though it wasn't snowing. And we were late. We came in about ten minutes into the first song, 'Food Glorious Food,' and we clumped down the long aisle in the dark to our seats in GG (7th row) on the aisle. I wasn't embarrassed about being late or disturbing anybody; I just remember walking down the aisle, mouth agape at that stage full of people, colour, action, movement, and music. I'd never seen anything like it in my life.

Willoughby Goddard, who played Mr Bumble and was singing as we came down the aisle, glared at us as we made our way to our seats. (Needless to say, since then, if I'm not at the theatre at least half an hour early, I start to sweat.) I watched the whole show mesmerized, and when Sean Kenny's set revolved to show the waterfront, I was stunned; when Nancy was beaten and killed, I was heartsick; when Fagan 'reviewed the situation' of his schemes and plans, I was delighted. I loved every minute of it.

Georgia Brown was cast as Nancy, and there was much publicity about this English woman. (She wasn't playing Nancy at my matinee. She was sick and her understudy went on. I remember being a bit put out at this, and thought that for this day, for my first show, the original lady playing Nancy should be there!) I didn't begrudge Rae Allen, who did play Nancy, the opportunity, but still, I bought the album of *Oliver*, and Georgia had a voice full of smoke and heartache. Fabulous. My whole life exploded open that day. But when we returned home, all I can remember is being horribly depressed because the event was over. I sat in the den with the lights off for at least an hour, feeling wretched.

Yet every Saturday afternoon, when there was a new play at either the O'Keefe Centre or the Royal Alexandra Theatre, I was on the bus and subway from the suburbs, heading downtown to the theatre.

One particular Saturday, I had a terrible dilemma: Do I go to the Royal Alexandra to see *Private Lives* with Paxton Whitehead or do I go to the O'Keefe Centre to see *The School for Wives* with Brian Bedford? Both were playing for only a week. I chose the O'Keefe, but always wondered what *Private Lives* would have been like. I went alone because school friends weren't interested; but I didn't mind, because to wait until someone came with me might have meant that I would miss seeing a show, and I couldn't bear that thought.

After I had learned how to drive, I discovered that I could go to the theatre more than once a week and not just for Saturday matinees. After that there was no stopping me. I read plays. I bought *Variety* every week to find out what was new in New York. When I got accepted to York University, I had to decide: should I be practical and study psychology or should I give into my passion, and study theatre? I followed my passion, and the euphoria when I made the decision was indescribable.

I had no talent for acting – too terrifying. I couldn't draw: designing was out. I thought the history, theory, and criticism part of theatre might be for me. One of my professors was Mavor Moore, who taught Canadian Theatre. I thought I had died and gone to theatre heaven having him as a teacher. What he hadn't done in Canadian theatre, his mother, Dora Mavor Moore, had. While Canadian theatre hadn't played a big part in my life up to then, I at least knew the name 'Mavor Moore.'

But it was Tennessee Williams who made me think I might have a future in theatre criticism. It was in a first-year theatre class, and the assignment was to write a character analysis of Amanda in *The Glass Menagerie*, along with a description of the set. I began writing and I was transported. My cheeks burned as the information poured out of me; I felt light-headed; I couldn't write fast enough. I knew this woman and her apartment; I knew what she looked like, what she wore, how she thought, how she ate or didn't, how she hounded her son. All the hints were in the text. I had found them. Tennessee Williams guided me to them.

I wrote reviews for the York University newspaper, *Excalibur.* I took a course in theatre criticism with Don Rubin during my last year. My first professional review was published in the *Canadian Jewish News* in 1972, a year before I graduated.

I also went to Stratford (Ontario) for the first time in 1972. Again, my mother took me. Another life-changing event. The play was *King Lear* with William Hutt. I can still see him, surrounded by his three daughters, who wore tall, white cone-shaped hats. He was majestic and unforgettable.

As well, I began going to local productions while in university. I can remember sitting in my favourite seat in the old Toronto Workshop Productions theatre watching George Luscombe's angry, inventive, political presentations. There were raw productions at Toronto Free Theatre, and earnest productions at Toronto Arts Productions. I learned about Michel Tremblay at Tarragon Theatre.

While in university, I began an independent project of my own: I decided to interview actors and actresses, passing through Toronto playing at the Royal Alexandra and the O'Keefe Centre, about their opinions of critics and criticism. I thought it odd that the critic tells the actor what he/she feels about the work, without the actor having a chance to reply in kind. I met fantastic people that way – Barbara Rush, Jane Alexander, Julie Harris, Kim Hunter, Hume Cronyn, Jessica Tandy, Sada Thompson, Angela Lansbury, and many more. Oddly enough, I interviewed few Canadian actors at the time. Did I get an earful about critics and their work from these actors, and an education too. I kept in touch with many of them long after they left town. I would go to New York to see their work when they played on or off Broadway.

Over the years, many of them became my friends and still are. Jane Alexander was one. She was playing Gertrude to Sam Waterston's *Hamlet* at Lincoln Center. I saw it over Christmas in 1975. When I saw Jane, I told her I was going to London shortly to see Albert Finney in *Hamlet*. She said, 'Let me know what you think.'

When a mentor who has shown faith in you asks you to let her know what you think, you let her know. I handwrote Jane a letter on one and a half sheets of 5" × 8" paper concerning that one play, about what the set looked like, how I didn't think Finney was up to the job, and about how many of the others were. Jane wrote back, commenting that my letter was marvellously detailed. That was the beginning of my theatre letters.

The next year I went to London again and wrote to Jane about what I had seen. This time there were more plays and shorter descriptions as I recall. It was still handwritten, but the letter was growing.

In the beginning, I would send the theatre letter, usually from London, to other actor friends as well. Jane always received the first one; I just photocopied hers and sent them to others. Over the years the 'London Letters,' as they were known, were typed on a manual, then on an electric typewriter, then on a computer. As my London trips included more plays, the letters became longer, overwhelming both me as the writer and those who read them. If I went to London for two weeks, I would consider a week's worth of plays to be a section, and it got to be that a section could be thirty pages long and describe twelve plays! A section might come out six months after I had actually seen the play. The silliest situation was that I might finish the London Letter for the previous year's trip just as I was getting ready to go to London again the following summer. Soon there were New York letters as well.

As friends passed the letters around, more people wanted to be put on the list to receive them, so I just sent out more. Douglas Beattie, director/producer extraordinaire (he produces the *Wingfield* series of plays, while his brother Rod plays all the parts in them), asked to receive the letters and was the first person to give me an 'honorarium' for the postage and printing. I was so overwhelmed with the list of people who were getting the letter (all for free to this point) that I had to say that no one new could be added to my list until someone on the list died, and they were all healthy at that point. When Pat Quigley, education manager at the Stratford Festival, heard about the London Letter (Martha Henry told her), the information on plays inside it, and how useful it would be to her, along with my statement 'No more people on the list,' Pat said, 'I'll pay.' She was my first real customer.

Cherry Jones passed part of a letter I had written to her, about a play she had been asked to be in, to the project's producer, Alexander Cohen, the dean of New York producers. I grew up watching plays he had produced when they toured to Toronto. He loved my analysis of the play, but in the end Cherry didn't act in it. He wanted to meet me when I was in New York next, and so we arranged a meeting. He asked about the letter, then took a look at it, was impressed, and suggested that I write a smaller version (instead of an infrequent thirty-page opus about a lot of plays), one that would come out monthly, dealing with five or six plays. I took his advice. When the Dean of Producers gives you advice, you take it. I changed the name to *The Slotkin Letter*, and Alexander Cohen became a paying subscriber to the new format. It has since mushroomed: actors, directors, designers, theatre-goers, and artistic directors now subscribe.

While I have always earned my living, after graduation, from administrative jobs, usually in education institutions, I continued to write reviews that were published only sporadically, and usually by papers that soon went out of business. Fortunately, this has changed. And while it was lovely to see my reviews in print, I felt more pleasure writing reviews in my own newsletters. I had as much space as I needed, and no one edited me.

Small reviews gave way to longer articles in glossier publications. *Performance Magazine*, the theatre magazine for the Royal Alexandra and the Princess of Wales theatres, published several of my articles. A year and a half ago, John Karastamatis, the director of communications for Mirvish Productions, did an interview with me about my *Slotkin Letter*. A producer from CBC radio saw that interview, and wanted me to come on the show she was producing (*Fresh Air*), to talk about my theatre passion and *The Slotkin Letter*. The host asked if I had ever wanted to be a theatre critic, and of course I said yes. The producer of *Fresh Air* recommended me to the producer for *Here and Now*, and Richard Ouzounian also recommended me to replace him. I auditioned and got the job. My first broadcast review was July 27, 2000. Since then, I have been interviewed in *Brill's Content* about *The Slotkin Letter*, which led to another radio interview, this time on the American NPR, plus an interview in the *National Post*. My head has been swimming since this all began two and a half years ago.

I have been asked how Canadian theatre has affected me on this journey as a theatre addict. An interesting question. If I were younger I might have said, without thinking, that in the beginning it hadn't had the same profound effect that going to other theatre events has had. I grew up on those touring American and British plays that passed through Toronto, or the ones I went to see in New York and London. I thought those plays were vibrant, angry, and full-bodied with larger-than-life characters. I thought our plays paled next to those. The whole notion of 'kitchen sink' drama comes to mind: I think I once wrote that Canadian plays usually took place in the kitchen, by the sink, where character after character whined about his or her lot in life.

Fortunately a wonderful thing happened that made me change my mind. I grew up and opened my closed mind. We have only been producing our own plays and writing our own stories in earnest for about forty years. We are so young next to those countries with long, established theatre histories – 400 years at least for England, 100 for the United States.

What we do have are writers who care for their fellows, especially the marginalized. If there is a person more calm or serene than Judith Thompson in her personal life, writing plays full of concern for her characters on 'the outside' of society, I haven't come across her. For me, Ms Thompson tends to load her plays with all the personal concerns of society, instead of cutting them down and focusing on a few. But, by God, there is a beating heart there and a champion. She makes the audience squirm. I like that. George F. Walker's plays also deal with the beaten down, the forgotten, the angry, but he writes about them with a vibrant, bellowing humour. Jason Sherman is not afraid of the huge subject. His mind is quick, as is his wit. He writes about Jewish subjects, characters who lack patience and kindness, people who look like they have it all, and don't.

Something I didn't have to grow up to realize is that our actors are second to none, *period*. To live in a country that affords me the opportunity of seeing Martha Henry, William Hutt, Martha Burns, Nancy Palk, David Storch, Jim Mezon, Susan Coyne, and Kristen Thomson (to name a few) act as often as I have and can is to have gold in my life. I was smitten with the theatre because I saw a touring show on its way to Broadway. I continued the love affair in large part because of the artists here in my country.

On June 6, 1992 Georgia Brown died, and that got me to thinking back to that first time, in 1962, when she wasn't there. I finally met her fifteen years after *Oliver* came to town. 'Where were you?' I asked. 'It was my first show ever. You should have been there.' It turned out she was sick that day – it happened so rarely that she could remember. But we had a laugh over it.

Theatre has taught me almost everything about life – except how to make my mother's chocolate cake, and she taught me that. Theatre has taught me about art, music, dance, performance, acting, character building, how far we've come as people, how far we have to go, how good we are, how evil we can become, how generous and open hearted we are and can be, how hard a heart becomes when love and kindness are absent from life.

I've thought a lot about that first play since I began this brief memoir, and about my theatre memories, especially since my mother was losing hers to Alzheimer's disease (she died in 1996). I think a great deal about her. My whole world opened up because of her, and over the last eighteen years of her life, while her whole world was shutting down, I couldn't do anything for her. Yet she took me to the theatre one day, and that has made all the difference in my life.

Inside Out: Notes on Theatre in a Tenderized, Tranquillized, 'Mediatized' Society

JOHN GILBERT

Theatre and drama should be unsettling, should make us 'un-easy' in the positive sense of the word, as should education. They should encourage dialectic and debate and not erase them through cosmetic manipulation. Too often theatre does the opposite, pandering to so-called 'certainties' and embedding unchallenged roles, boundaries, and thinking. In the classroom, drama and theatre offer space for the exploration of diversity. We have entered the Age of Mendacity where control systems, whether outright propaganda or misleading advertising and publicity, undermine the initiative to choose. Young people are especially vulnerable to such manipulative mechanisms. Theatre and drama risk becoming handmaidens to this development. Used properly, used educatively, drama/theatre creates a crucial space for scrutiny of the accepted and taken-for-granted.

The notes that follow have been prompted by recent experiences of my own, both as spectator and as performer. I think that they define the invasion of the factitious and mendacious in our society, especially as it concerns theatre and drama, and reaffirm the need for drama in education to pry open incarcerated thought and make available a means of breaking the silence on issues that remain trapped in taboo and stereotype.

'Look at me!' I am what the camera sees.

I pass City TV on Queen Street West in Toronto. A video cameraman attracts a crowd of young people jostling to be 'on camera.' Our society has become pervasively 'mediatized.' In other words, the visual media function as a mirror and determinant of representation. Under media influence, young people in particular seem to have acquired a new kind of 'self-consciousness' that is passed through the omnipresent filter of the image – specifically, the camera image. The myth of Narcissus has assumed a new configuration: fascination-control, domination, imprisonment by the 'look' – has become a device of tranquillization. French philosopher, J.-P. Sartre, who wrote of being captured by 'le regard de l'autre' – the look of the Other – could not have anticipated the extension his idea would have in our electronic, image-saturated age or the loss of freedom it entails. The process of self-creation, which is an integral part of acting (and action), is threatened in film and television and, more pertinently, in the theatre by the occult presence of the camera: self-creation and subject are reduced to subjection. 'I am a camera' becomes, more accurately, 'I am what the camera sees.' In a film I worked on recently, a young actress of some reputation made it clear that she did not want other actors in the scene to be behind the camera for 'eye-line,' preferring to be alone in her one-on-one relationship with the camera. No interaction but self-reflection and self-fixation, subjection.

Composed at All Times

Audition for a TV movie. In the waiting lounge with several young actresses, dressed more or less the same, 'composing' themselves in front of mirrors, obviously reaching for more or less the same idea of the character. They are, I discover, fifteen or sixteen years old but looking nineteen, and trying to rediscover what it was to be fifteen or sixteen, as the part demanded. 'Composing' here had taken on not only the added meaning of achieving some sort of relaxation and concentration before their ordeal, but also the sense that they were composing surrogate selves based on a pre-existing persona, acknowledging a reference point in some film, TV-series, or media personality. They find refuge and achieve tranquillity in a second-hand self thereby 'losing' themselves, literally, in the part. I have heard it said that an audition and the selection of an actor for a given part takes place between the door and the audition-room chair. In other words, the actor has little control over the process of selection, but merely composes himself/herself to be frozen by the look of the auditioners upon entry into the room. No action is involved, only acquiescence. This is more a North American phenomenon, however; in Europe, the interview still prevails as an accepted way of making the selection – but for how long?

'All the World's a ... Camera'

Unfortunately, the camera has invaded the stage. From the moment the actor steps into the dressing-room he or she is looked at. And the resultant self-consciousness is apparent on stage, when preconceived personae usurp the character-building process; whence, no doubt, David Mamet's injunction in *True and False* to allow the text to do the job of characterization, instead of importing a 'ready-made.' It is not surprising that video cameras have encroached upon the inner space of the stage, sometimes to useful effect, in the instances when that inner space is not externalized by the 'camera.' More often than not, however, imagery is appropriated from the inner recesses of the imagination of the audience and externalized on stage. The imagination is tranquillized by the literal: in a recent production of *King Lear* in the United States, the storm scene featured 'real' rain, provided, no doubt, at great plumbing expense. This 'special effect' mentality robs the play of its metaphors. The storm within, Lear's struggle with his demons, becomes literalized. The weakness of special effects is that they rob the individual audience member of the imaginative challenge of finding his or her personal representations of the inner storm, just as representations of Martians, say, deny us our own fanciful constructions. In Harold Pinter's play *One for the Road*, the real torturer never tortures anybody, with the result that we are all forced to search for the 'torturer' in ourselves in order to 'see' the torture. We have to enter areas of our experience, which are prohibited or suppressed. Theatre, because it invites us to explore what is not necessarily seen or represented, should, at its best, oblige us, invite us to acts of creation and self-confrontation. Film and television in our time, more often than not, allow us no such space, tell us everything, give us everything; and theatre it seems is following in the wake of these other, more seductive media. As a result, theatre companies are noticeably tailoring their programs along film and television lines. Successful filmed versions of the classics seem to determine repertoire. The appearance of another Shakespeare film – such as *Titus, Romeo and Juliet, Richard III*, or *Hamlet* – thrusts these plays to the fore in the seasons of the big theatres. And marquee names adorn the posters. Theatre's unique ability to surprise and disturb sinks beneath a wash of familiarity and idolatry. Packaging and marketing strategies guarantee that there will be no surprises.

Bio-theatre

Examining the program on a recent visit to the theatre made me think that the actors' 'bios' seemed to be getting longer these days. The 'bio' has become a means of self-promotion and a way of assuring the audience that they are getting their money's worth, that these actors are not just any old actors but actors who have won awards, have long and distinguished careers, appeared in such and such a film, TV series, etc. – none of which, of course, guarantees anything. But one of the odder features of the 'bio' is the personal touch encouraged by some theatre managements – mention of the favourite cat – what I would call the *People* magazine 'take.' This approach serves, I suppose, to show the audience that the actors are like them, but it also marks the beginning of the 'actor as persona,' not to say 'personality.' So often, the intrusion of an actor's carefully cultivated persona directs our attention to the individual 'performance,' as opposed to the collective performance, which more aptly serves the play. If we need any evidence of this drive towards individual 'performance,' consider this: the curious phenomenon of an actor including in his or her 'bio' a dedication of their 'performance,' as if it were a solo turn, to somebody: a loved one, mentor, mum or dad, friend, etc.

Big Mac-Beth

We are witnessing the appearance of a kind of fast-food theatre. Theatre is now 'franchised' out. Productions of the *Lion King, Beauty and the Beast,* or *The Phantom of the Opera* are spread out across the globe, all remarkably the same whether staged in London or New York or Toronto. Through a system of 'swings' actors can be replaced at a moment's notice. They are literally slotted in to guarantee a consistency in the product, for that is what this kind of theatre is: product. Understandably, then, lighting, sets, costumes, and music assume unparalleled importance. Budgets reflect this attention to the 'presentation' of the spectacle. Lavish musicals have set the precedent that smaller theatres attempt to imitate at their peril. Technical runs happen earlier and earlier in the process because the show has to be 'dressed' before the fundamentals are in place. More seriously perhaps, the dressing frequently compensates for the blandness of the dish. Dress it with relish and the tenderized, insipid 'meat' at the heart of the show will be digested the more

readily. Among the priorities governing production, along with imperatives such as money (bums in seats), are the following: keep them awake;
make them laugh at all costs; fill in the silences – dead air can lead to
thought; and assure their comfort. The latter can be achieved by larger,
more comfortable seats. Accessibility, whether in physical or in textual
terms, must be guaranteed. Disclaimers and warnings accompany the
product, whether regarding smoking on stage, gunshots, nudity, or pro-
fanity. Keep them tranquillized. Casting also plays an important role in
the packaging, and here television seems to be a deciding influence.
Symmetrical youth is prized, and age, except as concocted with make-up,
must not be present in its natural form: the white hair must be perfect. A
more questionable example of packaging comes in the form of trim-
ming and shaping the play, especially great classics, to fit a particular
agenda. In a production of *Richard III*, the excision of crucial conflicts
that inform the political landscape of the play – in order to turn it into a
soft parable of the redemption of a little boy lost – strikes me as unac-
ceptable licence, especially when the 'corrected' version is accompanied
by wall-to-wall generic Gregorian chant and kitsch intimations of 'decadence' for 'atmosphere.' When treated in this manner, these plays can
be made to serve any master, as with the ending of Julie Taymor's film
Titus.

Shouting ... Not to Be Heard

The theatre is caught in a spiralling push towards greater lavishness.
Audiences, under the spell of the mega-musicals, have come to expect
greater and greater excess in staging, 'getting their money's worth'
simply because there is 'more' – the three-pound lobster instead of the
small one. The more they marvel at the lavishness of sets and costumes,
the less they are required to think. Theatrical hyperbole, excess in all
aspects of production, is like shouting when a whisper would be more
effective. Applauding the set, costumes, and lighting has become a
common occurrence in the theatre, like the applause that greets the
'great actor' or the movie star appearing on stage – and this before the
performance has actually begun and any real judgment can have been
formulated. Yet all this shouting covers the silences, the 'subtexts,' and
makes literal the metaphors. The textual 'score' is frequently obscured
by another score. As in the movies, music underscores the action, manipulating the emotions of the audience, taking the place of what is
generated by the play, narrowing the choices of the spectator. 'Atmos-

phere' – for this is what it is – is a term often used in movies, as is 'background' – smoke and extras – designed to colour the viewers' response and manipulate their feelings. Overstatement prohibits under-statement, and prevents us from ' hearing': voices, irony, innuendo, and so forth. What is happening on stage is turned 'inside out,' giving a new meaning to spectacle as something to be looked at but not thought about. Advertising accomplishes much the same thing. But this kind of theatre serves its patrons in a way that is more and more acceptable as diversion, a snack to pacify the grumblings of reality: aperitif or digestif theatre.

Before or After?

In a group interview, members of the Chilean theatre company La Troppa said that in Chile 'theatre has become an amusing aperitif before dinner. It generates no thought. Now that all rituals are dead, we [as a troupe] attempt to rediscover profound emotion.' In our country, where we eat earlier, it is often a digestif. One often gets the sense that theatre is for either 'before or after,' it is seldom the main course. It either whets one's appetite or aids one's digestion. But what about theatre as the 'main course'? Even in those instances when it is the main course, the main event, it is all too often made more 'palatable' by decoration, modernization, or the star system. For example, plays that are classics are often made to exploit nostalgia for the past and are turned into costume drama. Various types of updating – whether in the form of modern dress, gratuitously used, or of language modernized to remove the difficult words – simply pander to the audience's fear of estrangement and silence the more complex voice of the text. The star system too can induce silence: for example, what happened to David Hare's *The Blue Room* when Nicole Kidman starred in it? Through no fault of Kidman's, it is quite likely that her presence made the audience less receptive to the play and more open to star-struck fascination. It is stating the obvious to say that theatre has been invaded by the star system. Stars sell and money rules. It is an unfortunate circumstance that stars distract us from the play while making it more palatable, more appetizing. Lest this sound like a jeremiad on the part of one who wants things to stay the same, refusing to acknowledge that the theatre must come to terms with contemporary forms of conveying messages, which includes the star system, let me try to explain why I think the theatre is being turned 'inside out.' And here we have to deal with paradoxes.

The More, the Less ...

The more we see, the less we 'see'; the more we hear, the less we 'hear'; the more we are told what to think, the less we 'think.' In other words, the inviting blank to be filled, the fertile silence, the challenging ambiguity – everything that summons us inwards has been replaced by surface, noise, and plenitude. The outside obstructs our way inside.

Outwardness can take many forms. For instance, the young actresses composing themselves, mentioned earlier, are endeavouring to construct from the outside the instantly recognizable image that will get them the job, since television and film rely so much on a shorthand of recognition. The repertoire of signs is so limited in the average Hollywood movie or in bread-and-butter television that the audience is afforded the facile luxury of instant recognition. Ambiguity is the death of ratings. However deviously the signs are manipulated, the message must contain no troubling silences, or omissions. Plenitude replaces the fertile vacuum; dead air provokes anxiety – which is possibly why Pinter and Beckett insist on the pause being respected, and why there is such a sense of threat in their plays.

Outwardness can also consist of a superfluity of effects that draws the spectator's attention to the surface. Choreographed movement, the stage 'picture' (at the expense of the truly dynamic), over-production in costume, lighting, and music pulls the viewers' focus away from the play itself.

Didactic theatre is now scorned, yet a different form of didacticism has replaced it, in the form of toning down the message through excisions in the text, or lowering the stakes in given scenes by removing any unpleasantness, using a cosmetic wash to cover up the offending elements in a scene.

Inside Out

Much of what I have been considering here is in fact about marketing, and about how the pressure to entertain has compromised much theatre. To entertain means to engage agreeably and amusingly. Marketing has invaded the stage to the point where the peripherals occupy the centre and the actors become products; the look, the image, the surface. The screen has replaced perspective and depth (a 'bad' word these days); and acquiescence and quiescence stifle contradiction and action. Once theatre is shunted to the edges it becomes safe. Or, as the Chilean group La Troppa would say, it becomes a mere 'amuse-gueule,' an amusing aperitif, never the main course. (This brings back a personal memory of a workshop with a Guatemalan troupe years ago, where I learned of their nomadic existence in the time of the generals. Their description of constant flight from the authorities suggests perhaps that they were serving up a theatre that was 'in-digestif,' and not so easily passed through the system.)

In our education system, theatre and drama must preserve their urgency and become a place where self-creation, imagination, and dialogue are still possible; where the engagement of people in productive conflict and thought can be generated. The theatre must be guarded against the insatiable appetite of the ego, the pressures to be 'hip,' the demands of self-promotion (either through 'image' or the exigencies of the camera), and the pressures to be seen and not see. Theatre should, in education, afford a place of freedom, thought and creation, subverting the ever-increasing demands of product and commerce, and be a place of action and not submission. It must be an area where the dialectic of factitious and authentic can be played out, where the institutional pressures to conform are, however briefly, suspended.

Notes

I wish to acknowledge the work of Eduardo Galeano, in form more than in content, especially *Upside Down* (New York: Metropolitan Books, Henry Holt & Co., 2000). The quoted interview with La Troppa is from *Libération*, 11 May 2001; my translation.

Improvisation and Risk: A Dialogue with Linda Griffiths

LINDA GRIFFITHS AND KATHLEEN GALLAGHER

Kathleen. I want to ask you about your reaction to the title of our book and your initial thoughts when you received the letter about contributing, about being part of this book. And what is possible in this relationship between drama and education? I am talking about what is possible, in terms of both process and product, when, for instance, theatre conventions and improvisation become a part of how students construct their creative lives. Of course, given the political climate, and the current situation in education, where we are moving further and further away from anything which is exploratory, everything seems to be about arriving at a 'standard,' about conforming to a 'norm.' This has really serious repercussions, I think, for what is a burgeoning field of drama education. So in your view, Linda, what are the possibilities left to us? How should our learning and teaching proceed?

Linda. Drama and education. It's just that I've never had a good experience with the intermingling of those two things. In the past, whenever I've been near institutions, I just hate it. Recently I started teaching corporate people how to give speeches, and I also taught at a university for the first time. I've lived a life so separate from organized learning. Most writers teach to make money, but I did film and television acting for a long time; that was my economy. But you have to have a sense of upward mobility or at least care enough to put on high heels for an audition, and I found I just didn't. So I had to change and adapt. I was also interested in teaching, ready to teach, I think. But at first, I felt like a fish out of water, now I'm better but ... I had never been in a Bay Street tower until two years ago; I had never been in a university drama program, except as a speaker who comes in and talks for an hour about whatever. So I had a very strong and strange experience when I first walked into these worlds. For whatever reason, I've needed to find an utterly individualistic path through things, and that's caused me to be almost unadaptable to institutions. I was kicked out of National Theatre School after the first year. Paul Thompson used to say, whenever I didn't know how to do something, 'They taught that in second year, Linda.' Arne Zaslov, who was heading the school at that time, was a guy very into things like The Physical Theatre, dead into improvisation, but a very specifically based improvisation. Physical improvisation. Nothing with language. In a way, I was kicked out because I couldn't improvise and spent the next twenty-five years improvising in one way or another. In a weird way, I was seen as conservative because I wanted to be told why I was doing all this stuff. I could not relate to what was being thrown at me. No one told me why, there was no philosophy, no ideals, nothing that would appeal to my mind. And at the time, what was being thrown at me was considered edgy and all that. Since then I have gone so much past that. What happened wasn't that I was particularly rebellious, but that I started to disappear. I just became a ghost. I lost more and more weight and grew paler and paler, and just felt that the physical training was crushing me. It felt like boot camp. I hated the mask work; I just could not connect with the need for a mask or any other kind of disguise. There was a big thing about juggling. It was supposed to teach you the universe, but I could not learn to juggle; something in me resisted, not in an overt way, but in a covert way that was very injurious to me. They called me licorice because I was so thin and only had this one pair of black leotards; I must have looked like a piece of black licorice. Who knows. After getting kicked out, and that was a special piece of nineteen-year-old pain, I then went to teachers college. It was a tiny course that was still available at the time. You did a one-year training program, and after that, if you taught two years out of the next five, you were allowed to teach elementary school. Well, I took the course and never taught at all. I went for a long walk in the rain on St Laurent Boulevard and told myself that no matter how bad I was, I had to act and I would find some place that would take me. I started working in theatre then and never stopped. I still wanted to train and found different ways to study. I went to New York and studied with Kristin Linklater in a fantastic workshop situation for six weeks. I took another workshop with Joseph Chaiken, and a wonderful madman of a method teacher, Peter Kass. I later went back and studied with Kristin Linklater any chance I could. I always did vocal warm-ups. I always did some kind of physical exercise, but it was with intention behind it. That's what these people taught me. Then Paul

Thompson taught me, Clarke Rogers taught me. I just went away from the institutionalized educational struggle.

Kathleen. Let me ask you a gender question, then, as I am remembering your acknowledgment of Rosemary Sullivan in your play *Alien Creature.* On the question of women artists, what might be the particular challenges you met in what became your theatrical recreation of this woman (MacEwen), and more generally, what are some of the challenges that you have encountered or experienced as a woman in a community of theatre artists?

Linda. This seems ridiculous but I think, for a while, I was totally unaware there was a problem. Personally I was very unaware, and in terms of my work, at first I was very protected. When I talk to students now I want to say to them, 'I got a deal that none of you is going to get.' When I first started working, I got a living wage to work with a small company in Saskatchewan, Twenty Fifth Street Theatre. It was fantastic, something that young actors slaver over when I tell them. In Saskatoon at that time, no one was going to hire me for a movie. I got a kind of relief from the confusions of ambition and just thought that I could do it, whatever it was. In that way, I was into a professional world when I was twenty-one. It doesn't happen now; you'd have a day job now and be running the company as well. When I did *Maggie & Pierre*, people were saying I was young, but I felt like a veteran because I'd been through the longest tour of the West ever attempted in recent times. Sixty-seven one-night stands through Alberta, Saskatchewan, and Manitoba. And that was long. I had been in three or four collective creations; I had worked with a company. I didn't feel like *Maggie* was the first play that I had done. I don't know anyone getting that deal now. Semi-professional is what's happening. Semi-professional means you cannot live by what you do; you have to have another job. And I didn't for a long time, except in the summers, when I waitressed. I would go back to a company, with very subsistence wages, about $50 a week in 1978. Then we did a tour that gave you enough money to save a little. I was always part of a company, a 'two women–three guys' kind of company. After we'd been working for a couple of years, Paul Thompson came through with his company to do the West Show. I worked with Paul Thompson, Eric Peterson and David Fox and Miles Potter, Anne Anglin, Janet Amos, Ted Johns and the new person was singer/songwriter Connie Kaldor. Paul decided that he would direct two collectives at the same time: one with his own company, and one with the Twentyfifth people. At first it was awful. I felt voiceless and I think that was gender. Layne Coleman and I watched one of the West

Show's rehearsals and those guys were fast and funny and aggressive and competitive. I do think that often women work in different ways; you have to let us in. You have to help to create the material in a different way. Anne and Janet had been at Thompson for years to get him to find a way in the sessions to let them in, to acknowledge that while the boys were being so incredibly great, there was another part of things that had to be given room to grow. They were the vanguard, and bugged him so much he figured there was something in it. So when I came along, a little later, Paul was already on the lookout for a way to 'let the female thing in,' because it was not just a question of opening the door for us, but rather it was a different way that we worked. In the sessions with his company that I watched, the guys would go all day, crank everyone up; they were so funny. The women were trying to come in, deeper, quieter, but it would be hard to hold the focus. The improvising sessions that I saw were mad scrimmages. The women got in, and did great material, but they had to fight for that slower, deeper rhythm, and sometimes they lost.

Kathleen. Tell me about the pioneers before you, those who broke ground. How did they describe women's different ways of improvising?

Linda. Probably not as immediately fast and funny. A subtler, a more smooth way of coming in. I don't want to go on about clichés of men and women, but when Layne and I watched that West Show session, we were the young company who went to see the older guys who actually had kids, they were travelling with young children, like two years old. They had a nanny but still, the women were looking out for the kids. I watched them, and I saw the women do something very different. It was coming from, you could say, a more emotional place, and it was without the pyrotechnics and muscular will. But I found that I had a muscular will too, that I had a big male, very stereotypical male part of me that could leap into these situations. I didn't know that, because at first I was tentative, I was fragile, but I couldn't improvise that way and so the way I knew was being this monster, not letting anybody enter the improvisation, wouldn't stop talking. This was unusual for my sex at that time. I would leap in like a maniac. Very, very much like those guys. I thought I was a lot more fragile than that. My first improvisation went on for an hour. I improvised all of the movie *Jaws.*

Kathleen. How could you do that?

Linda. I did the whole thing. I did the shark, I did Richard Dreyfus, I did Robert Shaw, I did the whole scars scene, I did the explosion of the boat, I did the swimming, and at the end I did the shark's death. It was the first time this had ever happened to me. As a woman, in a way, it helped me to realize how aggressive I was. Not in the sense of power, necessarily, but in a challenging way.

Kathleen. What about your commitments to 'Canadian subjects' in your work?
Linda. Deadly. Right now it's deadly. Don't.
Kathleen. Don't do Canadian?
Linda. No. Don't say Canadian.
Kathleen. You've got to do Canadian-Universal?
Linda. Global, I think, Global. *Alien Creature* is set in a Canadian city, with a capital 'C.' If I hadn't used the 'C' word in the synopsis of the play in the press release, it might have been okay. But, immediately, the idea is 'It's local.' No one is going to admit to that and I could be wrong. But, my feeling was, if I use the 'C' word, it will not be seen as 'universal.' The whole idea that you talked about with this book, the specifics making it universal, the idea that you can extrapolate from specifics, doesn't, I think, still apply. It applies in truth, at the moment, but not in percep- tion. But, if it is global without a place, never a place name, and it's written by a Canadian, you can get away with it. And that's fine. For a while there I felt that to call up any Canadian specifics was a death knell. Then Michael Healey's *The Drawer Boy* comes along, set in very specific South Western Ontario and the world wants to do it, and makes a mess of that theory. That's the thing with theories and the theatre, they get buried regularly and that's where academia is always behind. I come from the swell of theatre that was considered Canadian Nationalist and that's been expropriated like everything. When you hear politicians say in this really smarmy voice, 'We don't tell our own stories,' I just about gag. As soon as they say it, it's dead. It's just that, every once in a while, with something like *Alien Creature*, I feel that it is springing from a true place, and that true place can echo into any place. I hadn't felt that in a long time. Then I heard someone say, about the tour: 'Why do we want to see a show about a Toronto poet?' That pissed me off. The tour went well, and the show went great and all that, but still, there was that prejudice about the specific. There's a desire to tie things up in a little knot – she does famous Canadian women. What a deadly thought. Then Wallace Simpson comes along and she's not Canadian, then Gwendolyn comes along and she's not really famous. So it's silly. Are the couple in *The Darling Family* Canadian? They're not famous either. For *The Darling Family*, it didn't matter. And that's the play of all my work – even more

than *Maggie & Pierre* – that's been most produced, three times in New York, in London, in almost every city in Canada, so maybe not being specific is useful in having a play done. A lot of young actors and young companies do it. But I don't deny the part of me that's almost diabolically Canadian. I couldn't lose this identity, or the desire to write from that place, for my life.

I have watched things change. I think a lot of ground in Canadian theatre has been lost. In 1980 to 1982, there was a lot of really interesting work going on that wasn't niched. You could actually speak to a broad audience, from the toffs to the groundlings, and now the audience for new work seems so neatly niched. I like the new work, but I yearn for plays that can speak to a wider group of people and still be innovative. *Alien Creature* found a certain niche, it was the art niche, and, in a sense, the Avant Garde festival niche, and I wanted to break out of that. I wanted to say, 'No, it's larger than that,' even though it's very hard for a play of that nature, about a poet, which is seen as elitist, to make its impact. The whole populist tradition that I am from is entirely in pieces now. Things are niched. I feel like in the time I have been around I have watched ceilings being put in place about what to write, and how often to write about subjects that are local. In terms of the attention from media, I had to photocopy some reviews from the eighties and I was struck that the pictures were physically bigger, the reviews were longer, that theatre in this country when nationalism was emerging as an issue, was given more space. *Maclean's* had a regular theatre column. They don't now. It has to be international. There's lots of theatre I like that has come out of the art niche, but I yearn for plays that can cross boundaries, especially of class. Not that I'm really writing them at the moment. I have watched ceilings come down again, and maybe it's opening up again. Maybe it isn't. I mean, if you keep your clothes from the 1970s they will be in style eventually. Yuck ...

Kathleen. I would like to ask you a question about your early life experiences, in school or in the theatre. What do you now cite as having had real impact on you? Not made you, but shaped you in some sense?

Linda. There is the piece in *Alien Creature* about being five years old, and dedicating myself to something I thought was God, and later felt was art. I can remember that moment so clearly. And then my boyfriend took me to a Shakespeare play, when I was 14 (he was older than me), and I saw, in Vermont, a really good, small company doing Shakespeare in the round. We were only four rows away from the stage; I had never seen a professional play. I was transported and changed. I loved it so much and afterwards, I just couldn't rest. And I made him take me back for all three plays. This idea is very much part of Paul Thompson's view of an audience; back to the idea that plays should be able to play to the fourteen-year-old girl who knows nothing about the theatre, and the jaded elite as well. The first play I saw I thought: 'I want to be in these; I want to do it somehow.' I saw *Winter's Tale*, and it wasn't that I was dazzled by the costumes, it wasn't necessarily a Stratford-level production, but the basic beauty of the stories, the emotional level of the stories, the wonder of that work really got to me.

Kathleen. It's amazing.

Linda. If the story is strong, and if the dramatic intent is strong, you can kind of lose a few lines and words. And so the epic plays that I write are really big; they have narrative lines, they have stories.

Kathleen. That clarifies things. I mean for someone who has been in the audience of your plays, I now see a real rootedness in a particular, in the story, in a 'local' feel, all of what that is.

Linda. Yes, but, you know, in *The Darling Family*, there's no local at all, there is no sense that it's in a particular place. In a city obviously; they are both city people. And again, the Wallace Simpson piece is not local. *Jessica* was, in a way, incredibly local, in the sense of entering the world of native spirituality, but it was also travelling because it wasn't my culture and the audience didn't know much of it either. So is local familiar? Not necessarily. Local is not always important to me. Groundedness is what I search for, and that groundedness is as much in the subject, in the content of the piece, as it is in anything else. And the content is really the story. Even with *Alien Creature*, it's a long, fragmented model, but there is a story to it. It's almost *The Rime of the Ancient Mariner*. I do use form. I do think in terms of form. I love to tell a story; to rivet the people. It's my life to tell a story because I need to and to say, 'You, in the audience, are going to hear it.' Those forms are my own inventions, but I also do think in terms of models, sometimes classical models. It doesn't look like that. It shouldn't look like that. If it looks like that, I have failed. But there are recurring themes in my work. There is almost always a point where somebody prays, for instance. In *Maggie & Pierre*, Trudeau gets down on his knees ... It is a point where the character is at an end and must reach beyond. *The Darling Family* is full of prayer, and this is, in a sense, spiritual, fantastical, and multidimensional. Gwendolyn MacEwen talked about entering a fourth dimension, and I thought, 'This is a gal after my own heart.'

Kathleen. That is a bit of a signature piece for you?

Linda. I guess it is. I don't know, I don't even know if there is going to be a prayer in my new play, *Chronic.* There was one and I cut it out. But I think it is like bringing the character, one of the characters to their knees. Even though *Maggie & Pierre* has a lot of laughs, it is very much a cross between something funny and something not. That's part of Thompson's Canadian Comedia that's so out of fashion now. Well, wait ...

Kathleen. You know it is interesting, I was going to ask you this question about pointing to a piece that you wrote ...

Linda. I think if there was a piece, it would be *Alien Creature.* That was like me coming out, that was me on my knees. It was the essence of what I believe in terms of what my life has been about. Almost. How I think it is stupid to have this kind of life in terms of prosperity and practical choices. It almost doesn't take energy to do *Alien Creature.* Even though I am somehow bringing the audience to a point where the character really does fall to pieces. It is acting and it is not acting. It is a joy to put on that mantle and, in a way, to hide behind it, in order to be able to speak. I try to be honest with it. I wanted it to be a touchstone just for myself for future work. I can't do that again, and I won't do that again. The next thing is so different you might not think it would be written by the same person. But hopefully if you look closely, you'll see ... I don't necessarily want an audience to look closely when they are watching, and say, 'Ah, yes this is a Griffiths play, because it has this, this, and this element, right!' It just won't be like that with me, because I choose these specific subjects and these specific stories and each one tends to look different ... You can't say, 'Ah! She is using this whatever technique.' But you will find an element of the other dimension, fantasy, the fantastic ... I have been thinking, 'Am I a fantasist? Is that something to call myself?' Yeah, you probably could, but it wouldn't really fit. Still there is an element of the surreal in *Maggie & Pierre*, and it is in all of the plays. But I like to disguise it; I don't like it to be out front. I want to win the immediacy of the audience just there, like it is the first play I have ever written, and they think, 'What's she going to do?' and 'Is she going to make it or not?'

Kathleen. I am coming back to the obvious connections I am drawing between your experience of writing and being a writer, and the processes and the experiences I have had in drama and education and, in particular, the learning I've had from a pioneer from the early sixties in England, Dorothy Heathcote. Certainly she is a teacher more than anything else, but she is also someone who worked in classrooms with drama in a way that had not been done, and has often not been done since. Yet her influence was great and her method, as you were suggesting about some of your experience, got commodified in ways that, of course, diminish. Because people want methods! And one of those ways was the 'Mantle of the Expert,' as it is called. This was about working with really young kids in most cases, different kinds of populations of kids in different contexts in England. But it was her way of having kids don mantles that they would normally never have and it was also about, in some ways, the central conflicts of the local situations that they lived in, places like Newcastle and Manchester. She was looking at miners' lives and other real concerns in particular locations and these kids wore those mantles that would be so removed from their actual lives in a classroom. It is something about the power that one feels about looking out and looking in simultaneously.

Linda. Well, when I played and wrote *Maggie & Pierre* (in collaboration with Paul Thompson, it's important to remember that), I donned the mantle of an expert and I think it did influence me. I became something so totally outside my experience: male, powerful, the Prime Minister of Canada. There were almost no women in parliament at that time and playing someone with enormous personal power, as well as political power ... I really believe that made me think that anything was possible, not just the success of the play, but maybe I did think that I was the Prime Minister. I still had all the scars of a young woman brought up to believe herself inferior. I believed myself to be inferior to men. I was taught that way. And hopefully I was the last generation that was ever taught that way. And so when I played men, or this man, it was like becoming the highest you can imagine. I mean, I could have been the pope. I could have been the president of the United States, which is most powerful but not necessarily most interesting. It was a veil of huge power and of huge intellect and self-belief. And when I donned that mantle, I had the power. I was self-effacing, and uncertain and insecure, then I would become Pierre Trudeau, and these other things would happen. I've started teaching in my own way, running my own workshop classes in improvisation, and I think it's actually something that I should do with my students. Play the most powerful person you know, big, obvious power. I find I have to invent my own exercises and I'm not necessarily good at it. I haven't been to school enough ... Sometimes I think all students do is exercises.

Kathleen. But it isn't in the exercises, of course. It's got much more to do with the imagination and with the complex negotiation of human relations.

Linda. Right. When I began to teach in university, I found I didn't know a lot of exercises. I wanted to do a play in which exercises were a part or a tool; I only knew how to make plays. I did not know how to do the exercises that everybody was talking about, because they had been taught how to do all these exercises and they did the exercises with each other and they would then become teachers and teach everybody else exercises. Where's the play?

Kathleen. Yes. Exercises. They are limited. They are good, but they are limited. In my situation, I'm teaching teachers, soon-to-be teachers of drama. And they want that bag of tricks. The politics of education, driven by political agendas of accountability, have created a terrible problem. The problem is that these tricks have become the substance, so everyone does the same exercises, we all arrive at the same conclusions and can all demonstrate the same skills at the end of it. No uncharted territory.

Linda. Yes, so that you get all these terrible things. 'Whose Life Is It Anyway?' Recycled 'real' stories. It's a trap without the imagination. I've found that there is a lot of clapping going on in school. They were delighted to do these games and my heart sank. I even had them do their own warm-up because I thought I don't know how to do warm-ups. So I watched them happily do all this clapping and stamping, but it never related to the work. Then I thought: 'The hell with this, I can do warm-ups.' And I led them through a few things, even some clapping. But I didn't want to be that kind of teacher. Instead, we risked everything to try and do a collective creation, but they didn't believe it would ever be good. It seemed banal to them. The real people they imitated seemed banal, but a 'truth or dare' exercise wasn't banal. Again, there was an escape into the physical that didn't lead to people talking, relating, even in a non-naturalistic way. I didn't know how to lead them well, that was certainly part of it. I went too fast, wasn't sensitive to where they were, asked too much and it spooked them ... And I think I needed to understand the system in which things are related to a mark. So, you do a certain amount of work like this and then you give a mark. Then you do a certain amount of work, and you get marked on that. It's very difficult. That's why I like the corporate world. Because the stick has already been wielded. You have to learn how to communicate better and if not, you're fired. It's all very clear. No one's pretending to be idealists.

Kathleen. Corporate teaching is the kind of teaching that artists sometimes find themselves doing?

Linda. It's a way to make a living and still have some juice left to write. My experience with corporate teaching was that I felt like I was crossing the boundary to another world that I didn't know about and I think it made me a better teacher. In a way, the corporate guys are very eager to learn, someone has paid for them to take these courses, to learn how to speak to people better, so they're good students mostly. I saw it as a new world, and that made me open to it. I'm a sponge and I was taught to be a sponge to new experiences. When working with Thompson, you go out, you see people, you listen to everything they say, you look at their body language, their voice, you suck them in as much as you possibly can and spew them out in rehearsals. That changed a lot when I started using myself, when I started just making things up, when I started leaping wildly off the base of any kind of subject. I stopped watching people the way you watch them when you're in a collective. Everything you see and hear is food, and you're often doing the collective about something you know nothing about and so you'd better learn about it or you'll suck in the play ... I stumbled back into it again by doing corporate teaching. In my new play, *Chronic*, I wanted a work environment for the character, and I would never have been able to write about a computer company if I had never been inside a real office building. *Chronic* is vaguely based on a B movie done in the fifties called *The Tingler*, about a creature who attaches itself to people's spines, and increases in size through fear, and to get rid of it, you scream.

Kathleen. This is what you are writing about?

Linda. Well, sort of ... The creature, in my mind, is an illness and people scream to get rid of it and it goes to somebody else. But what happens is this one woman is mute and she can't scream, so there is a process to operate and take out this creature that looks like a monster. I started to just feed in the things that were happening from the corporate teaching. I named the character Oscar, after someone that I taught. I told him that I was going to use his name. Why make up a name when you've got the real guy; and he conjures up a certain kind of person. We had a great time creating together and we taught each other.

Kathleen. I think many theatre artists are reluctant to think about what they do as 'educational' or as 'teaching' people. When you write a play or when you perform in a piece you have written or someone else has written, what is it you imagine you might be doing for or to people who are out there in the dark?

Linda. Let me reverse it. If I don't learn something when I watch a play, I'm not satisfied. Sometimes a play can seem like an elegant exercise. That's why I like content and story because I want to learn, but not in the sense of a documentary. Always, in the theatre, there should be an element of teaching. But also I am learning from the audience, and that's what I got from the improvisational experience, from honing plays in front of the audience. The audience teaches you as much as you teach them and that again is a more populist relationship to the audience ... So, yes, I am teaching, because I'm supposed to be the expert and I am, but I also want to learn from them. The minute I stop learning from an audience is when I think I start to lose what it is I am about. The audience is precious and they should be treated as precious. I don't know if they are my students. They are as much my teachers as my students.

Kathleen. And your audiences know what they want?

Linda. Oh, yes. And that's great. They know what works. When you hear that dead feeling in the room, or a lot of shuffling, coughing, and Halls Menthol Eucalyptus, you know you have to look at that part again. It's not specific what they want, they just don't want to be bored and I'm determined not to bore them. I want to challenge them. I think that doing that initial work that I did with improvised theatre gave me the respect and love of the audience. So I'm an addict for full houses. It is like with *The Duchess. The Duchess* was a bit of the old days in that we got houses without good reviews. I got huge publicity for *The Duchess,* which helped to reach the audience, but it was also the kind of publicity that sets you up for a smack in the face. It was one of those times when the critics and the guardians of the culture don't like something, but people do, and they show up in droves. Not through subscription, but people walking right in the door. When I played to whole audiences of students for *Alien Creature* they were the worst audiences though. They sat back from the experience, they'd been told it was good, and now they were going to analyse it ... But I especially loved playing to young audiences, especially young women. They were fantastic. Young women are forming my new audience and I think they're so great. But when groups of students came, I felt that I was the teacher and they were the students. No, no, you are the people, right! You are the people and I will challenge you, I will turn things on their head, but in the end, you are my judges.

You asked me about my reaction when I got the letter about contributing to this book. My heart sank and I thought: 'I'm not educated.' I can yack forever about these things and perceptions of my work and my work process and all those things, but at the end I think: 'That is all bullshit.' And it is my old prejudices again. I did not know how to make it right and I couldn't stand the thought of writing a piece about me in a book. I also

have read some of those books and I find that removal from actual experience, the lack of visceral connection to the work ... the language often
goes nowhere. I'm pushing against the academic; I am always pushing
against something. Now I am pushing against the arts festival style of
doing things. No it can be beautiful; you don't need to be dressed in grey,
and to look like a kind of android. I was watching Robert Wilson, in 1978
in New York. Now with the style of Avant Garde festival plays, people are
talking of being edgy! I want to push against it and I went into my teaching situation and said, 'We are all going to push against it.' Some of those
students I'm still in contact with, especially the one I made cry. I felt
really bad about that, but everyone I talked to said that will be the student
who relates to you the most and it turned out to be true.

I got a really good deal in terms of entering the theatre. I don't know
what it would be like if I was young now. I don't know if I would be able to
do it, without the kind of mentoring I received. I was supported as I
learned. I would get a play presented, and that was a good deal. I don't
know how I would have survived without these things. Now I'm running
a company. Now I've got all kinds of papers and files and contracts. But
then, I was another kind of creature, and that kind of creature is not
supported by these times. And that is *Alien Creature* all over again.

Linda. When coming from a collective tradition, content is important.
Each play is first about something, so each play becomes very different,
because you are actually coming from the subject, from the content of it.
I've been through a process of development that feels bilingual. From
actor/improviser who works on her feet with a group, to writing on
paper, to improvising alone, which is also called writing, and back to
writing on paper. And sometimes all of these processes go into one play.
Except I haven't been in a collective in a long time; maybe they're for the
young. It's too nerve-racking and soul destroying and ... fucking awful.
But when they work ...

I hate when my work is called biography or docudrama. It is never
docu-anything, but it usually stems from some content-like thought and
some things are safer than others. *Chronic* is about Chronic Fatigue
Syndrome, but it's not about Chronic Fatigue Syndrome. It's about the
people in the play; it's not a docu-drama about an illness, yet there is the
content of it, the 'about.' Maybe because I have this legacy/rock on my
shoulders called *Maggie & Pierre.* People who didn't see it thought of it as
documentary in some way, which it wasn't at all. It was an imaginative
leap off, with elements of truth.

Kathleen. I like that 'imaginative leap off.' It makes a lot of sense.

Linda. In a way I am grateful that nobody said, 'How can you take liberties with actual persons, when you have your own voices and perceptions coming through them?' And the only way to answer that is really something that Maria Campbell said when I worked with her on *The Book of Jessica.* Maria Campbell is a native activist and author.

Kathleen. What is the book called?

Linda. The Book of Jessica. It is very painful, to the bone: two people, Maria and myself, arguing about, and me defending, whatever the process of work was, which became something that I wrote in collaboration with her. And so at one point I say, 'OK, so I'm stealing,' and she says, 'Fine. Admit that you're a thief and give back tenfold.' That is what an artist does. All artists steal but they then have to give back tenfold. That's what I try to do when I take these huge liberties with real characters or stories. I have sincerely attempted to steal, transform, and give it back tenfold. People who write books get asked, 'Oh is it a real person?' And they always say, 'No, it's a conglomerate.' Well, maybe it is, maybe it isn't. But to name the person, and then to do a conglomerate, make things up about them as well, is pushing the boundaries. Maria Campbell was after me for stealing. She just wanted me to say, 'I'm a thief.' Then she'd say, 'OK, fine.'

Kathleen. I had this very experience, just last Sunday at Tarragon Theatre, where Judith Thompson was giving a monologue-writing workshop. She did something that I am sure you are very familiar with. Each of the eight of us revealed a kind of transforming moment in our lives. Of course, we then had to write a monologue about another's moment, not knowing each other, so I was concerned. To begin with, I chose to work with what I thought had been the least devastating story that had been shared and then created something which was, in a way, twice removed from the people who had been described in the story. And still I felt the need, as I read it, to qualify for the teller of the story that this was an invention. I was tortured, in some ways, by this process of knowing that I was doing exactly that, feeding on some very private, very powerful moment in her life, and at the same time exploring it creatively with my own voice. In academia you come up against this all the time in social-science research. You are forever 'capturing' human beings in interviews and they inevitably become not the human beings, but my picture of looking at human beings.

Linda. It's so weird, because I always feel caught, split in many pieces because the way I began inventing material was through myself as an actor, and I wasn't sure that what I did was legitimate because I did it with an actress mask, if you want to call it that. When I did *Maggie & Pierre* I did it on my feet. Working with Paul Thompson ... he likes to pretend that the printing press has not been invented yet. More than that, he likes to pretend that no one knows how to write because he hates that 'writery' thing, wordsmithy things, he hates the preciousness that can come into writing. He likes the gut-level populism that almost naturally occurs when you use real people. So I would pretend I hadn't written any notes for *Maggie & Pierre*, but I would go away with some things written down, and I would not tell him. Even then I was working with a combination of myself on my feet and 'writing.' People work differently, but the method I was taught suggests that it's in the moment; the writing happens in the moment.

Kathleen. And the writing may never happen?

Linda. Oh, of course, that's true for every method, I mean the blank screen. The blank page to me doesn't quite mean the same, because if you can talk your way out of it, then you are kind of safe. When people called me a writer I thought that I was not really a writer because I had done it on my feet and that was not really writing. So the next play I did, I deliberately did not do any improvising and deliberately it was not a one-person show. It had eight characters and it was totally different. I had no idea how to do that but again I was mentored by Clarke Rogers and he led me through the expansion of the piece.

Kathleen. So, the writer's voice is –

Linda. The writer's voice is in everything, but then I found that when people asked me about processes, they had a kind of a weird look, like, you don't really write, so what is it that you do? If I had no arms, I would speak into a tape recorder, the way I am doing now, and I would call myself a writer and someone would transcribe it, and I would put it together and it would be writing. But *Alien Creature* was written – about 70 per cent of it – through improvisation.

Kathleen. Really? I do have a question about form for you, then. Years ago I saw *The Darling Family*, and more recently *Alien Creature*, and obviously they are enormously different pieces and you are a different writer now, but I want to ask you particularly about what those different things are that fuel your solo writing (one-person shows) and your writing for plays with more than one character, and what compels you toward one or the other form. Or does the form, in a way, choose you?

Linda. In a way there is a kind of practicality. When writing for more than one character it usually sends me to what I call 'paper writing.' Although *Jessica*, which has five or six characters, actually ended up with a lot of improvising. Paul Thompson set that up. We had so many stages to that project. We had a stage where a bunch of us improvised, including Graham Greene and Tantoo Cardinal. Then there wasn't enough to make a show. So Maria, Paul, and I went into Passe Muraille's Backspace and they fed in, and I improvised all the characters. It was so nuts. That was the first version we did in Saskatoon. For the second run in Toronto, I then took the material and reworked and rewrote 'on paper.' And the story of it all is *The Book of Jessica*. So there can be a merging of processes, usually with one method being predominant. I think also that it has to do with the subject; the play, the content chooses the method. I was determined not to 'write' very much of *Alien Creature* at all because I was afraid it would get to me, the idea of writing about a writer. I was afraid it would become self-conscious and 'writery,' and I knew that if I did it on my feet, the character would be more likely to come through. In this process, the person watching is very important and that was the director, Simon Heath. You can't do it for nobody, or I can't. At least one person has to be watching, and that person is crucial to the process. In this case, we call that person the dramaturge/director, but with improvisation, the person watching is on the inside of the process. It's physically in front of them, being created; their input is often on an energetic level, in the quality of their listening. Is it hard work? Yes, but it also just happens. I hate to use alchemical language, but it happens in the moment; sometimes I think of it like a turkey-stuffing kind of thing. You stuff the turkey with as much material and images and experiences (especially with a real research kind of subject) and then material comes out. And I have never known how to actually describe it, the magic of the moment of improvisation. Then you think, well, is there any skill that goes into it? Is there any experience that goes into it? Where are the techniques that go into it? They are there. But what is so beautiful in working that way is you are absorbed into the moment. Eric Peterson had a great comment after he saw *Alien Creature*. He was speaking about when I do real people. He said, 'They don't haunt you, you haunt them.' I laughed but in some way it's true. Then, *The Darling Family* was totally paper-written; not a word of that was improvised. I wrote it very quickly, and it poured right onto the screen. I changed very little except for editing from the first draft. That is rare for me. With the play I'm working on now, *Chronic*, it will go through twenty drafts, I know it. And I have done some improvising. At one point, with Leah Cherniak's help, I realized that I wasn't finding the core of the play, the emotional core. I think I was just too lazy to go through the process of improvising. Then with Simon Heath watching, and Leah Cherniak there for some of it, we got a space and a camera, and I began improvising. It was a turning point for the play. Still, that aspect might be 20 per cent of this total piece. I did something different again in the process for *Alien Creature*. I was definitely determined not to have anything in between me and the very core, so I set out to do something that I have actually never done, which was to try to work something out in front of an audience. I'm often asked to do a piece for benefits and things, so I decided I would do some of them extemporaneously. I had an idea of what I would do, and some odd notes written down, and no previous improvising. So, a few times I went out there and really made it up on the spot. It was so terrifying, but things happened that wouldn't have happened otherwise. I still wasn't sure if I wanted to go to this dark place of emotional turmoil, but after a few of those pieces, I'd found my way in. That was good for *Alien Creature*, partly because it was a one-person play. It wouldn't work with *Chronic*. No one's going to see those improvs. With *Alien Creature*, I think I found a way to speak for myself and her, every once in a while; but she lived the life, you know. For me, Gwendolyn MacEwen was beyond inspiration, beyond 'subject.' She was the breath of the play. At one point, I started writing these little poem things, partly to explore the idea of her fooling with poetic language in a playful way, partly to get the play from one transition to another. And I thought: 'Oh no, how do I get away with this one? You are writing a play about a specific poet, yet you are not using much of her poetry, you are using your own poetry.' Still, I thought, 'Just give back tenfold, be as true as you possibly can, and somehow it will be alright.'

Toronto, 2001

IV. CULTURE, COMMUNITY, AND THEATRE PRACTICES

Seven Things about
Cahoots Theatre Projects

GUILLERMO VERDECCHIA

What the Hell?

The mandate of the company is to develop, produce, and promote new
Canadian plays that reflect Canada's cultural diversity. What exactly does
that mean? I wondered. What does it mean to develop? What makes a
play 'new'? What is a play? What forms does 'promotion' take and what
the hell is cultural diversity really? I'm not going to attempt to answer all
of those questions here; I'll simply focus on the notions of cultural
diversity and reflection.

Cultural Diversity. On the most obvious level, it seemed to me that we
were talking about the reality that many of us experience daily. Guillermo
Gomez-Peña, in 'The Multicultural Paradigm' (1989), put it this way:
multiculturalism is not an art trend, a grant language, or a new investment package for art maquiladoras. It is the very core of the new society
we are living in!

In Toronto, one of, if not, the most ethnoculturally diverse city in the
world – in Canada, one of, if not, the most multicultural countries in the
world – it made absolute sense that the theatre would reflect that reality.
It seemed, to say the least, odd to me that there would have to be a
company dedicated to that particular job. Surely, the task of the theatre –
or one of the tasks – is to reflect, in various ways, the reality we live. Why
then weren't other Toronto theatres 'naturally' reflecting the cultural
diversity that most of us experience daily? When I stop to think about it, I
am shocked by the unofficial theatrical apartheid that seems to exist in
Toronto (and elsewhere in the country). There are all sorts of reasons
for this, and all manner of excuses offered for the situation, but the fact
remains that, with very few exceptions, professional theatre for adults

rarely reflects or represents the complex and rich social mix we see in our major cities. Theatre for Young Audiences, such as Green Thumb in Vancouver and LKTYA (formerly YPT) and Theatre Direct in Toronto among others, are much more responsive and responsible to the diverse audiences they play to and for.

Given the under-representation of racial and ethnic minorities in Toronto's professional theatres, it made sense that Cahoots would continue to try to correct this imbalance by producing plays where people of colour and ethnic minorities were the subjects of the drama. Plays that made the lives of the 'under-represented' central.

Yet at the same time, it seemed to me that simply producing plays that mirrored the ethnocultural makeup of the city (this year a Trinidadian-Canadian play, next a Peruvian) was not a particularly inspired response to the company's mandate. Not only would it take us, at our current rate of production, about a hundred years to cover all the ethnic cultures in town, but also, more importantly, such an approach completely missed the more interesting aspects of the idea of culture.

Culture, after all, is a process, not a finished thing. Culture is a living system: open, dynamic, and responsive. Ortega y Gasset, if I can recall correctly, suggested that culture is the totality of answers offered in response to the questions posed by life. Naturally, those questions change over time and are subject to particular, local conditions. Thus, we can expect that the answers will change and develop. It seemed to me that Cahoots could address not only race, ethnicity, and nation of origin, but also gender and sexuality, self-identification, language, class, region, ability, hybridity, and all the really interesting inventions, concoctions, proposals, and definitions that human beings come up with as we negotiate our existential condition.

Reflecting cultural diversity, it seemed to me, meant not thinking of cultures as isolated entities that could be 'represented' objectively or scientifically, but rather looking at the fluidity of culture, the variety of responses to the questions posed by life. We could, I thought, look at the points of intersection, of overlap, of fusion; we should, I thought, focus on the shifting border zones. In this I was happy to discover that I was in agreement with Cahoots's founder, Beverly Yhap. A Chinese-Trinidadian-Canadian, Beverly has always felt (because of her triple hyphenated identity) that 'the question of community is highly charged.' She was then, and is now, very aware that communities change and reform, and that identity depends very much on context. A West Indian in the West Indies, for example, can become an Asian in Canada. For Beverly,

Cahoots was not about 'representing' or 'speaking for' specific communities. It was about creating opportunities for artists of visible ethnic heritage to practise and refine their craft. It was about bridging the gap between 'multiculturalism' and the professional theatre community. Similarly for Jean Yoon, Cahoots's energetic co-artistic director (with Linda Hill) in the early 1990s, the plays the company produced did not speak for or represent any community; rather they were particular visions – individual and personal responses to specific environments, situations, contexts.

It became clear then that the other central idea in our mandate – reflection – meant much more than producing likenesses or mirroring nature. It meant reflecting upon, reflection as in critical engagement. It meant perspective and opinion. It meant debate and dialogue. Our vision statement states in part: We recognize that people are complex creatures who define and invent themselves in multiple, dynamic, and ever-changing ways.

Cahoots Theatre Projects is committed to work that examines, with precision, discrimination, and theatricality, the complexities of our individual identities and our dynamic social relationships with one another. The writers and plays that we, at Cahoots, are interested in get to the difficult heart of what it means to live, work, play, love, and dream in contemporary Canadian culture.

Avoiding Multiculturalism

I've tried as much as possible to avoid using the words multicultural and multiculturalism when talking about the company and the work we do. Not because I object to the language or the policy; in fact I think the policy has much to recommend it. Unfortunately, the words (like the policy) remain grossly misunderstood. Multiculturalism is – generally speaking – misunderstood as a policy that aims to 'freeze immigrants in their way of doing things.' (I'm quoting Neil Bissoondath [1994] here, but many others have expressed the same opinion.) Multiculturalism, or the official policy of promoting polyethnicity, remains, after thirty years, misunderstood as the promotion and celebration of folkloric, frozen-in-time, cultures of origin. Multiculturalism, therefore, becomes something that applies to everyone else. Multiculturalism becomes a convenient little ghetto. On this view, 'multiculturalism' is the space where 'ethnic' artists do their thing and tell their stories – whatever they might be – probably about how hard it is to adapt to life in Canada – in their own language, to their own community; and no one outside those communities need ever attend because it OBVIOUSLY has nothing to do with anyone else; and as long as we (that's the dominant culture WE) throw them a little multiculti money every once in a while, all will be good and we can continue to do what we've always done.

Obviously this misunderstanding of multiculturalism has nothing to do with what we, at Cahoots, and many other theatres with parallel mandates are up to. I think that there are all kinds of audiences for this work that the label 'multicultural' might scare away. If 'we' expect or believe that a good production of a play by Congreve or Chekhov or Williams has something to offer just about everybody, why doesn't the same hold true for a play by M.J. Kang or Jovanni Sy or Padma Viswanathan? Too often the label multicultural, instead of meaning inclusion and diversity, means exclusion – alien and incomprehensible otherness.

Some years ago I saw a production of *East Is East* at the Theatre Royal Stratford East (about an East Indian family in London in the 1960s), and well, there were all sorts of white folks there. It was one of the most diverse audiences I've ever seen. Similarly, when I did *Fronteras Americanas* so many years ago at the Tarragon Theatre, I was thrilled to discover that my audience included the usual suspects, Tarragon subscribers, but also Latinos who had come to that theatre for the first time, young Asian kids, Black men and women of all ages, theatre professors from Guelph ... all sorts of people. I'm happy to report that our productions of Leanna Brodie's *The Vic* and Betty Quan's *Mother Tongue* have also played to visibly diverse audiences.

Gomez-Peña again: We want to be considered intellectuals not entertainers, partners not clients, collaborators not competitors, holders of a strong spiritual vision not emerging voices, and, above all, full citizens not exotic minorities.

So Much to Do, So Little Time

Obviously there were all kinds of things that could have been and should be done to express our mandate. Cahoots was founded in 1986, and was burdened, it seems to me, with the Herculean task of having to, in some way, defend, promote, train, assist, encourage, develop, and produce virtually all those professional and aspiring professional, visible, ethnic, and cultural minority theatre artists whom the mainstream theatre community consistently ignored and who couldn't find a home or employment at Native Earth or Theatre Fountainhead. There was all kinds of work to be done: scripts needed to be found, written, strengthened; actors needed work, training, encouragement; directors needed to be developed; critics, bureaucrats, and theatre officers needed to be educated; money had to be raised; connections and networks with other artists and activists had to be established; grants and articles for *Canadian Theatre Review* had to be written; shows had to be built, produced, publicized, and sold.

Somehow, previous administrations did all of these things. Not at the same time, not regularly, not always as well as they would have liked, but they did it; they made it happen, and quite often with very positive results. Since its inception, the company has played a significant role in the development of several now-established artists, including Daniel David Moses, M.J. Kang, Nourbese Philip, Linda Hill, Sally Han, and Rahul Varma. Cahoots developed or assisted in the development of Betty Quan's Governor General–nominated *Mother Tongue* and Florence Gibson's Chalmers Award–winning *Belle,* and produced the premiere of Marty Chan's wildly successful *Mom, Dad I'm Living with a White Girl.* In 1990, the company sponsored a national conference for visible-minority playwrights, 'Write About Now.' A few years later, the company sponsored a training project for directors called 'Setting the Tone.' It also held an annual festival of new work called 'Lift-Off,' sponsored play readings, published a newsletter, and organized great and groovy fundraisers called Kulchabash.

There was, however, a price to be paid for all this activity. Administrations tended to burn out in a few years; the company went into debt briefly; it was unable to produce regularly, and was, outside of a small circle of theatre workers, relatively unknown. When I took Cahoots on, I realized that I would have to pick my battles; I couldn't do everything. And I didn't have to do everything. The context that Cahoots operates in today is different in significant respects from the theatre ecology that existed in 1986. For one thing, both Theatre Passe Muraille and Factory Theatre under Laine Coleman and Ken Gass have made themselves available to us as producing partners, which cuts down significantly on our costs. While Theatre Fountainhead is gone, we now have Obsidian Theatre, whose mandate is, in part, to produce and promote the great (and neglected) works of the African-American canon, while supporting, promoting, and developing Black Canadian artists. There's also Buddies, Loud Mouth Asian Babes, Canasian Theatre, Caliban Arts, and Native Earth: companies devoted to reflecting accurately the reality of contemporary Canada. Just the other day I received a letter announcing the establishment of Rasik Arts, a company devoted to theatre and theatre artists of Southeast Asia. Nightwood Theatre, too, has played a large part in making professional theatre in Toronto more representative. Even Canadian Stage sometimes offers productions and commissions to visible-minority playwrights – yes, this may be tokenistic (and as Rahul Varma has pointed out, too often the high profile of one artist of colour or ethnic minority artist is used as a way to deny the diversity that exists in a community), but all in all, what it means for Cahoots is that we aren't all alone and that we can be a little more specific in our approach to making inclusive Canadian theatre. Since I've been at Cahoots, my focus has been on playwrights and scripts.

I remembered thinking at the symposium on non-traditional casting in 1989 that while it was important to get casting people and directors to think about the biases and assumptions that underlay casting decisions, that wasn't quite enough. Certainly, there was no reason that an Asian-Canadian couldn't play an FBI agent on an NBC movie of the week, and there was no reason why a Black actor couldn't play the doctor (even if the script didn't specifically call for a *Black* doctor); still, I wondered, was that what we/they really wanted? Is that what we were 'fighting' for? More important – to me anyway – than being considered for the role of Ax Murderer Next Door was the opportunity to take charge of the way I was represented, of the way my family, my friends, my worlds and cultures were represented. In other words, it seemed imperative that visible, ethnic, and cultural minority playwrights write out of their lives, that we tell our own stories.

I am aware that there are many ways to create, discover, and invent a story or a play, and I am open to the possibility of working in different ways; but right now, for various reasons, my focus is on scripts. I don't think, for example, that the conditions exist for a strong collaborative or collective creative process. I do feel that by working individually with playwrights I can most efficiently utilize the resources we have.

Previously, development took place under the rubric of the 'Lift Off' development series, an intensive, concentrated workshop period, which culminated in a mini-festival of public readings. Since becoming Cahoots's artistic director, I have decided to make play development an ongoing year-round activity so that the development process can be more flexible and specific to the needs of the play and writer. In my experience, festival situations end up being about the demands and constraints of producing a festival, however modest, to the detriment of the script and production. If there's one thing new plays need it's time; if there's one thing festivals are short on, it's time.

I divide development into two categories that are obviously interrelated, but can be usefully separated: (1) developing a writer; (2) developing a play. Roughly speaking, 'play' development is about addressing questions or challenges posed by a particular work. Play development can and should take many forms, depending on the particular questions and problems raised by the script under consideration. This kind of play development can be anything from regular one-on-one meetings between a playwright and me to a four-hour session with actors or a week with actors and a designer in a studio. We might bring in 'experts' as well as actors: a choreographer, a boxing coach ... We may need to look at complicated technical requirements (as is the case of a new play by Padma Viswanathan called *The Samba Prophet*, which calls for multiple video projections, live action, and puppets). A workshop situation allows us to experiment, muck about, get a sense of what is working and why, and to determine directions for subsequent drafts.

The second aspect of our development activities is our playwrights unit, which provides a critical entry point and access to the professional theatre for emerging writers often from communities typically not represented by the professional theatre in Toronto (such as the Southeast Asian and Latin American communities). The unit meets for a few hours every week to discuss theatrical concerns, ideas, and practices of interest to its members and to share and reflect on our work as it develops. We also invite guest speakers to share their processes and insights with us, and we read and analyse the work of (primarily) Canadian playwrights, looking for models, examples, and inspiration. I'm not trying to cook up plays for production; I'm trying to give playwrights some support, some practice, some help. The playwrights unit is about laying foundations, sowing seeds.

Anybody who submits a script to Cahoots will get a written response from me within a reasonable period of time. In this, I am following the example of the late Urjo Kareda at the Tarragon, one of the very few artistic directors in Canada who actually read the scripts that came across his desk. I remember how absolutely demoralizing it was to send scripts out to ADs and never hear anything back. Not even a form letter saying, 'We got your script. It stinks. Leave us alone.' I also remember what a tremendous difference it made when somebody did read my script (Bob White and Daniel Libman at ATP or Urjo at the Tarragon) and took the time to write a considered response.

I try to do the same at Cahoots. I read them. I write a letter. I try to point out what I think is working. I try to ask questions that will get the playwright thinking critically and creatively about the piece. I try not to make suggestions, though I will point out things I don't understand. Of the many plays I read or see or even hear about I choose four or five writers to join our playwrights unit.

Reader Response Theory

Jennifer Ross, Cahoots's general manager, and I spent a year off and on courting a patron for a substantial donation. He was, generally speaking, very supportive of the company and enthusiastic about the work I had done in the past. We were requesting, through a foundation he and his wife have set up, about 10 per cent of our operating budget, which we wanted to apply to our production of Leanna Brodie's *The Vic*, a play for eight women that we co-produced with Theatre Passe Muraille in the fall of 2000. Jennifer and I sent many friendly emails, met for coffee with him, sent him packages, budgets, and proposals. All was good. All was positive. He never baulked at the figure we proposed, but he did ask to read the script. So we sent it to him. Well, he didn't really like it – or rather it didn't move him, didn't speak to him. He did come up with money for a different production, however – a substantial contribution. We also received support from the Toronto Arts Council, Ontario Arts Council, and Canada Council. This patron recognized that the author had a right to write about whatever she wanted in whatever way she wanted to, but he was, in a way, concerned about the depiction of minorities as, in some instances, troubled or destructive or abusive. Part of his response may have had something to do with whom he imagined the play would speak to. He may have felt, I think, that the play misrepresented 'minorities' to the audience, which in some way represented the dominant culture that sat in some sort of judgment.

This sentiment still exists among some members of our audiences. There are certain things, certain subjects, that are not to be aired in public. It is understandable that a community or people who feel under siege to some extent by the dominant culture would want to present a united and 'positive' front to that dominant culture. Still, the work that artists working out of specific cultural communities and concerns are doing today is no longer about explaining the minority to the majority. The words minority and majority hardly apply. The act of staging the lives of the 'marginal' changes the terms of reference. One of the challenges of producing new work involves this question of who is listening, watching, judging. The answer is constantly changing.

Recognition

Charles Taylor (1993), among others, has argued that 'mutual recognition between groups has come to be a crucial issue in modern politics' (188). This 'recognition' involves 'the acceptance of ourselves by others in our identity,' or that which 'is important to us in defining who we are' (190). We can all understand this idea at the interpersonal level, in terms of child–parent relationships and in our intimate relationships with significant others and partners of all descriptions. Our sense of self, of worth is deepened and confirmed by recognition of our identity from our partner or parent. Conversely, recognition consistently denied is damaging to our self-esteem, to our psyche. Taylor points out that socially we may be recognized in some ways – as citizens, for example – but 'still be unrecognized in our identity' (190). Indeed, our identity may not only go unrecognized, it may be dismissed or 'condemned in public life,' and when 'this kind of denial takes place, or seems to do so in the eyes of a minority group it is hard and sometimes impossible for the members of that minority group to feel that they are really being given an equal hearing' (190). The consequence of this dynamic that Taylor describes is erosion of the 'common understanding of equal participation' that is central to a functioning democracy.

I think the theatre can provide both kinds of recognition: the personal or intimate and the social or public. Perhaps the first and most dramatic example of this recognition for me occurred during a performance of *i.d.*, a play that I and several other members of the Canadian Stage Hour Company co-wrote, based on the police shooting of Wade Lawson, a seventeen-year-old Black Toronto youth. One of the characters in the play was an outspoken Jamaican journalist, played by Damon D'Oliveira. Damon wore a tam and used a rich Jamaican accent. At one particular performance (I don't remember what school class was in attendance), he made his first appearance and a roar of approval, a mighty, defiant whoop, went up from the audience. They loved him. Every time he came on, whoops and cheers, and it turned out that for many of those students it was the first time they'd heard that voice in a public context. They told us that they were not allowed to speak that way in school, and so the experience of that performance was, for them, tremendously empowering. I've seen that recognition elsewhere – not so vocally perhaps – with our productions of *Mother Tongue*. And with *The Vic.* (A member of our playwrights unit, a young woman of Portuguese descent, told me that she felt validated watching the story of the young woman in *Mother Tongue*; the play – even though it is about a Chinese-Canadian family – was, she said, about her experience in a way that most theatre she sees is not.)

Those moments of recognition are tremendously powerful and satisfying. I try not to sentimentalize what occurs in the theatre or what we do as theatre-makers, but there's no denying those moments of connection, of community, however brief they may be. As much as I like the theatre to be about turning things inside out and poking holes and debunking grand narratives, I know that it can and should also create flash points of reciprocity and affinity.

The Magic If

If we had more than a $100,000 operating budget.
If we were paid more than $13.00 an hour to do the work we are doing.
If we had an office assistant to answer emails and respond to inquiries about auditions.
If we didn't spend three months (January to March) writing grant applications.
If we could also train or develop dramaturges and directors.
If we could tour; if we had a Theatre for Young Audiences (TYA) department.
If we were more than an office.
If sponsors and corporations would support *risk* half as much as they support classics.
If pigs could fly.
If there were more time.
If we had six opportunities a year to get it right.
If we had our own photocopier.
If our modem had a dedicated line.

Voices

I come back to culture, in a description from philosopher Michael Oakeshott that, to me, sounds a lot like theatre:

Perhaps, we may think of the components of culture as voices, each the expression of a distinct condition and understanding of the world and a distinct idiom of human self-understanding, and of the culture itself as these voices joined, as such voices could be joined, in a conversation – an endless unrehearsed intellectual adventure in which, in imagination, we enter into a variety of modes of understanding the world and ourselves and are not disconcerted by the differences or dismayed by the inconclusiveness of it all. (1989, 38)

Negotiating Drama Practices: Struggles in Racialized Relations of Theatre Production and Theatre Research

JANICE HLADKI

In this chapter I examine collaborative practices in two interconnected sites of drama activity: theatre production and theatre research. Through a particular focus on tensions in cross-cultural contexts, I explore the ways in which these sites of theatrical collaboration across social 'difference,' in particular racial difference, are negotiated through contradictory, uncertain, and conflicting social relationships. I focus on the racialized practices of theatre creators and researchers in processes of collaboration rather than on theatre texts or plays produced from collaborative artwork. My broad intent is to question 'how' we learn in drama, particularly across racial differences.

In her work on drama education, Kathleen Gallagher observes that 'how' questions – including interrogations about how practices are shaped and organized – are at the very heart of learning in/with/for drama (2000, 126). An emphasis on 'how' questions in education has been central to pedagogies that challenge the idea that the 'what' of a subject area can be universally and neutrally applied to all teachers and learners (hooks 1994; Spivak 1993; Trifonas 2000). These pedagogies ask questions about what knowledges are produced, by whom, and for whose benefit. Thus, they recognize the significance of social differences such as gender, race, sexuality, class, nationality, and disability for how learning occurs. Similarly, drama in education is concerned with thinking through how people learn and teach differently and with examining how the 'what' of drama is shaped by social differences (Gallagher 2000).

I will argue here that one of the meaningful ways that drama educates us is through the understanding that theatre is a social site of contested interaction and complex responsibility. In examining the struggles and tensions of racialized relations in collaborative theatre production and theatre research, I challenge the usual emphasis on harmony and unity that typically shapes theories of collaborative arts practices and participant research. Communicating with others, understanding social relationships, and building communities are central to dramatic learning (Gallagher 2000). My purpose is to complicate these key pursuits. These areas of education need to be rethought by recognizing the complex entanglement and struggle of theatre processes and of learning through theatre.

The import of such an understanding of theatre can resonate into the world at large, into 'the condition of complicated entanglement in which we find ourselves' (Ang 1997, 57) in the twenty-first century. Both 'difference' and 'collaboration' are at the heart of an understanding of 'education' (Jipson et al. 1995) and of what 'we' means in practices of working 'together.' These issues are particularly pressing and difficult in our contemporary world. An examination of power relations within theatre collaborations and collaborative research offers insights into 'one of the most urgent and complex political predicaments of our time ... How, in short, can we live with difference?' (Ang 1997, 57).

I foreground the importance of race for investigating these complications in relation to theatre and education. This chapter should also contribute to race research from a theatre and education perspective. Kay Anderson (1996) observes that there are few attempts to unsettle us/them or self/other frameworks in research on racialized relations. I hope to disrupt these binaries, since they obscure the complexity of racial identities, which are multiple rather than fixed and undifferentiated. Collaborative theatre production and theatre research are educational sites that can enable understandings of how identities are made complex and negotiable in racialized relations.

Collaborative Practitioners

Working with a feminist post-structuralist approach, I examined my interviews with indigenous theatre artist/activist Monique Mojica and her reflections on her theatre/performance collaboration with Djanet Sears and Kate Lushington. Conjointly, from my position as a white, feminist researcher, I questioned how I might ethically represent Monique in relation to how she identifies herself in her interview narratives. Race has been, and continues to be, significant in shaping practices in activist theatre communities in Toronto, and it is central to the theatre writing and collaborative practices of Djanet, Monique, and Kate. In addition to the research relationship across racial difference, I have a layered connection with all of the research participants, since I am researcher, colleague, friend, and co-member in a Toronto arts/activist community. I thank these women for complicating my understandings of, and for challenging my assumptions about, racialized social relations in theatre. Interviews and personal communications with all three women have helped me to interrogate my conceptual perspectives and theoretical positions by thinking about particular contexts and working practices in theatre. Thus, the research has been a process of education. Learning that emerges from power and struggle (Foucault 1980, 1982) in collaborative theatre activities across difference centrally informs what we mean when we ask, 'What is drama?' I want to emphasize that this question is necessarily attached to further interrogations: for which subjects? in what particular conditions of practice? and how do we come to know, through negotiating with 'others,' what drama is about? These questions embedded in 'What is drama?' are central to this chapter.

In profile materials provided to me, the women of the theatre collaboration represent themselves in the following ways. Djanet Sears self-identifies as an African-Canadian playwright, actor, and director. Monique Mojica names herself Kuna and Rappahannock, adopted into the Bear clan, Cayuga nation, of the Hodenosaunee Confederacy, and as an actor and playwright. Kate Lushington positions herself as a white Jewish woman who writes and directs in film, performance, and theatre. As for contextualizing my own location, since my collaborative work as a theatre researcher is addressed in this chapter, I am a white woman with a working-class background. I have a long history as a recognized artist, and more recently I am an academic who researches issues of cultural production and reception.

Monique, Kate, and Djanet are well known for their contributions to the arts in Canada. They have acted in a wide range of theatre, film, and television productions, and are recognized for their playwriting and for their challenges in their work to understandings of racial identity, racial relations, and racism. Djanet has written plays that speak to African, African-American, and African-Canadian identities, including *Harlem Duet* and *The Adventures of a Black Girl in Search of God*. Kate has written a play entitled *Fraud*, about women who struggle with issues of Jewish identity. Monique is known for her play *Princess Pocahontas and the Blue Spots*, and its focus on Native women who resisted colonial and imperial domination. All of these works have a poetic and a volcanic quality in terms of how they educate with respect to social identities. Throughout their history as colleagues, the women have made contributions to each other's work in the roles of dramaturge, performer, and director. They continue to seek out new occasions for collaboration. In their individual and collective endeavours, the representation of race and gender has a strong significance.

In 1993, the women came together for the first time as co-authors for the performance/theatre work *Onions, Strawberries, and Corn*. They continue to collaborate on the ongoing development of this play. The play's title refers to activities of food preparation and cooking that occur throughout and that represent a shared interest of their friendship. The types of food also represent the racial differences narrated in the text, with 'onions' as Djanet's food, 'corn' as Monique's, and 'strawberries' as Kate's.

Kate, Monique, and Djanet experienced a rich process of development on the script and the performance, one that involved various forms of improvisation and scene development. They worked with a facilitator to identify their individual writing and performing styles, particularly as they understood these to be shaped by racial identity, and to address the implications of these styles for collaborating across their racial differences. The play traces the interrelationship of friendship and racial identity: through story, song, poetic text, autobiographical narrative, gesture, and movement, the women explore their separate and linked histories and their practices of negotiation across racial differences of blackness, whiteness, and indigeneity. The play has neither a linear story nor characters that enact that story, but is instead produced as a series of moments where Kate, Djanet, and Monique, as themselves, or as a range of characters, perform what Gallagher calls 'workings of art' (2000, 116). That is, they work through the struggle of learning about and understanding their friendship and their racial identities. It makes sense, then, that the women speak about their play as being in a constant process of development.

The struggle of their social relations is described in the script as 'forbidden territory' (Lushington, Mojica, and Sears 1993, 1). They imagine themselves as crossing the 'borderline' of this terrain in order to create a story of what it means to 'know' the 'other.' This process of knowing and negotiation is articulated as 'walking on eggshells' and as 'swimming in treacherous seas' (24). These descriptors in the play underline serious, difficult, and fragile bonds, but *Onions, Strawberries, and Corn* is also celebratory and humorous. In addition, Djanet, Kate, and Monique are remarkable performers, and in the video recording of the production, it is evident that they take pleasure in working together on stage to enact their complicated professional and personal relations.

Theatre, Activism, and Education

The theatre work of these women can be understood as 'activist' and as a form of education. Their artistic practice is related to social change, social justice, and the enhancement of learning, particularly in terms of gender and race. They address issues of 'difference' and identity in their work, and offer challenges for understanding the complications of racial relations for friendship and for working collaboratively in the arts. Djanet, Kate, and Monique explore how artistic practice can be a vital component of social engagement and how social issues can be integrated into artistic practice. In this sense, their theatre practice is a form of social intervention that becomes theatre. In addition, as a mode of education that seeks transformation for artists and audiences, this form of theatrical collaboration is linked to what writer, activist, and teacher bell hooks (1994) calls 'teaching to transgress,' whereby learning and pedagogy interrogate systems of domination, such as racism.

Performance artist Guillermo Gomez-Peña (2000), who has a long history of collaborative production with many artists, writes and performs about what he terms the contemporary crisis in communication and the need to articulate the unspeakable in activist art that seeks social change. In their play – and in their interviews with me about their collaborative practices – Monique, Kate, and Djanet address the zones that they call 'forbidden territory.' Their activist art, as reflected in their production and their process, provides knowledge about this territory: how we learn across racial differences, which can often be experienced as unspeakable; how we can effect social change; and what 'we' means in working 'together.'

Onions, Strawberries, and Corn, the ethnographic data about collaborating on this play, and my analysis of my research relationship with Monique all suggest that collaborative practices in theatre across racial differences involve contested interaction and complex entanglement. Yet as this chapter makes clear, these sites of theatre practice are also about building community and establishing communication with others, creating the potential for artistic and social alliances, and developing new learning in terms of what it means to do drama. Thus, negotiating drama practices is about a combination of conflict and cooperation, connection and disconnection, and association and disassociation. It is struggle.

Collaboration as Links/Separations

I move now to a particular consideration of Monique Mojica's interview and her reflections on indigeneity and conflict in the social relations of the collaborative theatre project. I focus on Monique's observations because they help me understand differences of social identities and their implications for theatre and education. Her thinking about separations and links in theatre collaboration provides understandings about the tensions of collaborating across racial differences in the two cultural sites I address here: theatre production and theatre research. Monique underlines the complication of communicating with, and learning about, 'others.' In my talks with her, I am compelled to face 'both the possibility and necessity of communication between differently positioned subjects and the inevitable limits of any such communicative acts' (Felski 1997, 66). I am also invested in considering how, in communicative interactions across difference, 'each of us confronts our respective inability to comprehend the experience of others even as we recognize the absolute necessity of continuing the effort to do so' (Brodkey 1996, 113). This points to the impossible/possible dilemmas of such practices.

Some feminist and drama theorists might argue that emphasizing difference and tension undermines opportunities for affiliation and alliance. However, I am interested in questioning how cultural projects and activist art can proceed *with* conflict and *with* limits of communication. Under these conditions, communication may entail 'moments that go beyond rational argument, and ... that are, in some fundamental way, unspeakable, expressible only circuitously' (Ang 1997, 60). Engaging with Monique's reflections and with the rich complication of Djanet, Kate, and Monique's theatre collaboration helps me to consider the dilemmas of impossibility and possibility in the practices of drama production and drama research and to explore the consequences for education through theatre. I breathe into the tensions of Monique's work with her colleagues and into my struggles around representing Monique as an act of breathing into the heat of blown glass: with amorphous shapes, tensility, fragility, and entangled elasticity.

**Separations/Links: 'Different Parts in the Triangle'
and 'A Native Woman's Point of View'**

Monique foregrounds the simultaneity of linking and separating in the social relations of the collaboration:

Sometimes it's hard because you know I have these allies and then all of a
sudden there is a point where we all retreat to our different points in the
triangle. And there is a point where I know I stand alone with a Native
person's point of view. And it's around ... I was about to say it's around land.
It's around ... is it around land? It's around ... [*long pause*] who's here first?
[*laughs*] You know? That sounds, it sounds really juvenile, but it always
comes down to [*loudly*], 'WE WERE HERE FIRST! We were here! We were
here before anybody! We were here!'

Monique narrates a context of 'different experience' from her colleagues, and this is a position where she must 'stand alone.' Her observation that the women 'retreat to [their] different points in the triangle'
signals an irresolvable tension in the communicative practices of the
collaboration. This tension would appear to suggest particular dimensions of power, including colonialism, territorialization, and ordinary
issues for First Nations peoples. The tensions between Djanet and
Monique and between Monique and Kate are produced through ideas
about indigenous identities.

When I read this section of the transcript and when I listen to the taped
interview, I hear Monique's lyrical, dramatic, and quietly intense vocaliza-
tion. This is a voice I enjoyed listening to so much in the interviews, and I
have also taken pleasure in Monique's voice in her acting work. I hear her
mobilizing what I would call a poem/song of indigenous perspectives on
the relation of humans and land and on the sacred importance of 'the
land,' particularly for Native women (Acoose 1995; Anzaldua 1987; Brant
1993; Welsh 1994). In Monique's words (from one interview):

land
this side of the ocean
elsewhere
people who came from elsewhere
our land
you came from elsewhere
it's around land
it's around
is it around land?
but it always comes down to
WE WERE HERE FIRST!
we were here
we were here
we were here

With the differences between herself and Djanet and Kate in mind, Monique uses the image of a triangle to express the divergence, yet possible convergence, that marks difference in the collaboration as a matter of practices of communicative interchange. Monique names her identity as an indigenous woman as a key marker of difference, and she does so through an emphasis on territorial and ideological boundaries that cannot be crossed by her non-Native colleagues. The figure of a triangle suggests relation and connection, yet its points represent the different racialized positions of disconnection. The women may work as 'allies,' but they also stand 'alone.'

Land is a key idea through which Djanet, Kate, and Monique are situated in the triangular working relations, as Monique fashions them. First Nations artist Doreen Jensen reflects on the significance of land in relation to First Nations cultures in this way: 'Our art is our cultural identity; it's our politics ... Our culture is this land. Whether you acknowledge it or ignore it, the land and the culture are one. Land claims have to be settled' (McMichael 1999). In Christine Welsh's film *Keepers of the Fire* (1994), a number of Mohawk, Tobique, and Haida women emphasize that with 'anything to do with land, you have to take a stand,' and that this action is a 'sacred responsibility.' It is possible for Monique to mobilize her particular Native identity through ideas concerning land, originary habitation, and a distinct and oppositional identity from Europeans and all people 'from elsewhere.' This negotiation of her identity is political, for '[m]embers of embattled communities have to "theorize" about identity everyday: they have to circulated [*sic*] how they are viewed by others and how they view themselves' (George Lipsitz, in McLaren 1997, 158). Furthermore, if the telling of an individual narrative requires telling the stories of the collective (Visweswaran 1994), then Monique's individual narration about her 'self' requires a telling about her relation to 'others' situated in First Nations collectivity. In Western traditions, moreover, the individual is the basis for human relations, and those relations are seen as being in opposition to nature and the land (Smith 1999). Yet for many non-Western and non-white cultures, identity may be constructed through relationship to others, to land, and to nature (Flax 1993; Smith 1999). Monique underlines this knowledge. Her emphasis on indigenous survival through connection to the land and on standing 'alone with a Native person's point of view' may suggest another interpretation of the title *Onions, Strawberries, and Corn*. Representing the corn in the title, Monique could be described as 'indigenous like corn' and as 'tenacious, tightly wrapped in the husks of her culture' (Anzaldua 1987, 81). Monique's narration might be read as negotiating an idea like 'Indians endure' (Gunn Allen 1990, 299) in relation to her non-Native colleagues, Djanet and Kate.

Ideas about land, place, or geography reference the violent histories through which Native lands and bodies have been brought under colonial control and the ways in which the bodies of colonized women and colonial women are related in complex patterns of power through the 'vast, fissured architecture of imperialism' (McClintock 1995, 6). Monique is positioned in a discourse that articulates how colonialism functions through the usurpation of land. Young suggests three implications of territorialization within colonialism, and I read Monique's interview narrative as related to these activities: the seizure of land or space, including cultural space; the formation of the state and state controls around land as private property; and, in territorial contexts, the violences perpetrated on bodies required as labour for capital (1995, 172–4).

When I ask Monique if/how a breakdown of communication might materialize during work on the play, she discusses how that occurs differently with Kate, her white friend and colleague, than with Djanet, her African-Canadian friend and colleague. Monique terms the breakdown in communication with Kate as a 'point of discord,' which would appear to resonate around originary habitation as a particular mobilization of indigeneity.

> For me that happens with Kate too in a different way ... in that she sees a tremendous difference, having grown up in England, between European culture, British culture, and North American culture. Where to me, it's all European. So that's a Native person's point of view. You're all Europeans. I don't see much difference between Americans and Canadians or Americans, Canadians, and Brits. You're all Europeans. And that's a point of, of discord. [J.: Hm, hmm] Because Kate does insist that there's a difference, there's a whole part of North American culture she knows nothing about or didn't participate in because she was in England. But, you know, I don't care! That's recent! You're all Europeans! You did not come from this continent! You came from elsewhere.

Kate, according to Monique, might 'insist' there is a difference between North American and British white cultures, but for Monique it is important to be able to claim, 'We were here first,' in opposition to 'Others' who are 'all Europeans.'

While Monique also makes a distinction between her 'politic and position' in relation to Djanet's, it seems Monique is less emphatic in her expression of what she calls the 'difficulty' between them. Difference is again situated in opposition and between 'indigenous people and people who come from elsewhere.' However, I hear Monique struggling to work out her understanding of Djanet's 'politic and position' with regard to people of the diaspora. She says:

> Hmm ... [*long pause*] Sometimes Djanet and I have had some difficulty around me trying to explain the difference in politic and position if you're talking about indigenous peoples. And sometimes that has been difficult because if you're on this side of the ocean and this is our land, there's a very different ... position from being part of the diaspora. The indigenous and diaspora are polarities ... And I make a distinction between ... First Nations people and people of colour ... But I think that ... sometimes that position is difficult, difficult for Djanet. What she's expressed to me. Indigenous people and people who came from elsewhere, but she doesn't see herself as coming from elsewhere ... Herself ... Because African peoples are also indigenous peoples ... I think it goes around something like that.

Following from my interpretation of these two interview excerpts, I understand Monique to be engaging with perspectives on indigeneity and difference and to be situating the social relations of the collaboration through an indigenous/non-indigenous emphasis.

Although all three women share a commitment to anti-racism in their work, Kate, as a white woman, might be positioned as linked to a history of white colonial forces in relation to First Nations people. Djanet, as an African-Canadian woman, might be associated with peoples who have experienced imperialist domination and oppression. In terms of First Nations women and African-Canadian women in contemporary Canadian society, there are a range of shared racisms that Djanet and Monique may be said to experience. Yet there are specificities in those experiences that would suggest a range of different injustices, violences, and risks. It seems to me that Monique insists on the differences between First Nations people and people of colour, while she makes a point of recognizing and working with how she situates Djanet's views. Once again, Monique is unsettling self/other oppositions. Djanet's identity might be understood in relation to the following: 'Black and female identities are not simply figurative or superficial sites of play and metaphor, but occupy very real political spaces of diaspora, dispossession and resistance. What is complicated is the simultaneity of suffering and power, marginalisation and threat, submission and narcissism, which accrue to Black and women's bodies and representation in racist cultures' (Kanneh 1995, 346). In working with 'difficulty' (in terms of her relationship to Djanet) and 'discord' (in terms of her relationship to Kate) as descriptors of different forms of collaborative tensions, Monique maps out how power circulates through relations of gender, race, nation, class, territory, and birthplace.

The demarcation of Native women, white women, and Black women into 'analytically distinct oppressed groups' can serve to support the construction of a unified, oppressed Native constituency that can fight racism (Knowles and Mercer 1992, 122). Thus, a group, however small, organizes around specific issues and demands, temporarily drawing support from various constituencies. In addition, the group or community may become undifferentiated and essentialized. However, as Rey Chow argues, 'pressing the claims of the local ... does not mean essentializing one position; instead it means using that position as a parallel for allying with others' (1992, 114). This view necessitates a continual examination of what is possible in/for alliance, coalition, kinship, and collaboration. It speaks to what may be sites of struggle in activist art: there will always be connections and disconnections that make the creation of that art complex. Monique's interview narratives suggest a negotiation of racialized relations at the points of tension in negotiating drama practices. She makes claims of commonality for Native struggles in general while simultaneously situating the specific political conditions that might provoke a particular expression and moment of allegiance and resistance. Monique refuses oppositional perspectives and, instead, negotiates an integrative approach that can juggle, strategically, the notion of a linked community identity and tradition with the idea of differentiated community knowledges and processes. Thus, in terms of the theatre collaboration, Monique recognizes the complexity of learning about 'others,' about the 'how' of drama in relation to the 'what,' and about the contentious ways that theatre practices are sustained *and* made fragile.

In like manner to Monique's emphasis, Stuart Hall, recognized as an important theorist for questions of difference in education, suggests two different perspectives on cultural identity (1990). One view emphasizes the notion of 'a true self' that is part of a shared and unified collective culture. This is an identity of recuperation such that marginalized peoples can resist, reinterpret, and reconstruct histories of domination. Hall's other version of cultural identity underscores difference, discontinuity, and the idea of identity as process. He does not place these perspectives in opposition, in that each is recognized as necessary. Yet he does not suggest that they might operate *simultaneously*, and I believe it is the simultaneity with which Monique struggles as a Native woman, as 'a provisional, contingent, strategic, constructed subject' (Lather 1991, 120). The constitution of identity through an opposition to all others provides a means whereby a community functions with knowable boundaries, definitions, and practices. This negotiation offers indigenous peoples survival in the face of historical and contemporary terrors, dangers, violences, and genocides. Monique underlines the importance of a collective cultural identity, while recognizing the limitations of a view that establishes an aspect of 'identity as an irreducible category of existence' (Richards 1993, 50). She reworks and reflows a negotiated identity: a movement of affirmation/interrogation, interrogation/affirmation ... the movement of a loom: pause, set, weave, pause ...

Monique articulates an engagement with the complexity of what it means to be 'allies' with Djanet and Kate, and she points to how she connects and disconnects with each of her colleagues differently. The tension is embedded in a politics of difference and, simultaneously, a separating of self and other and an aligning of self with other. Trinh Minh-ha's notion of the 'outside in inside out' underlines this complication: 'She is this Inappropriate Other/Same who moves about with always at least two/four gestures: that of affirming "I am like you" while persisting in her difference; and that of reminding "I am different" while unsettling every definition of otherness arrived at' (1991, 74).

Trinh's idea of a subject who struggles for connection and recognition while simultaneously holding on to a position of separation and difference is important for learning in theatre. Theatre practitioners work in a social situation, and they attempt to negotiate their relationships through various forms of language and different modes of communication. Gavin Bolton (1984) argues that learning through dramatic action is a process of separation as well as one of connection and interaction. Learning in a site of theatre collaboration involving communicating across different racial locations requires an understanding of the 'other' as simultaneously separate and attached, similar and different.

A Feminist Reworking of Theatre Research: Performing an Accountable Positioning

In this final section, I point to some new directions for interrogating my theorizations about Monique's interview reflections. I focus on Monique's use of the term 'half-breed' to name her identity and on my interpretation of her self-representation. I begin to open up the ways that racial difference, particularly my positioning in whiteness, shapes my interpretive frames. The significance of Monique's identification as half-breed is central not only in her discussions with me about her working relations with Djanet and Kate, but also in *Onions, Strawberries, and Corn*. Monique developed a character called Savagina Halfbreed Jones, who rages against white dominant culture.

In my collaboration with Monique, as a white researcher working with a Native research participant, I struggle with ongoing issues about representational practices in art and research and with questions of ethical practice in qualitative inquiry in the arts. Importantly, I address the implications for communication and understanding in working with 'others' in drama and education. Thus, my focus in this section is about 'accountable positioning' in theatre research, and it is shaped by concerns of language and power in relation to how a researcher represents a research participant, how an academic represents an artist, how a white woman represents a Native woman. In the previous section, I discussed how Monique articulates the complexity of collaborating across racial difference in a theatre project. I now turn to this complexity in a theatre research relationship.

Interviews and conversations with Monique provoked an interrogation of how academic theories – and my investment in those theories – about identity, 'otherness,' and difference have been developed predominantly in relation to non-indigenous subjects. When Monique and I met to discuss my interpretive work, we talked about my writing and about language. We considered the term 'hybridity,' which is central in postcolonial theory, and the ways in which my application of that theoretical language as a response to her use of the term 'half-breed' might fail to take account of racial terminology. For theatre researchers, it is important to develop responsible and accountable writing about artists' identities. This is particularly the case when working with research participants who are activist artists and for whom anti-racist practices are central in their plays and their working processes. The questions behind such a goal include, How does a researcher learn in theatre research? and How can writing practices in theatre research be negotiated when racial differences shape different conceptual frameworks for researchers and for research participants?

Monique's interviews indicate how she situates herself racially. She names herself as 'half-breed' and articulates this Native identity through drawing on competing regimes of bridging and separation, symmetry and asymmetry, fragmentation and coherence, and stability and tenuousness. In the interviews Monique suggests that her identity as a Native woman connects her to Djanet through Djanet's Arawak (African Native) background. Her Jewish heritage connects her to Kate's Jewish identity. Yet, as I have mapped out earlier in this chapter, Monique also believes that she 'stands alone' from her fellow artists. Following from these complications, Monique has to negotiate with her colleagues when it comes to writing about race in their play and to collaborating across their racial differences. Implicating ideas of nation, territory, culture, and blood to articulate what it means to be a half-breed, Monique says:

How do you live with that identity
when you are always trying
to balance
the sum of many parts?

cause all of those
all of those individual little pieces –
and even the Native part which is, you know, my identity,
is two different,
[J.: Hm, Hmm]
two different
nations adopted into a third

and, you know, living in a family of a fourth
and in the territory of two others.
[*laughs*] I mean
what I do
and what I live
comes from all of those.

But it's not compartmentalized
in the living of it.

I hate that about being a half-breed,
about being that bridge, because
you're always the one
that, that things pull on.
The bridge

between two cultures
living in two worlds,

I have had the experience of someone who is mixed-blood, who is

a child
of a Holocaust survivor
and the child of ...

a mixed-blood Native person who ...
despite all odds
forged
an identity as an indigenous person of this continent
... And that's weird.

It's very complex.

'Half-breed,' the term Monique uses to name her 'mixed-blood' indigenous identity, surfaces rich knowledges about racial identity and histories of racism in Canada. These embedded knowledges are crucial to the collaborative theatre process and the activist art practice of the three women, in that Monique's, Kate's, and Djanet's work focuses on how identities are forged and claimed. In their play and in their working practices, they constantly ask what it means to be a white woman, an African-Canadian woman, and a Native woman. In *Onions, Strawberries, and Corn*, autobiographical narratives and created characters speak to their individual and related identities. In the interviews, they relate stories of how they understand their racial locations and the implications for collaborative practices.

'Half-breed' references normalizing regimes and mechanisms of power and language including, for example, Native contact with Europeans; state-legislated definitions of 'Indian' and indigenous theorizations of 'Indianness'; miscegenation and the myths of its dangers, degeneracies, deviations, and moral disorders; eroticized and exoticized racialized 'others'; the licentiousness of classed and raced bodies; and racialized heterosexuality (see, e.g., Gilman 1997; Kulchyski 1992; McLaren 1997; Stoler 1995; Threadgold 1997; Trinh 1991; and Young 1995). 'Half-breed' may also connote histories of Native resistances, protests, accommodations, survivals, and genocides. Monique's use of 'half-breed' points to the mechanisms of power that determined who could be accorded the status of 'Indian' in Canada. Historically, the Canadian government fostered animosity against half-breed and light-skinned Indians through systemic Indian-against-Indian regulations and structures. Monique brings all of these meanings about power and colonialism to her use of the term 'half-breed.' Her language is political, and it shapes the kind of education that Monique, Kate, and Djanet bring to their activist art: an interrogation of racially organized systems of domination.

How did Monique and I negotiate a collaborative research process? How did I learn through theatre research across racial difference? In a draft of my writing, to which Monique responded, I suggested that 'hybridization,' as a term underlining struggle, opposition, and negotiation (Ang 1997; Bhabha and Hassan 1995; Trinh 1991) and emphasizing the 'unassimilability of cultural differences' (Ang 1997, 62), might be a way of understanding Monique's identity as half-breed in relation to her colleagues. Following from my discussions with her, however, this idea provokes concerns for me. There is a tendency for hybridity to refer to an equal mixing of parts. Yet there are power differences in hybrid positions. The white and indigenous aspects of Monique's identity are not equivalent or parallel: not equally negotiable or equally in opposition. Monique clearly refuses whiteness in her interviews, and in her representation in *Onions, Strawberries, and Corn,* she names herself as a Native woman who is a half-breed. She narrates a different story from my emphasis on hybridity and my underlining of a mix that positions whiteness in balance with indigeneity. My theoretical lens can be read as underlining the authority of whiteness and its influence in shaping my interpretive practices.

When I met with Monique to discuss my writing, she observed, 'I have a reaction to the word "hybrid"' (personal communication, 25 February 2000). Monique and I began a discussion about the power of language, the historical roots of language, and how terms applied to indigenous peoples have developed through racist and colonialist ideologies. She was interested in an examination of how her reflections on her 'political position' might challenge my suppositions: 'Some of the places I talk from are opposite from academic assumptions about identity, nationhood, and citizenry' (ibid.). From her position as an activist artist, Monique questions how my academic theoretical constructions of difference may meet their limits. She brought a book about racial terminology (Forbes 1988) to my attention, and together we looked up the word 'hybrid.' The author examines the meanings of racial terms and concepts and their historical and contemporary application to African-American and Aboriginal mixed peoples. Both Monique and I learned that the term 'hybrid' is attached to wild animals. Her view that the term 'hybrid' positions mixed-race peoples as non-human was reinforced by the author's research on a range of cultures where 'hybrid,' referring to wild animals, holds racist connotations. The author also notes that such terms as 'hybrid' and 'mulatto' were 'designed to identify and to limit, to control, *and*, by and large, *to exclude*' (ibid., 130). Through colonial and imperial force, terms were used to categorize racial difference. Monique's concern with my use of hybridity and hybridization underlines the replacement of, or the erasure of, her term 'half-breed,' which she politically recuperates 'in defiance of the historically derogatory implications of the term' (personal communication, 25 February 2000).

Monique's language for her identity is integral to her work with Djanet and Kate, in both the text of the play they produced and in the project's working relations. As a theatre researcher, I can negotiate an accountable positioning by recognizing the significance of Monique's identity claim of half-breed. The significance of her naming of identity and its importance for activist art is clear in an interview comment, where she speaks to the assimilation, dispossession, genocide, *and* resistance of Native peoples: 'Everything I do as an artist, whether consciously or unconsciously, I do as a memorial to that survival, I do as a memorial to that genocide.'

Negotiated Positions in the 'Hows' of Drama

We need to see what race means and does in those institutions that play so large a part in defining what counts as official knowledge and in helping to form identities around those definitions.

(Apple 1993, viii)

When I first addressed the negotiation of drama practices, I worked with Monique's reflections on her work with Kate and Djanet to produce theatre. I read Monique as constituting the working relations of a collaboration in an activist theatre project through narratives of association and disassociation and of shared and conflicting histories and experiences: 'Respective experiential worlds are not easily reconcilable and mutually translatable into one another's discursive registers' (Ang 1997, 61). Monique's idea of the 'different points of the triangle' as a descriptor of the working relations signals a geometric or territorial figure of boundaries that suggests the simultaneous vibrations of disparate points *and* connected lines. She and her colleagues are invested in being allies in cultural production, and she connects and disconnects with each woman differently. However, the ideas about indigeneity through which

Monique self-identifies are constructed as an oppositional space in which she stands alone.

In discussing the negotiation of drama practices, I reflected above on how my conceptual categories define and constrain interpretation of the practices of a theatre artist. My theoretical applications have met their limit in how I take up Monique's naming of her identity – an identity that is so crucial to how she works as an artist. I have attended to these challenges as an attempt to make visible my positioning in whiteness and the consequence for my research practices, to map out my learning in theatre research, and to examine particular aspects of the collaborative relations between a research participant who is a theatre practitioner and myself as a theatre researcher.

By troubling the significance and implications of racialized relations in theatre production and theatre research, I hope to suggest that relations and practices in drama activities are negotiated in contentious, mutable, and complex ways. Attention to the possibilities and impossibilities of theatre practices informs any deeper understanding of the tensions and conflicts of the 'how' in drama. The problematic of the 'what' of drama and how it educates us becomes a complex interrogation of power and responsibility in human communicative exchanges. One of the most important ways that drama can educate us is through studying theatre as a social and cultural production that is organized and negotiated through racialized relations of struggle.

Drama through the Eyes of Faith

WALTER PITMAN

The mention of drama education conjures up the image of a group of children or young people in a classroom engaged in the study of text, or better, acting in a scene of a play which they themselves have written. We tend to dismiss adult drama education, particularly that taking place outside the institutional framework. It is perceived as peripheral, even trivial, when set beside the serious work of child and youth learning, which is the basic business of the school, the college, or the university. I wish to address this strand of drama education in the context of the informal adult learning that takes place throughout our lives outside the standard venue of the classroom, both connected to our personal human needs and on a world stage, intervening in the very events that decide the life chances of millions of people. I do so without embarrassment as, on the first point, there has been a good deal of research on the extent to which each of us is involved in a variety of educational projects at any one time in our lives. The decision to attend a play after preparing oneself mentally and emotionally for the occasion, reflecting and contributing to a greater individual and societal understanding of the play's theme, is an example of such a project.

I also do so in the knowledge that Canada is recognized throughout the world as a nation on the pinnacle of both the theory and practice of adult education, largely as a result of the work of Ted Corbett and, particularly, Roby Kidd, who died some years ago after decades of writing and direct, 'on-the street' involvement, but not before placing Canada in the forefront of the adult education movement. The fact that the offices of the International Council for Adult Education are to be found, not in New York or Geneva, but in Toronto indicates the leadership that Kidd provided over several decades, even before he took on the chair of the

Department of Adult Education at the Ontario Institute for Studies in Education in the 1960s.

Can we, as teachers, accept the fact that most drama education, both informal and adult-oriented, takes place after 10 pm in theatre foyers, on the street outside the community's theatre, and in nearby bars and restaurants? It goes against the grain for most academics whose lives are spent watching students learn in a formal setting and judging the quality of the experience in the marks achieved in tests and examinations that determine the retention and understanding of a particular body of material. Yet, in a city like Toronto, with its dozens of theatrical perform-ances every night, this informal learning network involves many thou-sands of adults, old and young. How can these learning experiences be discounted? It may be that some of the discussions are casual and unfocused, but in my experience they are more likely intense and even confrontational. A major problem for the educator's point of view on the process's legitimacy is that the 'class' secures its information about the play and its schedule of performances from the entertainment section of the local newspaper. At least in North America this learning is thus characterized as 'entertainment,' even though the subject matter of the play may concern the fragility of relationships that keep families to-gether or drive them apart, the perceptions of race and gender that destroy civil society, the greed and violence that threaten the very future of humankind. It is the largest, most consistently pervasive, and most continuing form of drama education to be found in our society. It may not fully correspond to our definition of what drama education should be within the context of a formal curriculum and the normal relation-ship of instructors and students, but it nonetheless deserves our atten-tion, even though, ironically, this contemplation and discussion of a theatrical presentation may not be perceived as 'education' by either the purveyors of professional theatre or the clientele to whom they 'pitch' their message of enticement. The reality is that part of what we do in the formal classroom and call 'drama education' comes down to a process devoted to understanding the complexities of life through the minds of great playwrights and their interpreters on stages to which we look for insight and possibly, on occasion, transformation. But the informal proc-ess is engaged in precisely the same task.

For the last number of years, the author of this chapter has been involved in gathering together a group of theatre-goers, very much the same kind of people who can be found discussing the play in the foyer, the street, the bar and the restaurant, and seeking to bring some form to that discussion. The venue for the group is a church reception room with a fireplace, easy chairs and couches, and access to coffee for those so addicted. The group do not share job or life experiences, but they are on a shared-faith journey. They have committed to buying a subscription, in this case, to the Toronto CanStage line-up of plays at its Front Street St Lawrence Centre Theatre space. [This series was selected for its presentation of a broad variety of productions from the classics to the contemporary, from Canadian to works from Europe and the United Kingdom, and even translations of plays from languages other than English.] The participants would regard themselves as an 'ordinary' group of people who share one enthusiasm: a love of drama and theatre and a desire to find meaning in what they have seen on stage. It may be a comedy that seeks mostly to amuse or a tragedy that shakes the very being – each receives a serious viewing. We share a small planet in a vast universe with these playwrights, and that very fact is reason to expect drama to express ideas and emotions that are worthy of our attention. The fact that one, ten, or twenty of our terrestrial colleagues on this crying earth have put enormous energy and intellectual rigour to the task of conveying that message on stage is surely enough to give us pause and encourage us to join them 'beyond the footlights' in the intellectual struggle they have endured on our behalf. Normally, we do so after the play has ended and the theatre is darkened.

That a group of theatre-goers should think it appropriate to come together in a church may be disconcerting to those who believe that 'religious folk' are single-dimensional, bent upon prayer and worship, and isolated from the 'cut and thrust' of the world (at least on Sunday morning). Even those who can get past that stereotype would suspect that the religiously oriented would, as well, find modern plays with street language and explicit sexuality quite unnerving. In fact, my experience with this group not only leads me to the observation that the participants are connected with all the 'drama' of everyday living, but that these elements of realism that pervade the contemporary stage neither shock not titillate them. All they ask is that the realism have legitimacy and integrity. One might observe that there is as much sexuality, mayhem, and violence in the Holy Scriptures than could ever be portrayed either on Front or Berkeley Street.

More important, drama and religion have, down through the ages, been inextricably linked. There are many theories about how humankind came to 'present a mirror to nature' on a risen platform for fellow citizens to contemplate. The Greek dramatists may be the earliest examples we have that seem closest in their expression to our twenty-first-century experience, but most scholars find drama emerging from ritual that sought to understand a complex universe many thousands of years before an itinerant actor named Thespis stepped on an Athenian stage in 534 BC.

Although, for the casual observer, church drama may be seen as the annual depiction of a stable scene in bathrobes and towels (most hilariously depicted in John Irving's novel *A Prayer for Owen Meany*), the Christian worship service in the mainstream religious traditions as well as the Christian liturgical year have a dramatic construction that makes a program of shared intellectual exploration around theatrical experience quite appropriate. There is a weekly drama on Sunday mornings that commands the attention of a significant minority in our society. A word about the particular church in which the 'drama education' takes place is necessary. Lawrence Park Community Church, though it was multi-denominational in its beginnings shortly after the Second World War, has for some decades been associated with the United Church of Canada. It is not unusual in its congregational demography from most other parish churches, although its location in a well-to-do North Toronto neighbourhood would seem to suggest a higher than normal income bracket for most of its members. Nonetheless, these theatre-goers are engineers, secretaries, teachers, and homemakers. None would perceive themselves to be theatre people in the professional sense, but all share, as well as an interest in the spiritual, an enthusiasm for the theatre experience.

A participant in the discussion, the Reverend Dr Lillian Perigoe, the church's minister, regards theatre as the way the human spirit connects with the divine. She believes that a faith that perceives itself as incarnational must seek an incarnational worship medium and that drama is indeed the way the 'living word' can become blood, flesh, and emotional involvement. In a preaching ministry, she is aware that the theologian can become too theoretical. She sees the dramatic moment as a marvellous tool for the preacher, an opportunity to give life to 'the word' and connect it to people and their lives. Admittedly, not every church is as consciously aware of its theatrical roots as the one in which this congregational group meets. Certainly every service contains dramatic tension and resolution, and that is, in part, the unique contribution of Lillian Perigoe, an avid playgoer, indeed a generous supporter of the Stratford Festival and, more significantly, a former English teacher with a distinguished career as both teacher and department head before choosing to take up this new vocation. She was able to bring all the insights and skills of her former profession to her new work as a United Church minister. One example from the worship service may suffice. When the time comes for the reading of scriptural passages, she is comfortable in ignoring the lectern, on which a huge open volume containing Holy Scripture rests, and placing a simple wooden stool as close to her congregants as the architecture of the sanctuary will allow. She then introduces her 'by-heart' recitation of that Sunday's passage with a simple, 'Let me tell you a story.' The anticipatory tension is palpable in the sanctuary. Very simply, she recounts the 'story' contained in the lectionary reading, with all the shifts it contains, until it reaches its dramatic climax. Her stories for children contain every nuance of theatrical skill one could expect on a stage. However, she is conscious that being too 'dramatic' may bring down on her head the charge of being too 'theatrical,' by definition, in the minds of some people, 'irreligious,' or at least highly suspect. In this church the chancel has recently been redesigned and rebuilt; some would say, not so much as a place of sanctity, but as a stage on which children and parents, singers and instrumentalists, yes, even dancers, express sadness and despair, love and hope. Sanctity and drama become one. It was her inspiration that led to the title for the theatre program: 'Drama Through the Eyes of Faith.' She insisted that these gatherings would be part of the educational development of the congregation rather than a 'precious' little group far apart from the main thrust of the church's normal activity.

The purpose of the program was very clear from the outset. It would encourage a love of the theatre as a legitimate source of knowledge and understanding. The process would lead to a deepening comprehension of the human condition, in all its glory and its failings. Both were appropriate subjects for any faith community proclaiming its confidence in a compassionate divinity and beginning its creed each week with the assertion, 'We are not alone, we live in God's world ...' Most important, there was recognition that these plays were not presented in a Christian or Jewish or Buddhist context, but within a secular, materialist society. The presentations were not morality plays, and theatre-goers had no reason to believe that their particular faith and beliefs, or their ethical and behavioural understandings, should enjoy any more credence on the stages of the twenty-first century than any other faith experience and belief pattern, or indeed a legitimately atheistic point of view. Theatre confronts, but it also reflects the world around us, and it was essential for this group to realize the implications of living in a society in which no organized religion has much resonance with the majority of people, either in the theatre community or beyond. The philosophy or theology, or the absence of either, on the part of the playwright, as exposed by the drama, had to be recognized and respected. However, the right of the audience member to agree or disagree, and to do so strongly and with conviction, was a basis for an experience that has turned out to be most rewarding.

One might consider the discussions that have erupted around the plays presented by the Canadian Stage in the 2000–2001 season as examples of the struggle that takes place among these playgoers. Carol Shields's *Larry's Party* inspired Richard Ouzounian to adapt the novel into a piece of musical theatre that received much negative critical comment, but very accurately followed the author's story. It revolves around the efforts of 'Larry' to find himself within the metaphor of the garden maze, a construction that captures his attention after a visit to Hampton Court in the UK, and provides him with both his vocation and his reason for living. He becomes successful, planting mazes in the gardens of wealthy clients, and his career and comparative prosperity are assured. The discussion, while focusing briefly on the creative work of the playwright and the strong direction of Robin Phillips, soon concentrated on the development of 'Larry's' character, the circumstances that led to the breakdown of his relationships with his wife, the disintegration of his family, and the implications that all this had on the people around him. The set was a constant reminder of the main theme ... the degree to which we all sense life as a 'maze' and find our way to our 'centre' with a myriad collection of personal strategies, including intellectual grasp and spiritual development. In every way, the play, in spite of one or two silly and trivial songs, did remind the audience that we live in a world that is itself a maze of disorder and chaos demanding our efforts to bring form and order to our own experience and understanding. (The recent events of September 11th, 2001, have been a revelation to those who thought that living on the North American continent was a sure defence against the horrors faced by those who inhabit other parts of the world.)

The participants offered thoughtful observations on the degree to which the play itself lost its own way, perhaps through too closely following the text of the novel, but there was as well an appreciation of the integrity of the production and the skill of the actors who had brought the piece to life. (The creativity of the author and those who have been part of a production are worthy subjects for a group of people who believe that 'creativity' itself is a divine gift and that its use perhaps brings us closer to our Creator than does any other human function.) This musical had an intensity that few musicals achieve and a powerful climax that moved some members of the discussion group to tears. The discussants struggled to analyse the elements of Larry's character that had led to his pain and broken relationships. Yet, there was reason to celebrate the developing sensitivity, compassion, and forgiveness that had marked the conclusion of the play. The man had grown as a human being, long-standing conflict had been resolved, and a restoration of a positive and loving relationship had overcome the self-centredness that had emerged from the experiences of his early childhood years including those that transpired within his own family. The play and the subsequent discussion revealed the enormous pressures that modern life places on each of us as we seek to find our individual response to the drama of our existence. There was no attempt with us to find easy answers based on a 'Have you been saved?' solution that surfaces in more evangelical religious communities. We recognized the terrible 'maze' of our own experience and the enormous challenges we must overcome in order to enhance our lives and dwell abundantly on this planet.

Another play, *Wit*, was surely one of the most powerful theatre pieces written in recent years. It is almost a 'one-woman' show, with the Toronto production featuring a Canadian, Seana McKenna, playing Vivien Bearing, PhD, in a superb performance that left the audience in virtual trauma. The central figure is a serious scholar with an extraordinary mind and a breathtaking command of language that expresses her 'wit' assuredly, but her fear as well – her horror, her sense of helplessness, her pain in the knowledge that she is dying of ovarian cancer. She appears on stage in hospital garb, impatient and angry about her treatment by both the hospital and life itself. Her barbed tongue intimidates most of her health-care workers and she exhibits initially an attitude of defiance at her fate as a patient at the mercy of forces quite beyond the command of her sharp mind and devastating articulation. The interchanges with her doctors and nurses reveal a life filled with satisfaction as a scholar but, in retrospect, exhibiting little concern for the needs of others. Her students were obviously terrified by her expectations and she had shown little compassion for the crises in their lives. The tension of watching a death take place before one's very eyes is more than upsetting, it is numbing. At one performance, an audience member collapsed and there was a fifteen-minute delay while her physical needs were addressed. There were, as there are in most good plays, multiple messages that engaged the theatre group in a series of debates: the question of euthanasia as a legitimate alternative to the excruciating pain we had witnessed and the loss of dignity that the medical procedures had brought upon the patient; the right of the medical profession to treat patients as research objects in spite of all the discomfort and humiliation involved. Perhaps, most important of all, is the depiction of a brilliant woman who has lived out her life 'in her head,' specifically with John Donne's metaphysical poetry, and has lost all the balance of mind, body, and spirit that allows humankind to live with some integrity.

However, most of the discussion revolved around questions of life and death. One could have expected a simple answer from a faith group that recognition of a divine presence in the mind and spirit of Vivien Bearing could have solved the terror and despair we had witnessed. That was not the case. In fact, the severest criticism was of what appeared as a kind of spiritual transportation of a now dead human body that shook off the attributes of humanity, along with the hospital dress, to embrace a simplistic life everlasting in a cloud of water vapour and a blaze of overhead lighting. (One member of the group did see meaning in an image that reminds us that we arrive in the world naked and alone, and leave in exactly the same state.) There was more interest in the authenticity of Vivian's interaction with her mentor, a professor who had inspired her career, and in the realization that *she* had retained her enthusiasm for others around her – her grandson and her family – and had a capacity for compassion that Dr Bearing had obviously lost. This woman had somehow combined her passion for intellectual challenge with her concern for those around her. The group found compelling the depiction of a quality of caring that would teach us how to die.

At the end of the play a shaven-headed Seana McKenna received a standing ovation every night. More important, there followed a period of quiet reflection as audience members showed a reluctance to leave the theatre with their thoughts and emotions. Each member of the discussion group remembered clearly his or her reaction to the impact of the play. Each had nurtured their thoughts for some weeks, yet each, one by one, was able to articulate the meaning of this dramatic presentation with passion and emotion. Viewing the play 'through the eyes of faith' had not brought easy comfort, but another level of interpretation of the human experience and its connection to 'abundant' dying.

There is a broader issue in this matter of drama education from a faith perspective. As one looks at the impact of fundamentalism (to be found in every religion) on the world, one realizes the horror and pain over the centuries that can be attributed to the narrowness and intractability of a faith that recognizes no ambiguity, fosters no tolerance, and assigns much of the rest of humanity to a state beyond the pale, and therefore identifies those beings as legitimate victims of hate and even genocide. If people of faith can be brought to read the great dramatic literature of the ages, see and hear the irony of the human condition played out in whatever venue can be found, that is surely the ultimate vindication of drama education on a grand scale.

Indeed, one might translate drama education into a strategy for human survival. One debate on the world diplomatic scene, now that the Cold War is over, is around the issue of 'humanitarian intervention.' It is hard to believe – the Western media being of no assistance – that there are forty wars going on as these words are being written. They are not, however, the old conflicts of nation against nation. Most are internal wars that pit tribe against tribe, ethnic minority against ethnic majority. The United Nations, the world's best hope for a peaceful planet, was not organized to prevent these kinds of wars. National sovereignty is the very basis of that organization and the right to intervene in the internal affairs of other countries on the 'pretext' or the reality of human suffering at the hands of fellow citizens was never contemplated in 1945. Only now, in the new millennium and with the images of the collapsing towers of the World Trade Center forever in our minds, have we realized that a world collectivity alone can cope with terrorism. Yet we are conscious of the fact that small wars kill citizens – 90 per cent non-combatants, mostly women and children – and can escalate into full-scale conflicts that might ultimately involve nation states and the most deadly of weapons. Though the old nuclear stand-off may have disappeared, the weaponry of that era still exists and is now in the hands of governments that are substantially less responsible and stable. More to the point in these zones of conflict, the small arms in the hands of children-soldiers who have no restraints to overcome in their use are more powerful than those carried by seasoned troops in the Second World War. Until September 11th we took little interest in these 'foreign affairs.' Now we may be forced to confront the question of what indeed produces terrorists and terrorism, and the answer of a limited faith experience may not be nearly enough.

What has this to do with drama education? Simply, humanitarian intervention after conflict has begun is a questionable concept. Two examples suffice. The Rwanda massacre took place because the West was not willing to intervene; hundreds of thousands of women and children were slaughtered. The intervention of NATO in the Gulf War took place through high technology, which 'protected' the innocent by bombing them and had motives that were far from humanitarian. It is highly questionable whether any military intervention is sufficiently benign to be of great use. Only one form of intervention has the support of many who have considered these matters. It is the intervention of peace building in places where the tension can be identified long before the fighting has broken out.

Of all the strategies that will foster understanding and tolerance, encourage negotiation and accommodation, there is nothing that works more effectively than drama education, the intervention of 'live' theatre. Where lectures and slide shows do not work, drama does, often through the simple technology of the battery radio.

That is surely the ultimate expectation – that drama education could be an effective mechanism for saving the human race – a suggestion that should bring a smile to the lips of any observer who has listened for too long to the exaggerated claims and expectations of educational leaders on 'state' occasions. Obviously any hope of pre-conflict resolution will depend on a whole arsenal (to use an inappropriate word) of methodologies and strategies to reduce hatred and intolerance and find common ground for mutual security. Nonetheless, drama education is one of them and its power has matured over the centuries, particularly in recent years in Central and South America, in Africa and Asia. There is now a considerable literature that examines its beneficial effects. Gifted instructors can use the world's great dramatic literature to explore those elements of human psychology that allow conflict and violence to be the answer to every difference. Even more powerful is the invitation to potential members of opposing armies to create their own plays, making use of their own anger, fear, and desire to confront rather than talk or understand. With these considerations in mind, there is good reason to retain and expand the commitment to drama education in our schools. The young people sitting in our classrooms face a dangerous world, and while those hours in drama class may well prepare them for a life on the stage, they may also give them the skills to create a culture of peace.

In our faith community, drama education is celebrated among adults who care about theatre and their world, and wish to discuss what they have heard and seen. This experience of many thousands of adults in informal learning environments needs to be recognized and valued. These are people who see the irony of human existence and the complexity of every philosophical conflict, and can see through the simplicity of attitudes and articulations that lead to violence and death. One Canadian writer has stated that the twenty-first century will move from an obsession with an economic paradigm that has resulted in a world of very rich and desperately poor people, to one focused on cultural considerations that will put the highest priority on economic and social justice. Every environmentalist and social worker now threatened with burnout, teachers at every level, and young persons confronted with a fence in Quebec City in the spring of 2002 realize that the status quo cannot answer the deepest desires of humankind. Drama education is an important part of the spectrum of hope that allows men and women to 'soldier on' in the face of those things that seem to be disintegrating, undermining, and eroding all that is the best of the past and offering an illusory picture of prosperity for all in the future.

Drama education, a powerful mechanism for encouraging young people to confront their own demons as well as providing a lifelong strategy for confronting the problems they will face, comes to have global significance in a world that young people find hostile and unresponsive. This is a sobering thought for teachers who are themselves faced with enormous pressures and sense little public understanding of their particular challenges. Perhaps a dedication to a process that has such enormous possibilities can be a comfort to the profession and a motivation that is strong, vibrant, and dynamic, far more powerful than the pathetic 'slings and arrows of outrageous fortune' that beset them everyday. For all our sake, one hopes so!

As the World Turns: The Changing Role of Popular Drama in International Development Education

LORI MCDOUGALL

The use of drama to impart new ideas and challenge old beliefs is increasingly popular in international development education. In many developing countries, live folk theatre has been a key tool for assessing social problems, raising awareness about issues, and mobilizing public support for change. This mode of theatre is necessarily participatory in nature, relying on a collective process of learning between community members.

India, like many developing countries, has seen in recent years a mushrooming of community-based organizations, many of which have sought to use popular theatre as a tool for development education. Many such groups have sought to tie drama to specific social-development objectives, such as raising awareness of domestic violence or the importance of female empowerment. Performance methodology may be more or less participatory in nature, depending on the supporting organization and the scale of the program. Grassroots organizations tend to undertake small-scale activities that give equal weight to the 'means' (collective analysis) and the 'ends' (community mobilization). Meanwhile, larger organizations such as government departments may conceive of folk theatre as a form of mass social advertising, in which drama is used to illustrate specific developmental themes and messages in a popular fashion.

As folk drama grows in popularity among development agencies, both governmental and non-governmental, relatively few popular drama experiments have been undertaken by the mass media. Development educators have tended to view TV and radio as expensive, inflexible, and elitist formats in comparison to 'interpersonal' live theatre, performed in local dialects using local situations and idioms. At the same time, many media organizations have shied away from incorporating social messages into popular entertainment, fearing that audiences will sniff out anything too 'worthy.'

A new study from India compares the impact of education delivered by live folk drama with that delivered by the mass media. The results challenge the supremacy of live theatre and suggest a great untapped potential of TV- and radio-based drama for effective development education. Meanwhile, opportunities abound for synergies between the mass media and live drama, particularly with regard to participatory formats and processes in areas underserved by the electronic media.

These changes may have implications for educators and policy-makers in Canada and other developed counties, where the potential of TV-based drama for education may also be underutilized, and where geographically remote or socially excluded communities may benefit from such new approaches in popular education.

From Social Analysis to Social Advertising

The use of drama to inspire and educate is time-tested in the developing world. In conditions of illiteracy, poverty, and social inequity, folk theatre has been an effective form of social analysis and protest. Drama has grown beyond its classical, mythological roots to bolster political reform movements and to tilt at the failures of social and economic development. In a world where caste and political networks conspire to suppress marginal voices, folk drama has offered new avenues for democratic participation – be it on issues of political corruption, communal violence, gender inequity, or environmental destruction.

Recently, protest drama has given birth to a pragmatic new form of action-oriented drama. The social-action groups and rural movements of the early 1970s have spawned a multitude of large and small non-governmental organizations (NGOs) that now offer financial and organization support for popular drama. Today's performances use professional marketing techniques to promote highly targeted developmental change: song, dance, drama, mime, and puppetry are used to 'sell' social-development messages to audience members. Taking their cue from advertising and popular films, scriptwriters employ comedy, melodrama, suspense, action, and fantasy to entice audience interest and effect positive behavioural change.

The spread of drama-based 'social advertising' is indeed very different from the highly participatory drama of the 1970s (Deshpande 1997).

Today, folk drama is a standard tool in the social advertiser's bag of tricks – an increasingly popular alternative to billboards, wall paintings, or radio advertisements. Indeed, it is not uncommon to see newspaper advertisements from government agencies offering contracts for folk drama performances, with bids to be evaluated on the basis of cost and technical capacity. This is not surprising, given that the government of India's own 'Song and Drama Division' currently performs more than 45,000 shows per year and strains to keep up with demand from both government departments and private development agencies.

Whether efforts tend toward social analysis or social advertising, there is little doubt that today's development education has moved far beyond the moralizing messages of years ago. Audiences are entertained and persuaded, rather than subjected to dreary, didactic commands about the use of condoms or the need to boil drinking water. The merging of drama and education has opened new vistas for social development.

Inviting Participation

Live drama is clearly an effective means of bolstering knowledge and encouraging informed public choice. Live performances, staged in the foreground of the village school or administrative office, have long been associated with the virtues of 'interpersonal communication' – the notion that friends, neighbours, and relatives are the most valued source of information because they are known and trusted.

Village plays are designed to use local idioms to tell local stories that, in turn, promote community discussion and action. They may or may not involve local actors and locally written scripts, but they are witnessed by neighbours and friends and family, who may discuss them afterwards and adopt certain knowledge or attitudes as a result of this exchange. For that reason, TV and radio programs have often been considered a 'second-best' option in development education: too impersonal, unreflective of local sentiment/language, and too formal and distant in nature to provoke real attitude and behavioural change (Gumucio Dagron 2001).

Yet can this distinction be sustained? Can TV drama create characters and situations that seem just as trustworthy as the friends and relatives in one's own life? Can this 'virtual intimacy' translate into low-cost, mass-scale developmental impact? Does live drama lose its cachet when villagers begin to attach more modernity and authority to media celebrities than to once-revered community elders? And can live drama be culpable of delivering performances that fail to provoke and persuade because of a failure to invite meaningful audience participation? Indeed, one may question what is more important – the medium itself or the power of drama to provoke questions, reactions, and discussion, regardless of format.

TV Drama vs Live Drama: A Case Study

The hegemony of live drama has been challenged by the findings of a recent study comparing the educational impact of live drama with that of TV/radio. This study examined knowledge, attitudes, and practices toward leprosy in rural India following an intensive educational campaign using both live theatre and TV/radio (ORG 2001). The campaign was undertaken by BBC World Service Trust, the NGO arm of the British broadcaster's external services. It was designed to raise awareness of leprosy symptoms and to increase early detection and cure by attacking the age-old myths and social stigma associated with the disease.

The campaign involved a mix of social-advertising techniques: short, repeatable TV and radio commercials ('spots') and five-minute dramas, posters, and village plays with varying degrees of audience participation. The TV and radio programs were produced in partnership with Doordarshan, India's state-owned broadcaster, which gave a generous amount of free airtime for the programs in exchange for production funding and technical training from the BBC, which was in turn supported by the British government's Department for International Development. Since Doordarshan enjoys a terrestrial monopoly in India, most of India's poorest communities do not have regular access to any other TV channel. As a result, the leprosy programs enjoyed strong reach in rural communities. Even so, the live-drama component of the campaign was felt to be particularly important given the continued lack of access to TV and radio among some of the most marginalized – and leprosy-prevalent – communities of the project area.

Surprisingly, the quantitative study showed that the drama-based TV/radio inputs outperformed the live drama inputs by a statistically significant margin. For example:

- When asked about symptoms of leprosy, 54 per cent of respondents exposed to the live drama programs, but not to the TV/radio drama programs, reported awareness of a 'non-itchy skin patch' as a symptom of leprosy. This compared with 65 per cent of respondents who had been exposed to the TV/radio inputs but not to the live drama inputs, and with 52 per cent among respondents not exposed to either the live theatre or the TV/radio inputs.

- When asked about beliefs about leprosy, 30 per cent of respondents who had been exposed only to the live drama inputs, but not to the TV/radio inputs, said they believed that leprosy is caused by a 'curse of the gods.' This figure compares with 17 per cent among respondents exposed to only TV/radio and not to live drama, and to 56 per cent among respondents not exposed to either. Similarly, 33 per cent of respondents exposed only to live drama said they believed that 'all leprosy patients can pass the disease to others,' while just 23 per cent of respondents exposed only to TV/radio programs said the same. For those not exposed to the media inputs, the figure was 41 per cent.
- When asked about their behaviour toward leprosy patients, 33 per cent of respondents exposed only to the live drama shows said they were 'not willing to sit next to a leprosy patient.' This compares with 22 per cent among respondents exposed only to the TV/radio programs and 66 per cent among respondents not exposed to the media inputs.

Such results point to the remarkable power of both live drama and TV/radio to exert a positive impact on knowledge, attitudes, and behaviour on social development issues. However, in comparative terms, it is also apparent that TV/radio outperformed live drama by a clear margin, despite the reputed interpersonal advantages of live theatre. For example, the live theatre shows were often performed in local dialects, while the TV/radio shows were broadcast in standard Hindi. Most of the live theatre shows involved the participation of a health worker who could advise on diagnosis and local treatment facilities, while the TV/radio shows did not attempt to give specific addresses/locations of treatment clinics. Further, 79 per cent of respondents who saw the live theatre shows said that they found them 'very interesting'; this compares with a similar approval rating of 75 per cent for the TV/radio spots and dramas.

Cumulative Effect

Why should TV- and radio-based drama outperform live drama, despite similar audience approval ratings and the localized advantages of live drama?

One answer may be that TV and radio programs can be highly repeatable, creating a cumulative educational effect in a way that a one-time drama show cannot. For example, the BBC's leprosy spots and dramas sought to build in as much entertainment as possible, so audiences would tolerate frequent repetition of the programs. The scripts echoed those of Bollywood films, and were packed with family melodrama, singing and dancing, and action-adventure. They also starred some of India's most loved film heroes, comedians, and sports celebrities. Finally, a rhyming jingle and theme music was used at the end of each spot and drama to repeat the key educational message and to act as a unifying force for the campaign. This created strong public appreciation of the programs, encouraging the broadcasters to schedule the programs more often, which in turn translated into a greater level of educational impact. Indeed, repeatability is the chief advantage of drama-based formats compared with non-fiction programs, such as documentaries or instructional programs.

The cumulative impact of this reach cannot be underestimated, enabled as it is by the massive economic efficiency of TV/radio-based education relative to live theatre. When analysed on a per-viewer basis, TV and radio programs are far more cost-effective than live theatre shows, which are naturally more limited in audience size. During the BBC leprosy campaign, the cost per viewer reached of the TV/radio programs was many times cheaper than that of live theatre shows – less than Cdn. $0.01 (0.18 rupees) per person compared with $0.22 (6.4 rupees) per person reached by live theatre.

Apart from the quantity of exposure, the quality of the productions, and the ability to 'standardize,' the educational content has also played a key role in the success of the BBC electronic media programs. TV and radio programs can be rerecorded, edited, and perfected before broadcast, and each broadcast will be identical to the one before. By contrast, live theatre performances can be highly uneven, with educational themes delivered with greater or lesser clarity by performers who may be struggling with their own prejudices and myths about the subject matter, which can in turn be reflected in their dramatic interpretations and their on-stage confidence. Of course, highly professional stage direction and strong pre-performance workshopping may assist in improving performances, but standardization across a large number of troupes and performances is rarely possible given the limited resources of most development-education programs.

Finally, the educational muscle of the electronic media relative to live theatre may be rooted in changing public tastes. TV, in particular, appears to represent a new form of moral authority and modernity in rural India, especially in the eyes of adolescents and young people. This may make messages delivered by traditional forms of media, like village theatre, seem less interesting or important by comparison because the messages tend to be de-linked from the things that TV audiences have come to associate with upward mobility, notably, wealth, urbanity, youth, and education.

TV access continues to spread like bush fire across the developing world. TV audiences in India have increased five-fold over the past ten years, rising from 110 million people in 1989 to 280 million in 1993 to more than 500 million by 1999 (Singhal and Rogers 2001). This has significant implications for traditional social patterns and modes of education. The traditional moral authority of the village headman or family elders may pale in comparison to that embodied by India's top cricket hero or action-movie hero. Glamorous drama serials may promote consumer aspirations while devaluing traditional village life, leading to rising rates of rural-urban migration, intergenerational conflict, and greater personal dissatisfaction. On the other hand, strong TV role models can offer new vistas for gender equity, influencing both male and female viewers to accept the notion of female employment outside the household and increased male domestic responsibilities.

Indeed, group viewing of such popular serials can promote lively discussion among family members about the issues raised, leading to the erosion of traditional barriers, among young and old, men and women, and even members of different castes living in the same community (Johnson 2000). Just as live theatre relies on interpersonal effects for impact and authority, drama-based TV programs can create a similar effect by creating positive and negative role models that stimulate discussion and collective learning among community members.

All this would suggest that the vehicle for development education – live theatre or the electronic media – may be somewhat less important than public perception of the quality and authority of the drama showcased on stage, and also less important than the triggers provided by each for participatory discussion and analysis – be it on an individual level (i.e., the para-social interaction of character and viewer) or a collective level (i.e., viewer to viewer).

Bridging the Electronic Divide

TV drama may be an important new vehicle for development education, but what of communities and individuals that lack access to the electronic media? Much has been written of the 'digital divide' – the notion that electronic-based education may accelerate the creation of an underclass who lack the money, social connections, literacy, and geographic ability to access electronic-based education, whether it's delivered via the Internet in Canada or across TV screens in rural India. Indeed, almost every village in India may have a TV set, allowing a broader spread of education than ever, but audience characteristics still tend to reflect certain gender, caste, spatial, and income divisions.

These realities would suggest that a multiplicity of vehicles will continue to be necessary to ensure that a degree of educational equity is promoted. To this extent, there will always be a role for live theatre in delivering development education in India, as long as villages remain unelectrified and poverty keeps TV ownership out of reach for all. Improved targeting of live performance locations would seem to be increasingly important, so that such performances can be planned for communities with the least access to the electronic media.

There may also be synergies to be realized between drama-based TV and live drama. One wonders about the possibility of combining video screenings of high quality drama-based TV programs with participatory drama/discussion exercises linked to the video program. This approach could deliver the best of both worlds: standardized high-quality education with community participation. Indeed, this is an approach that is now being tested by the BBC World Service Trust's current media campaign in north India, tackling HIV-AIDS (2001–3).

In general, TV producers would do well to recall the traditional virtues of live theatre in creating more participatory program formats that invite direct audience involvement in the storyline. This could be done by asking viewers to write or phone to 'vote' on the resolution of a storyline, which can then be shaped accordingly. Or producers could invite live phone calls or audience letters/interviews at the end of each program, to be handled by one of the drama's key characters, who comes 'to life' to anchor this portion of the show, and thus encourage audience members to further identify the actor as a friend or confidante, whose character on the show is reinforced as a positive role model for real life.

Conclusion

Popular TV-based drama is a promising tool for development education, particularly when it can be combined with interactive discussion and applied to remote or socially excluded community members. As the gap

narrows between the once-opposed notions of 'interpersonal' folk theatre and 'non-personal' mass media, new space is created for participatory TV formats whose characters invite emulation, respect, and pro-social
modelling. Such an approach opens up the corresponding possibility of
new synergies between video screenings and live discussion/drama in
areas with low access to the educational possibilities of the mass media –
whether in the developing world or in Canada itself.

Many thanks to Sharad Agarwal and Smita Choudhary for their insights
and analysis of participatory communication methodologies during the
BBC World Service Trust leprosy media campaign.

The Other Side of Alternative Theatre: An Interview with Sky Gilbert

SKY GILBERT AND JIM GILES

I've always tried to encourage the idea that theatres are modern churches. Of course I have a huge distrust of conventional, homophobic religion, but I think that people need places to worship – to feel inspired and divine ... I want to go to the theatre and laugh, but also be touched by the depths of anger and sadness.

(Sky Gilbert, *Ejaculations from the Charm Factory*, 28)

Sky Gilbert, as artistic director, was the controversial force behind Buddies in Bad Times Theatre for eighteen years, a theatre he founded in Toronto dedicated to gay and new Canadian works. Its name is taken from the title of a poem by Jacques Prévert, which recounts the story of a theatre company's struggles to pay the bills because it chooses to produce artistic instead of commercial works. Gilbert's honesty, commitment, and belief in what he does have had a lasting impact on Canadian theatre. His work has enabled gay playwrights to 'come out of the closet' with pride and honesty. He continues to challenge the status quo in mainstream and avant-garde circles, providing new opportunities for confronting conventional thoughts, values, and beliefs.

Jim. What are your earliest memories of going to the theatre?
Sky. I don't remember anything from childhood. I do remember as a teenager going to Stratford with a group of other students. I don't remember anything about the play. I was chasing after a girl(!) who was scorning me. That I do remember. I remember going to see a play at Stratford with my mother and sister and a teenager that had Irene Worth in it – it was *Hedda Gabler*. I remember very distinctly saving up my money to see *Private Lives* with Brian Bedford and Tammy Grimes at the Royal

Alexandra Theatre. I also remember enjoying the play very much –
living on the excitement of it for weeks – and her dresses.

Jim. Can you discuss the first play that had an impact on you as a gay man?

Sky. It's hard to talk about early plays and being a gay man because I
didn't come out until I was 28 years old. Though I had struggled with
being gay before that, of course, I actually hated 'gay' plays because I was
in the closet and I hated myself. I saw Lindsay Kemp's *Salome,* for
instance, when it came to Toronto Workshop Productions, and Paul
Bettis's *Jekyll Play Hyde* (I talk about both of these experiences in my
memoir *Ejaculations from the Charm Factory,* by the way). What made the
productions gay was that they both featured male nudity and at least the
suggestion of male-on-male sexual contact. But I cursed both productions and made fun of them as pretentious claptrap. Reading plays by
Noel Coward inspired me as a teenager. I think I was able to get off on
the gay sensibility without admitting it to myself. *Private Lives* was an
entrance to a glittering world where people were articulate and entertaining, and their insights were profound. Looking back on it now, I can
see that part of the appeal was also that the men were not acting very
much like normal straight men, and the women were bucking the
patriarchy. At the time I just thought I liked these people, and I'd rather
spend time with them, or the characters in *Hay Fever,* than with my
boring high school contemporaries.

Jim. What is your definition of 'gay theatre'?

Sky. Theatre with significant gay subject matter. This, of course, is necessarily distinct from theme. The definition is made in a homophobic
culture and is shaped by that homophobia. Even to this day, we rarely see
plays in which gays or lesbians are the leading characters and live their
lives in a realistic manner; that is, without the details being censored.
The reason I make a distinction between subject matter and theme is
because I think that any good theatre has 'universal' themes. Art is about
two things ultimately: love and/or mortality. So is gay theatre, or Jewish
theatre, if it is good theatre. But what makes universal artwork gay or
Jewish, in both cases, is that in a culture which doesn't allow such
detailed stories to be aired, finally someone manages to portray these
details. The subject matter is specific, but out of that specific comes a
universal, if it is art.

Jim. Can you comment on the history of gay theatre in Canada? What
shifts, in your opinion, have been made?

Sky. John Herbert: First pioneer. Gay is seen in the context of prisons. A
brave attempt, but gayness is still something that the audience can see as

being a result of the prison experience. Larry Fineberg and John Palmer: identified themselves as bisexuals (at least Larry did) and wrote wild sexual plays in the sixties, which were produced and directed mainly by straight men. Their work stretched the boundaries, but the subject matter was viewed as sixties decadence. In Michel Tremblay's *Hosanna*, a drag queen is allowed to take centre stage and tell her story, but she stops being a drag queen at the end of the play and leaves gay culture behind, as does her leather-clad lover. The play is viewed as a metaphor for Quebec, which excuses the subject matter. Sky Gilbert and Brad Fraser: blatant sexual queer subject matter in the plays.

Jim. What's happening now in gay theatre?

Sky. Lots of AIDS plays of various types. The theatre which I started, Buddies, is doing AIDS plays and or non-gay stuff and or stuff that is supposed to appeal to a middle-class audience. I consider AIDS plays mainly to be homophobic. There are now gay movies. These movies feature either gay men in ungay situations (marriage, children, family, work) or in semi-tragic, unflattering circumstances acting idiotic in gay culture (*Queer As Folk* American version and *Gypsy Boys*). Gay theatre, when and if it appears, seems to be following this general conservative trend. There is a new play at Summerworks, for instance, about a young gay man's right to be conservative and accept what I consider to be straight values (marriage and religion) and to reject (quite specifically, apparently) me. This seems to be the horrifying future of gay theatre. Of course, it's horrifying to me; others might consider it growing up and getting away from all that nasty blatant sex.

Jim. How do you think theatre educates an audience?

Sky. To me it is through an ineffable experience. The audience connects with the characters/story/poetry/images, identifies and has some sort of emotional experience (sometimes called catharsis), which can be positive or negative (involve ecstasy or fear or anger). This emotional experience causes the audience member to:

a) (most significantly) unconsciously confront aspects of life – emotions, situations, primal experiences – that he or she has avoided, or has not consciously confronted in that way before (this makes theatre dangerous: the Platonic mode, the Artaudian mode);

b) turn back to the ideas in the play and mull them over, which can lead to conscious thought and discussion of ideas. I am more suspicious of this more obvious and Shavian aspect of theatre education (this keeps theatre safe: the Aristotelian and Brechtian mode).

Jim. How do you think gay theatre educates a straight audience?

Sky. On a conscious, literal and obvious level, it gives details of gay life and gay culture which audiences find surprising and interesting. If queer characters are honest about their lives, then straight audiences are bound to be shocked and, through that shock, educated.

Jim. How do you think gay theatre educates a gay audience?

Sky. By giving them role models. This does not necessarily mean positive ones. Since queers never get a chance to see how queer lives are lived – in fact, have no narratives on which to model their lives – they often live helpless and confused existences. Straights have very specific narratives (marriage/children or the lack of) that, though they cause enormous pain, at least give people measuring sticks against which to examine themselves and their actions (they can even reject these models, but at least the models are there). When queers at last see themselves, in realistic detail, presented on stage, then they are able to think of possible narratives for their lives. They can reject these narratives or not. But at least they have a starting point. Detail is important for the following reason. When an effeminate little gay boy sees the hero rescuing the girl in straight drama, he plays the girl in his fantasy. But he is also acutely aware, at some point, that he is playing the wrong role, and that this can't be applied to his life (without people ostracizing him – 'Hey, you're not really a girl' – the detail traps him). When the life of a drag queen is presented onstage (and it rarely is) in detail (even if it is a tragic story, and the drag queen is an example of decadence or misguided excess), the drag queen viewer has a way to position and think about his life without a nagging voice saying, 'That's not you at all.'

Jim. What is it about gay theatre that delights you?

Sky. The honest details of our lives revealed.

Jim. What is it about gay theatre that angers you?

Sky. The honest details of our lives hidden and glossed over by queer writers and artists due to their own hypocrisy (and careerism).

Jim. Can you talk about your own tastes as a theatre-goer?

Sky. I'm doing a thesis on Noel Coward because I'm a fan of comedy of manners. Historically, I like Oscar Wilde's *The Importance of Being Earnest* and I get a real thrill from seeing Joe Orton's *What the Butler Saw* being done real well. It's easier for me to get into stuff that was before 'Out' gay theatre happened. I have criticisms of 'AIDS' plays such as *The Normal Heart, As Is,* and *Angels in America.* I feel it's close to what I'm doing but I feel they make too many compromises.

Jim. Christopher Newton commented that you're asking too much of your audience in your early work. What do you think he meant by that?

Sky. I always thought it was my job to challenge the audience. What I was doing at the time was a kind of non-narrative, non-linear style with lots of queer sexual in-your-face content. Newton thought it was too much to get the radical form and the radical content at the same time, and perhaps I could have hit them with one or the other. This is one of the reasons I wrote *The Dressing Gown*, which is based on *La Ronde* and had a clear structure, and *Drag Queens on Trial* and *Drag Queens from Outer Space*, which were like little fables and fairy tales. Even though they were very queer, they were very accessible – and hugely successful. I didn't want to abandon my subject matter. I've always swerved back and have done plays that were less accessible. My most recent play was quite weird and people came out of it upset and confused. But I have to do it because it's something that I'm interested in doing. I'm not interested in doing something tried and true. I definitely could have continued to work in a certain mode and probably gotten much more successful.

Jim. Do you think of gay theatre as alternative theatre or does it stand on its own?

Sky. I think that my theatre is alternative theatre, but I don't think a lot of gay theatre is alternative. Because I dared to suggest that Edward Albee's *Who's Afraid of Virginia Woolf?* was really written for a drag queen, John Clum found my position to be militant. I don't think we ever see the way I approach drag anywhere in the theatre. We may see some of drag in Genet or John Waters, but we don't see them as happy sexual people in the mainstream. My characters are about going out and getting laid, which is the reality of the world. For me that's how queer alternative theatre is involved with actual alternative lifestyles.

Jim. How important is the alternative artist?

Sky. What is happening now is very interesting. Real alternative artists (and it's happening in every area – it's happening in feminism, anti-racism) are actually silenced by the mainstream. For example, you have a black television station, so 'we've got the blacks covered now.' And when we get a gay network, it will work against our cause in a way because the homophobes will say, 'Now that they've got a gay television station, what are they whining about? Why do we have to worry about their rights? Why do we have to give special treatment to AIDS? ... They've got their gay television station.' So what I'm saying is that this co-opting has meant that the something we see as gay theatre, or women's television, implies that we're getting our liberation, but we're actually getting something that *quiets* actual liberation, actual discussion. It's a Noam Chomsky thing – the actual discussion is not occurring because another discussion has been put in its place.

Jim. How do you see yourself as a member of the gay community?

Sky. A few years ago I came to terms with my counter-culture status and I decided that if I wanted to write about certain kinds of things and be a certain kind of artist, then that is what I would be. I think it rather sad that my views might be considered so radical within the gay community, but they are. It's a diverse community and to make generalizations about individuals from an idea of community is wrong. Generally speaking, right now it's a conservative community about marriage and babies and supporting AIDS causes. It's not about sex or drugs and rock and roll. There are people who support my position of being more honest about things, but there's a big fear that the straights won't like it. My theory is that the ones who don't like it won't like it even if we get married. I don't think trying to please the straight people works. I think there's a status quo, just as I think that there is a gay culture, even though I don't think that everybody participates in it. I call 'drag' and 'leather' and 'camp' gay culture, and I get in trouble for saying, 'That's gay culture,' which doesn't mean that everyone who is gay is into 'drag' or 'leather' or 'camp.' Just as black culture is 'rap,' there's lots of black people who hate 'rap,' but somehow out of black culture it's irrelevant. Lots of black people repudiate 'rap,' but it doesn't matter. It's just like black tap-dancing, or black basketball players; it's all going to happen because of repression and a culture that was created under repression. I feel the same way about community. There are notions of community and notions of consensus within the community that come out, even though there are many individuals with different views.

Jim. What are your thoughts on Buddies in Bad Times now that you are not part of it?

Sky. I think it was good to make a clean break. One of the reasons I left was because I recognized that I'd have to do more middle-of-the-road stuff in order to stay there. I've been criticized (and I'm used to it) for doing 'those weird plays that nobody will understand.' I'm fond of Christopher Newton's line 'The middle of the road is where you get run over.' I do think it's a dangerous place to be. Instead of doing what you believe in, or what you want to do, you try to please a nebulous audience. There are places that do that well and can do research and spend like Disney to find out what pleases the masses. But for some little theatre that's trying to please a more general audience, you're liable to end up going nowhere. I also didn't feel that the gay community was really behind Buddies in Bad Times. When we started in 1981, there was excitement. What we were counting on was a contingency of extreme queers and radical straight people who were behind us. But radical artists didn't have money and also there weren't a lot of them. By the end of the eighties, the community was sort of saying, 'Why gay theatre?'

Jim. What will the history books say about Sky Gilbert's impact on theatre?

Sky. What a horrible question! I guess I'm pretty certain to be known as a gay activist for many years, and not as an artist at all. I think we live in pretty homophobic times, and my honesty (frankly) completely over-shadows the possible aesthetic impact of my work. I think this will go on for a while. Eventually, I hope people will be able to stop being shocked by the honest details of gay life that I present, and respond to the work aesthetically, as art. But I won't be around to hold my breath, thank God!

V. THEATRE FOR AND WITH YOUNG AUDIENCES

Theatre for Young Audiences and Grown-up Theatre: Two Solitudes

MAJA ARDAL

The following thoughts have been formulated on the basis of my experience as artistic director of Young People's Theatre (1990–8), which was housed in a permanent facility in the heart of downtown Toronto. One of the first actions I took when I assumed the artistic directorship was to institute a 'Pay What You Can' performance for every production. Over two hundred seats were made available to members of the public, and this fluctuated in response to demand.

A great deal of my development as a writer comes from my years working on plays for young people. Young audiences had very clear demands from the plays we developed and produced at Young People's Theatre. The story was everything. We had to captivate our audiences with powerful tales, whether they were drawn from the classics or created from scratch. We were making theatre during a time when action-packed television, film, and video games were a rapidly increasing element in children's lives.

So I had to be an expert, not only in the making of plays, but also in what the competition was. And when I studied the entertainment world of children, I realized that most young people watch television passively and play video games competitively. Movies for young people are captivating, either as animated musicals or as explosive space-age films. This left a wide-open path for us theatre people to tread. We were action-packed and musical. We often had fantastical characters. But our action was more emotional than war-like. And our plays communicated with the audience, with an immediacy that left no misunderstanding as to how much, or whether, we were being enjoyed!

Today, I write mostly for adults, but I am still guided by the days when I tried to reach the imaginations of children. And I always want to be. The adult theatre world can benefit from more captivating stories of dream and fancy.

Having spent the last three years in the world of adult writing, however, now I feel distanced from the work that is being created in theatres for young audiences. I seldom run into people who are working on stage or in schools for children. There is a gulf between theatres for young audiences and the adult theatres in our community. We perform at different times of the day, but adult theatre-makers do not mingle often with 'daytime' artists. It is partly because of different schedules, but also because the adult theatre world, the press, and the regular theatre-goer do not show enough interest in Theatre for Young Audiences (TYA) as a valid contender for equal status with the mainstream theatre community. And because they do not know much about TYA, they care less about young-audience theatre than I believe they should.

Much as TYA has enriched the lives of children, it should also enrich the general world of theatre. Educators have made great strides in defining the value of the theatre experience for students, and even greater strides in embracing the contribution of professional artists. Drama in education has proved itself repeatedly to be a major and empowering program that enriches the educational system as a whole, while generating in young people a combination of self-realization and love for theatre.

Professional touring productions are a wonderful marriage between schools and theatres. 'Issues' plays, performed in the student environment of gyms and school auditoriums, was where it all began. The school tours tackle subjects of particular interest to the curriculum needs of the student. Educators attempt to recruit the finest-quality productions for this purpose, and over the last twenty years the calibre of these productions has risen in quality and sophistication. Funding bodies have finally recognized the equal value of professional TYA writing, directing, and producing, and we now have advocates in that area at all levels of funding. Theatre for Young Audiences in the schools is an example of how artists and educators can work in harmony. And Canadians do it as well or better than most. Yet touring shows are quite different from the plays produced for young people in our theatres. My concerns are about the *theatre* experience for young people and the challenges we face when we produce work on stages dedicated to schools and families. These two distinct kinds of TYA happen in distinct worlds. In the *school* the artist is a guest of the educational world. In the *theatre*, the educational world is a guest of the artist.

These are important differences that I have nagging questions about. The relationship between TYA theatres and young people is still not perfect. I don't know who coined the term Theatre for Young Audiences, but I believe it has done as much to hinder as to help. This very specialized world has, by its nature, become a separated one.

Playwrights for adult theatre write plays from a very personal perspective. We express a view of the world, and do so in our own voice. For TYA, we have to anticipate that it will be largely children who appreciate our play, and so our 'voice' is focused on appropriate age groups, and we have to find a way to story-tell that has integrity and is accessible.

But what happens when the production is for people who are not in charge of buying the tickets? for young people who do not have information and income at their fingertips? when the play is written for young people whose choices are controlled by guardians of their cultural interests? And what happens to a theatre company whose sole source of ticket revenue is parents and teachers? How does the playwright straddle the world of adults and the world of the child, and still retain her own singular voice? This is not a problem in the plays that tour to schools, because the artists (the guests) have a built-in agreement to tailor their work to issues that bring a message to the student and conform to the school system.

Sometimes parents and teachers are made aware of an adult theatre that has a play of special interest to young people. And this kind of situation does occasionally occur, when a playwright has written a piece that resonates with a remarkably broad age range. The play will be promoted in the regular seasonal brochure, which is tailored to an adult audience. Parents and teachers will be drawn to the play, which is offered in a theatre they already come to for their own enjoyment. They will decide to bring children to the play, based on descriptions and sometimes reviews. The theatre may often have a higher profile in the community than any TYA company. In this situation the theatre will have a richer and more age-diverse audience experiencing a play not tailored to children, but valuable to them nonetheless.

In the case of Tarragon Theatre's production of *I Claudia* by Kristen Thompson, Thompson created a work from the depths of her passion and imagination that happened to connect with a broad range of ages. She did not *plan* the production for young people, and so her material was never tailored or compromised to attract and suit students and families. It simply did. That is the perfect scenario, yet I believe it is almost impossible to achieve in a theatre that only has a relationship with parents and teachers, because the TYA theatre is utterly *dependent* on the attendance of young people. TYA theatre is one giant step removed from the very audience it seeks to reach because the ticket-buyers are parents and teachers, on whom the theatre relies to bring their young charges to the plays. And they have to seek the approval of parents and teachers if anyone is going to attend their theatre at all. And yet, unlike in the case of Thompson's play, TYA theatre's entire focus and efforts are for children.

Just as TYA is at the height of success in specializing in excellent plays for young people, it seems clearer than ever that we have created two forms of theatre, adult and TYA. And I believe that this separation causes fewer adults to understand and enjoy plays created in the TYA sector. This is a problem because I believe *all* society should have an interest in children, especially in their imaginations and perceptions of the world around them.

Yet it is not only the adult and child audiences who are separated by the two forms of theatre. So also are the artists. In the adult theatre world, we explore all ideas and express them, generally, free of any restrictions to theme and language. But in a theatre dedicated to young people, writers, directors, and actors are bound by the age and vulnerability of the child, and by what the adults in their lives deem to be appropriate. This seems reasonable, but do the expression of the artist and the expectation of the parent or child ever come into conflict? And if so, how and why does this happen? Are we devaluing theatre for the young by separating it so thoroughly from theatre for the adult? Sometimes adult theatre is not for children, but in my opinion children's theatre is *never* not for adults!

Several years ago, when I was artistic director of Young People's Theatre in Toronto, I produced and directed *Two Weeks with the Queen* (co-produced with Alberta Theatre Projects). This beautifully written Australian play dealt with issues of childhood cancer, homosexuality, and AIDS. The central character is a twelve-year-old boy, and during the course of the play he becomes disillusioned with the monarchy, makes friends with a gay man, learns about AIDS, and comes to grips with the impending death of his little brother. The play had been a huge hit with all ages in Australia and Great Britain, and was still running in both countries. We promoted its world success to our Toronto audiences. We were honest about the subject matter and enthusiastically described the balance of tenderness and humour. And barely anybody came. Bookings were dismal from both families and schools. Parents and teachers expressed concern with the subject matter. For the most part, parents said they did not want a theatre experience to be the way their child first learned about gay people, AIDS, and terminal illness. Teachers also did not want to get into trouble with parents for taking their students to a play with such material. In addition, teachers had difficulty justifying bringing students to a play that did not connect somehow to the class curriculum. This was a problem that YPT had been seeing increase yearly, as class pressures increased and funding decreased in Toronto schools.

We did everything we could to encourage attendance. The theatre invited educators to see a preview without their students. The talk-back was rich and feedback was the best we could hope for. Still, although they were as upset about the situation as we were, very few of them booked the show. They knew a fine production when they saw one. But teachers, like artists, are caught in a trap of trying to enlighten children without enlightening them 'too much.' How on earth do we figure out where to draw the line? There were, of course, parents and teachers who were particularly attracted to the play, and brought their children, trusting that YPT would provide the wonderful experience it had promised. These people found the play a wonderful way to open doors of discussion with their children about tolerance and acceptance. We received wonderful letters from many of them, thanking us for opening doors of understanding in such an enjoyable way. But they were simply too few.

Two Weeks with the Queen was recognized by our colleagues in Toronto with seven Dora Award nominations. Yet thousands of young people did not get a chance to see it. However, when the YPT production moved to Alberta Theatre Projects, an adult theatre, as part of the subscription season, something extraordinary happened. Adult subscribers were delighted to see a play they could bring children to and had booked well in advance. They came flocking. And when the press gave the show attention, the theatre was filled to the rafters. Adults and children sat side by side in the audience. Many gay people came, and sat with their lovers, their children, and others' children, grandparents, uncles, aunts, and parents. Some educators came and some students came, but the variety of ages in the audience was constant. The city of Calgary was represented at the theatre! This was, in my opinion, the perfect theatre experience.

The reason for the play's success everywhere but at YPT is disturbingly simple. Painful though it is to admit, the play was successful *because* it was produced by adult theatre companies. The adult theatre world did not have a protective layer around it when it came to buying tickets. It became a 'Theatre' and not an 'Educational' experience. I was thrilled for ATP, but devastated for YPT. By producing *Two Weeks with the Queen* at YPT, I believe we inadvertently hurt its chances of reaching a broad public. This production alone lost over $50,000 for YPT, and we were in danger of becoming a hesitant and careful company in the future, choosing rather to follow marketing directives and ceasing to produce material that was challenging and innovative. The fear of losing money could become the defining factor in selecting future seasons. YPT faced a philosophical crisis that jeopardized its position as a leader in TYA. Meanwhile I wracked my brains to come up with some answers, answers that could promise our writers a future creating original plays for our main stage, and that could attract adult ticket buyers to unknown and sophisticated plays. But all I had were questions.

Were we, at YPT, only supposed to be predictable and familiar in our work, and steer our artists away from challenging subjects and towards safe, recognizable ones? And if that was the case, did it mean that YPT was supposed to give parents and teachers what they asked for, rather than developing in them an interest in and curiosity for trying new material in new ways? How was I to face my writers if I had to ask them to tailor-write stage plays in order to meet parameters of expectation from parents and teachers? What was I doing for the development of the creative process under these circumstances? And if a mixed audience is such a perfect experience, why are we then relegating our young people to a 'children's' experience, and controlling every detail of the work on stage as if the fabric of their moral lives is going to be destroyed if they see something that is not literally 'telling' them how to think at every turn?

Children are not as literal-minded as many would have us believe. They understand metaphor and they understand imagery. They understand that theatre is an experience to reflect upon, not to obey, that theatre is an imaginary world of 'what if' and not the 'only world.' They understand that there are more people in the world than just the 'good' guys and the 'bad' guys. They know that there are grey areas, when good people do bad things, and that people who do bad things are not automatically bad, or tidily redeemable.

We need to show children the messy aspects of life. As artists we are not here to answer. We are here to question, and to invite our audience to question with us. In the end, do young people not prefer to see theatre that everyone else, regardless of age, sees? Do they really want to sit in the theatre just with their own age group? Do they want to sit with 400 other children and feel like a pack rather than individuals?

Overall, the biggest question remains: by specializing in producing theatre for young people, have we broken the direct line of communication between the voice of the artist and the young audience member? In this tangle of fretfulness, I came to this conclusion: I no longer feel that it is of value to have theatres with stages that exist exclusively for children. I believe, rather, that more theatres in Canada should merge with the TYA companies who produce stage productions. At the very least, they should integrate more productions for children into their own seasons. They should cross-pollinate artists between TYA and adult theatre. And they should introduce small children to theatre companies that could very well still be in existence for them when they become adults.

If adult theatres merge with TYA companies, people of all ages will enhance the atmosphere of theatres. Children will be able to graduate to seeing adult plays in the theatre in which they have grown up. Plays for families and young people will be offered as part of the theatre's season. Artists can flow from adult to young-audience plays. The profile of the children's plays will become mainstream, and theatres will become a true mirror of the whole society around them.

Theatre for Young People: Does It Matter?

LARRY SWARTZ

Desmond Davis, founder and artistic director for nine years of Carousel Players, one of Canada's most successful children's theatre companies, opens his book *Theatre for Young People* with the following insight:

> It is no coincidence that the word for the main activity of childhood is the same as the word for what is done in theatre. Children play games and playwrights write plays. The artists who recreate plays for the delight of adults were called players long before it was called theatre – at least in our language. The exercise of the imagination is much the same in the child's creation of play and in the creation of the theatre. Even the same means and conventions are used. And most vitally the same human needs are satisfied. (1981, 1)

What are your first memories of going to the theatre? Were you taken by a family member? Were you part of a class excursion? Were you sitting in the gymnasium of your school? Can you remember the actors, the colour of the set, the place you were sitting, the title of the play? Can you remember the experience with the same detail that Frank Rich, chief drama critic of the *New York Times*, describes in his memoir *Ghost Light*, recalling his first visit, at the age of seven, to Washington's National Theatre to see *Damn Yankees*:

> The lights shining on the curtain dimmed, plunging the theatre into complete darkness. Then just when the suspense became overwhelming, the whole audience holding its breath, the curtain did rise, ascending heavenward so fast (where did it go?) and revealing such an explosive cacophony of light and costume and people singing and dancing that it was more than

I could absorb. The whole whirligig of sights and sounds and bodies rushing forward seemed to be aimed directly at me. And there was no letup. Each moment that followed passed too quickly, each shock of delight slid instantaneously, cruelly into memory – a pileup of double-edged sensation turned instantly into a kind of sorrow.

If only there was a way to hold each moment, to freeze it in time and put it in my pocket and preserve it forever, before it was hopelessly lost. (2000, 19)

Frank Rich's parents were avid theatre-goers and would bring home new recordings of musicals. He took refuge in these re-creations of the shows in his imagination, scene by scene. It was Broadway theatre that gave him salvation from his parent's divorce and from everyday life in Washington. His theatre fanaticism grew as a result of being taken to see plays and later working at Washington's National Theatre, a site he described as his 'saloon until I reached drinking age – the one place that promised me surefire intoxication' (242). Although it may be desirable that children should have exposure to the theatre, most do not – a minority have the opportunities that I had and fewer attend with the passion and regularity that Frank Rich describes. Who will take students to the theatre? Will engaging students with plays produced specifically for young audiences make them life-long theatre-goers?

Theatre for children is a special art form, different from adult theatre, with its own dynamics and rewards. To gain an enthusiasm for reading, children need a variety of books that appeal directly to their world, their interests, their fears, and their experiences. 'In a similar way,' says David Wood, 'children's theatre can open doors to a new world of imagination, excitement and thoughtfulness' (Wood and Grant 1997, 5). In the afterword to his anthology *Around the World in 21 Plays*, children's theatre advocate Lowell Swortzell (1997) tells the story of Alice Minnie Herts Heniger and her Children's Educational Theatre, which had operated in New York City from 1903 until 1909. Heniger wanted to fulfil a demand for engaging entertainment for young people; audiences came largely from the immigrant and tenement populations, with limited English. Heniger presented a production of *The Tempest* that established her playhouse as the first significant theatre in the United States operating specifically for young audiences. Trusting great literature, Mrs Heniger believed that these plays could reach every child who spoke little or no English. When Mark Twain, whose *The Prince and The Pauper* was dramatized for this same audience, became a member of the theatre's board, he declared children's theatre to be one of the great inventions of the twentieth century. He predicted that its 'vast educational value – now but dimly perceived and but vaguely understood – will someday presently come to be recognized' (ibid., 678). Swortzell tells us that playwrights as well as audiences have been liberated, so that today's theatre for young playgoers is a more accurate, compelling reflection of the world in which we live; more varied and more inventive and more provocative than Mark Twain could have imagined almost a century ago when he predicted a bright future for young audiences.

For many children, the first experiences of seeing live theatre take place at the schools they attend. If teachers can't take the children to the plays, then they can bring the plays to the children. I can't blame my school teachers for not exposing me to plays – what theatres or theatre companies were available for them to choose from? In the past fifty years, the children's theatre industry has grown and many schools can now choose to invite a number of professional companies and artists to perform for audiences of children. Richard Courtney (1991) makes reference to the work of Holiday Playhouse in Vancouver under the direction of Joy Coghill and Myra Benson, as well as to the national tours led by Brian Way, as pioneers in educational theatre troupes from the 1960s. Today, Prologue to the Performing Arts organizes over 2400 school visits for approximately three dozen performers and theatre companies throughout Ontario.

In my twenty-five-year career as a teacher, consultant, and drama instructor, I have been acquainted with several educational companies. I have served on the school arts committee and arranged to have plays, dancers, storytellers, musicians, and opera performances at the school. One of my first experiences was with Golden Horseshoe Players, under the direction of Sharon Enkin, a pioneer of children's theatre in Ontario. The company's production of *The Peacemaker* by David Holman addressed cultural issues and dealt with the question of brotherhood in the story of two warring peoples, the Blues and the Reds. This play exemplified the company's mandate to address values in education by giving children the opportunity to examine their own attitudes to equality, conflict, and change. More recently, Puppetmongers, by the brother and sister team of David and Ann Powell, came to my school to present *Cinderella in Muddy York* and the children were able to learn about the history of Toronto through a version of the popular fairy tale. Their entertaining work also provides children with skilled models for manipulating puppets with which they can later experiment in their world of play and drama.

In my own teaching, I have been fortunate to work with principals who advocate for strong arts programming, and who commit a portion of their school budgets to the performing arts. We were able to organize a program where each student in the school paid a one-time fee, thereby contributing to the arts budget. Arts mattered to these principals, to the teachers, and to the parents' councils. For most children, such performances in the gym, with poor acoustics, minimal lighting, uncomfortable seating, and powerful theatre are perhaps the only ones that they will experience in their lives.

Many of the plays chosen for school audiences are considered not only for their intent to entertain, but also for their mission to 'educate.' David Craig and Robert Morgan, formerly co-artistic directors of Roseneath Theatre, have been creating and producing plays for young audiences for over twenty years, and have won awards for many productions, including *Morgan's Journey*, *Napalm the Magnificent*, and *Dib and Dob and the Journey Home*. In 'The Importance of Children's Theatre in Elementary Schools' (Giles 2001), Craig and Morgan claim that children's rich emotional lives are often ignored or played down in popular entertainment. Although limited by their age, children experience life's joys and sorrows as powerfully as many adults do. Thus, Craig and Morgan have committed themselves to writing plays that engage the mind, body, and spirit of their young audiences, plays that demonstrate respect for different points of view, for problem-solving, and for risk-taking: 'Feast – not fast food. Simple – not simplistic. Involve the audience, don't distract it. Emotionally powerful – not watered down. Talking to – not talking down to. These are the tremendous challenges that face us as we create a production' (ibid., 12). Craig believes that imagination is what makes theatre – particularly theatre for young audiences – a potentially powerful educational experience. Students are hungry to experience this rich, multi-layered expression of life. Good theatre respects integrity, imagination, beauty, balance, and humanity – often through a construct imagined not only on the part of the playwright, but also by the audience that enters this world. Robert Morgan insists that we cannot underestimate the impact of live performance. To be engaged as an audience member in a theatre experience can help us participate more completely in other aspects of life, for theatre is an experience of community. We gather together to watch something about ourselves. Moreover, theatre demands high-level thinking, mainly because it asks members of the audience to sit in judgment of the play's characters as they make choices within the context of the drama. Craig and Morgan create dissonance by getting children to question character's values, behaviours, and choices.

The interaction between the audience and the characters is active, which makes it a captivating way for children to experience these issues.

Amah Harris, the artistic director of Theatre in the Rough, an educational company that has been performing in schools since 1985, follows a mandate of the harmonious coexistence of peoples as the foundation of her work. The thrust of the company's work comes out of the Caribbean and African communities. Harris believes that it is important to know who people are and how they function in their home country in order to understand how and why they function the way they do in Canada. In this sense, her live theatre can give children an opportunity to see how different nationalities articulate their culture through theatre. One of Theatre in the Rough's school plays, *Kwakoo Anansi and the Rescue in the Kingdom*, tells the story of two different-looking ants in conflict because they mistrust each other. Eventually the characters come to realize that their differences can be harmonized, and in so doing they help each other. When I asked Amah, 'What do you think children learn from watching this play?' she answered:

> It's really not about two ants; it's about anti-racism and conflict resolution. I believe strongly in recognizing differences. If a million people sing the same note, you cannot have harmony, but if two people sing different notes, you have harmony. When people understand the beauty of harmony and how powerful it is – and not just sing a melody where everything sounds the same – they are saying it's okay to be totally different from each other. Differences complement. That's what I hope the Anansi play says to young audiences, because the ants have to live together, just as we have to live together in Canada, in the world. The children seem to understand the message instantly. They get caught up in the music and the costumes, but they come to know what we are trying to say about living in harmony.

Teachers who are concerned with the arts may choose to take their classes to see plays that are performed locally. I have taken my students to live performances at Ryerson Theatre, Harbourfront, the children's festival at the Living Arts Centre in Mississauga, and neighbouring high schools. I recall the time I took the children to see a performance of *The Hobbit*. One of the boys, who was struggling with literacy skills, was so impressed with the experience that he spent one hour in the classroom the next day recreating a drawing of the set, and beamed when he came to my desk to retell the complete story of the play. Also, as an uncle, taking my nieces and nephews to see plays was a ritual I always enjoyed. I remember sitting beside my niece Rachael when she was six years old and consoling her when the lights went up at the end of *Jacob Two Two Meets the Hooded Fang*. She thought that Jacob, gone from the stage, had disappeared from the world. A colleague also described taking a teenage hockey team to see a community production of *Julius Caesar*. One boy commented, 'You know, this stuff is exciting when you don't have to read it!'

Recognizing a need to engage young adolescents with theatre-going experiences, actress Martha Burns developed a program called *Way To Go*, which organizes volunteers to chaperone young people from inner-city Toronto to see such plays as *Dancing at Lughnasa* and *Hamlet*. The students, through workshops and discussions, can look deeper into the plays they experience. An initiative such as this is significant for providing youth with financial support, adult accompaniment, and frameworks for responding that help make the play-watching experience a positive one.

Each year as a classroom teacher, from grades two to eight, I took my classes from Mississauga to Toronto to see a play at Canada's largest theatre for young audiences, the Lorraine Kimsa Theatre for Young People (LKTYP), formerly Young People's Theatre (YPT), which has been producing innovative plays for children of all ages and the adults in their lives since 1966. Each year over 150,000 young people come with their schools and/or families to see plays produced for audiences ages four and up in both the Mainstage theatre (Susan Rubes Theatre) and the Studio theatre (Nathan Cohen Theatre). LKTYP is committed to presenting top-quality productions that reflect and celebrate Canadian culture and further the development of new Canadian plays and artists. Each year LKTYP gives voice to issues and concerns relevant to Canadian youth, bringing literary classics to the stage and commissioning original plays that explore exciting and diverse performance styles. *The Nutmeg Princess*, a musical play based on the Caribbean story by Ricardo Keens Douglas; *Whale* by David Holman, about an enormous media campaign to rescue whales; *Two Weeks with the Queen*, based on the novel by Australian Morris Gleitzman that sensitively deals with the experiences of cancer and AIDS; and *Old Friends* by Ronnie Burkett's Theatre of Marionettes, which gave a compassionate look at the lives of older people, are examples of the range of stage experiences the LKTYP provides.

Patterson Fardell, educational services director at the LKTYP for the past twenty years, believes that the theatre's school programming is a vital resource for the educational system, reaching students from the inner-city communities across Metropolitan Toronto and welcoming them alongside the more advantaged. Fardell, who conveys a passion for the arts as a vital and integral part of every child's education, feels that theatre is a shared experience that helps build community.

The Lorraine Kimsa Theatre for Young People is dedicated to creating and producing professional theatre of high quality for a diverse audience of young people. Its vision supports the belief that 'theatre should make children proud to be children, and proud of their heritage, citizenship, and accomplishments.' These experiences can offer younger children a sense of wonder about the magic possibilities of theatre and an understanding that it can be exciting and entertaining. Such plays as *The Very Hungry Caterpillar*, by Eric Carle, and *The Paperbag Princess*, by Robert Munsch, are examples of familiar stories that are intended to delight children with rhythmic language and large comic characters. Some plays are drawn from the classics of world literature (*Oliver Twist*, *Jane Eyre*, *The Secret Garden*), while others give children a fresh perspective on Canadian history. Recently, *Ghost Train* presented audiences with an account of the contribution of Chinese workers to the building of the Canadian Pacific Railway, as told by contemporary Chinese-Canadians. Also, celebrations of the life stories of people whose dedication to principles of social justice (e.g., Louis Riel, Nelson Mandela) have made them outstanding role models of our time offer another kind of theatre aimed at older students. Finally, LKTYP often attempts to provide fresh interpretations of theatre classics such as *The Diary of Anne Frank*, *Macbeth*, *A Christmas Carol*, and *The Miracle Worker*, staged specifically for the young audiences who fill the theatre.

One of the themes of a recent season was 'YPT plays for a better world!' The company's theatrical productions are intended to open young minds and hearts and validate the common experiences and challenges of today's children, who are growing up in an increasingly complex world. Theatre is an outstanding teaching tool to motivate student learning, stimulate an interest in reading, and get young people thinking and talking about themes, issues, and values that are important in our lives as Canadians. The theatre experience offers young people a great opportunity to think about sensitive issues, because they can be dealt with in the safe zone of 'the world of the play.' These life experiences, represented by the characters in a drama, can subsequently be discussed in the classroom after students have seen a production. Good theatre opens doors rather than providing answers; it is not prescriptive. Over the past years, plays at the LKTYP have addressed media literacy, bullying, alcoholism, poverty, divorce, racism, teenage dating, violence and abuse, the immigrant experience, and other issues.

On a recent trip to New York, I went to see the Pulitzer Prize–winning play *Proof*. During intermission, a father and his two sons, of about eight and ten years old, were standing behind me in line to buy a snack. As Act One had ended, moments earlier, one of the characters revealed an unexpected secret and several members of the audience gasped. As I waited in line, I heard the father comment to the boys, 'Wow! Did you hear the audience?' The boys, however, were only interested in their M&M candies and didn't seem at all interested in the father's question. I wondered why the father would bring such young people to see what was really an 'adult' play. Out of the many Broadway and off-Broadway offerings available, why would this father pay almost $100 per ticket for such a mature play when he could have chosen *The Music Man, Aida,* or *Beauty and the Beast*? Perhaps the father wanted to see the play so badly that he decided to drag the kids along, or perhaps he was stuck with two extra tickets and decided that the boys might just get something out of the play. Who knows what the children 'got' out of the experience. Of course, whatever they took away was different from what an adult audience would take. Yet I'm also sure that I took from *Proof* different things than the European woman who sat beside me. The reactions, connections, and responses were unique to each of the 800 or so who sat in the theatre with me during that Sunday matinee. I am guessing that this wasn't the first theatre experience that these young lads would have had. For all I know, they had just been to see *Annie Get Your Gun* the day before.

Do we take youth to see plays because it's good for them? For young children a play, a song, a painting, a poem, a trip to a museum, a family picnic, a parade, a boat ride, a baseball game, a subway ride, the birth of a calf, a funeral are all life events that add to their emotional and intellectual understanding of the world. What makes theatre-going important is that children come to experience an artistic representation of the world. They can witness, as Antonin Artaud states, 'life lived on purpose' (1958, 73). They can experience the ritual of sitting in the audience, being quiet in the dark, and watching others work in the world of pretend. The more often they go to plays, the more they learn about the conventions of being an audience member. The more plays they see, the more they come to learn about different styles of theatre, different uses of sets and props, different ways of bringing actors on and off the stage, and different techniques of manipulating time. They learn about costumes and music and laughter and gesturing and silence and intermission and applause. They learn about having conversations, telling stories, getting along, arguing, and loving.

When children are exposed to the theatre, they can learn to develop their responses, learn about the responses of others, explore their interests and learn about the interests of others. The more they are taken to live performances, the more their insights are honed, the more their appreciation can grow, so that, as they mature, they can become their own best critics of the art form:

> Yes, children are a critical audience, but they have only one real criterion – that their attention be held. *Boring* is nearly the only natural term of criticism in a child's vocabulary. They will accept all kinds of meretricious material provided it is diverting. Easy proof of this is found in the bulk of their television viewing. Fortunately, acceptance does not mean preference. They can be taught and encouraged to prefer quality entertainment to cheap entertainment. It is the responsibility of all agencies providing theatre for young people to ensure that their entertainment is of quality. They are all responsible for educating though they may hopefully not try too hard to teach. (Davis 1981, 164–5)

There is no guarantee that attending a performance will create a lifelong commitment to theatre-going, but those children who are involved in theatre, who experience the thrill of a play, may come to foster a curiosity for, a tolerance of, and a greater understanding of this art form called theatre.

The Incredible Adventures of Mary Jane Mosquito: Lyrics to 'Patty Cake'

TOMSON HIGHWAY

Introduction by Patricia Cano*

Working with Tomson Highway is a little taste of heaven. Theatre heaven. Or, at least, it is what I, a young theatre person almost out of university, envision every actor's dream gig to be like. He is an honest man with a brilliantly active mind, and he balances beautifully between professional-ism/perfectionism and just plain old havin' fun!

Putting together *Mary Jane Mosquito* was therefore a breeze, a breeze with punch, that is! Tomson challenged me with a wonderful repertoire of music that explores many different styles, stretches my range some, and trips my tongue even more (Cree words and the fast pace of one song in particular twist the tongue). More importantly, however, he gave me the gift of a simple script with a huge message – the universal kind – to share with my audiences. Now, this presented an even greater chal-lenge than having to learn Cree and adopt its tongue-twisting rhythm, for how was I to speak the language of both adults and children? While I worried, Tomson just laughed and said it would work, and my director, Tom Osborne, simply offered me the following advice: 'If you just talk to them' – meaning both children and parents – 'it will work.' Talk to them, eh? Sounded easy enough ... and it was! As Mary Jane learns in the end, and I did too along with my audience: when one shares his/her gift with the world, the world gives back ten times ten times ten.

My final thoughts? Tomson's script is a beautiful, perfectly packaged example of his gift to the world. He is, above all else, an exemplary human being whose voracious thirst for life and happiness is contagious

---

*Patricia Cano played Mary Jane Mosquito in the world premiere of the play.

(WARNING ... You *will* laugh and feel good if you meet this man). His works are therefore expressions of this 'joie de vivre,' and, when read or heard, resonate within us all, male, female, child, adult, brown, white, because his joyous soul is in his work and therefore speaks directly to our souls.

I met him when I was about six years old and knew him only as 'tomson. l'indien, ami de raymond.' Who knew that we would later meet, fall in love – because that is what happens, one falls in love with Tomson Highway – and perform together? Lucky for me, somewhere a star was thinking of me and wishing me a happy life. He is my friend, my mentor, and a huge-hearted man. A gift to us all.

Patty Cano

MARY JANE
(*As piano music crescendos, Mary Jane first talks over the music and the children's voices*)
And *this* is the song Ms. Maggie-May Ditchburn would make us all sing, three, four. Hup, two, three, four. Hup, two, three, four ...
Sings: 'Patty cake, patty cake, baker man,
Bake me a cake a-faster than you can;
Tommy-let, Tommy-let, take your pan,
Make me an omelette that's bigger than a man;
Daddy cake, daddy cake, take your van,
Take me to the beach for a real fine tan;
Little tick, little tickle, daughter of the man,
Give me any lip and I'll put you in a can.'

You see, for some reason truly dreadful, truly sad,
Miss Maggie-May Ditchburn, the first chance she had?
She'd take Mary Jane and shove her to the stage,
And show her to the class like a budgie in a cage,
A kitty in a cooler, or a puppy on a page,
Throwing words into the song intended to enrage,
Miss Mary Jane Mosquito, Miss Mary Jane 'the bore,'
Why? two, three, four?

So the other little bugs would a-giggle and a-roar,
So the other little critters would a-titter to the core,

At Mary Jane's expense, yes, at *my* expense!
She was jealous, she was jealous, I ain't dense;
Miss Maggie-May Ditchburn was as jealous as a ver*mine*
Jealous as a snake, jealous as a swine,
And you wanna know why she was jealous as a vermine,
Jealous as a snake *and* a-jealous as a swine?
Cuz deep down in her heart, in her tired old heart,
She knew I had a future she couldn't dream a wart,
She knew I could become, knew I *would* become,
Everything she'd dreamt of, everything and some
But she never would attain, never would become,
Like sing on every stage in all of kingdom come,
Like fly down to the south for a real fine tan,
Like buy a little nest in Man-hat-tan;

She was jealous, she was jealous and I well knew it,
She was out to get '*la moi*,' and more than just a bit,
Can you imagine anything so foolish, so unwise?
So Mary Jane Mosquito I strongly you advise,
'Soon as you can do it, a-quicker than a deer,
Grab yourself a bag and get on out of here,
Fly away from here, leave Petit Petit,
Yes, fly away from home, leave it with a bee';
I'm saying to myself as I'm marching in the line,
I'm saying to myself in this little heart of mine,
As Maggie-May Ditchburn is a-bangin' on her kitty,
And I'm a-singin' and a-howlin' and a-wailin' right along,
Miss Maggie-May Ditchburn's simple little ditty,
Miss Maggie-May Ditchburn's simple little song:
Hup, two, three, four,
Hup, two, three, four.

'Patty cake, patty cake, baker man,
Bake me a cake a-faster than you can;
Tommy-let, Tommy-let, take your pan,
Make me an omelette that's bigger than a man;
Daddy cake, daddy cake, take your van,
Take me to the beach for a real fine tan;
Little tick, little tickle, daughter of the man,
Give me any lip and I'll put you in a can.'

'Patty cake, patty cake, pag'wee-siganis,
Pag'wee-siganis and pag'wee-siganis,
Tommy-let, Tommy-let, sasapi-skisa,
Sasapi-skisa and sasapi-skisa;
Daddy cake, daddy cake, ootapanas ootin,
Ootapanas ootin and ootapanas ootin,
Little tick, little tickle, pooni-nagamoo,
Pooni-nagamoo and pooni-nagamoo.'

'Patty cake, patty cake, baker man,
Bake me a cake a-faster than you can;
Tommy-let, Tommy-let, take your pan,
Make me an omelette that's bigger than a man;
Daddy cake, daddy cake, take your van,
Take me to the beach for a real fine tan;
Little tick, little tickle, daughter of the man,
Give me any lip and I'll put you in a can.'

'Patty cake, patty cake, pag'wee-siganis,
Pag'wee-siganis and pag'wee-siganis,
Tommy-let, Tommy-let, sasapi-skisa,
Sasapi-skisa and sasapi-skisa;
Daddy cake, daddy cake, ootapanas ootin,
Ootapanas ootin and ootapanas ootin,
Little tick, little tickle, pooni-nagamoo,
Pooni-nagamoo and pooni-nagamoo.'

Hup, two, three, four,
Hup, two, three, four
Mary Jane scats ... End music. Silence.

The Land inside Coyote: Reconceptualizing Human Relationships to Place through Drama

CORNELIA HOOGLAND

Drama underlies my work as an artist, teacher, and scholar. Drama's investigative actions and its storytelling conventions, such as plot, character, setting, and metaphor, facilitate the exploration of facts, ideas, and feelings in each of my forms of inquiry. Drama's ability to inquire into a topic as well as touch a subject's emotional heart make it pedagogically suitable for my study of human relationships to place. In this chapter I am interested in a specific aspect of place, namely, the natural world – the non-human world of plants, animals, rocks, sky, weather; in other words, the places and things that envelope human life in rural, urban, and wilderness landscapes.

I haven't always been aware of the usefulness of drama in teaching and learning. Until feminist theory brought the body into theoretical view, I did not appreciate the body's contributions in making sense of experience and in creating understanding (Hoogland 2000a). Although I've been a practising artist for longer than I have been an academic (Hoogland 2000b, 2001), I did not understand how my practice was inextricably fused to my scholarship, and how my poetic and dramatic writing informs my research and teaching. As an ecofeminist, I view my own connections to my body and to the earth as the basis from which to understand relationships that are commonly presented as dualistic and contradictory; namely, those of body/mind, woman/nature, and culture/nature.

I present my work as narrative accounts that form the two main parts of this chapter. The first is a general discussion of human alienation from place; in particular, how most children are unconnected to their local geography, and its flora and fauna. I assert the value of place and community and the natural world as a source of authority and meaning.

This *meaning* is more than personal; I believe our survival as a species depends upon reconceptualizing our relationships and acting upon a dynamic in which the human is but one voice among many.

In the second part I describe my research that explores the ways in which artistic approaches can increase children's awareness of the natural world and their place in it. I use drama to help kindergarten children make connections with the place in which they live and go to school. As the children in my research study became more comfortable with and knowledgeable about the natural world (its paths, contours, creatures, and plants), they made observations and told stories. Their texts – words, phrases, and sometimes stories and drawings – were dictated to the attendant adults and taken back to the classroom to be used as the students' 'fieldnotes' in writing and acting out their own stories. Drama has been instrumental in shaping my research and in helping children to articulate their experiences. A notable by-product of the study was the illumination of the processes of literacy as the children's experiences were mediated through artistically informed symbol systems.

Drama as Methodology

Drama constitutes my methodology. Its forms and conventions are particularly suited to creating, recreating, and deepening experience; to using alternative spaces as teaching sites; to negotiating gender and cultural differences; as well as to meeting the needs of special populations. I'm particularly interested in drama's narrative structures (a plot's beginning, middle, and end), in suspense, storytelling, and setting (place names, creating a sense of place), and in character (non-human beings as characters with intention). I'm also interested in the ability of the language of poetry, myth, and stories to create an ethos of relatedness and an aesthetic connection between humans and the more-than-human-world.

Environmental drama has conventionally used issues-based structures in which, for instance, questions of the responsibilities of different community organizations with regard to environmental and health issues are examined (see, e.g., 'Drama Structure 2: Black Spruce Narrows' in Clark et al. 1997). While I am interested in such an approach, I am concerned here with a conceptual framework that supports drama activities that can help students extend the perceptual boundaries mandated by their culture, and enable them to make contact with meanings, feelings, and power in the land; or, more exactly, in their own backyards. I envision backyards (where people live and work) as places of theatre that become sites of exploration. These techniques are derived from oral cultures, in which experiences in and of the land are a valuable source of knowledge (as discussed below). I proceed on the premise that environmental education, on the broadest scale, is failing to alter the tide of ecological damage that threatens our world. Believing that the arts can address the emotional and imaginative connections missing in much environmental education (and in curriculum generally), I explore a groundwork for a dramatic program (and not the replicable program itself) that enables people to make aesthetic connections between themselves and the land they inhabit. The modest, hoped-for consequence of this chapter is that, when its concepts are applied to a curriculum, students will be more strongly connected to the place in which they live.

Students of a Technological World View

My research is premised on the need for students to experience the physical world in order to better understand their place in it. Yet contemporary students rarely walk to school or play outdoors, let alone explore any *wild* places in their neighbourhoods. Rather, their experiences occur within a technological world view that posits a transcendent narrative of satisfaction through consumerism and technology. Television and computers offer mediated versions of nearly every aspect of life. While I acknowledge the positive aspects of postmodernism, my research challenges its excesses, manifest in such things as the privileging of manipulated and deceptive images, ironic distance, and deconstruction.

So what do contemporary students experience of the non-human world? What settings and adventures were part of their early experience? What can they remember? How can they be helped to remember further? How can they create not just the settings but also a close identification with nature? What sort of identification is meaningful to contemporary students? Or does the natural world even play a formative role in their lives?

I'm reminded of an illustration in a children's book called *Quail Song* (Carey and Barnett 1990). A coyote who has tried very hard to learn another creature's song has ended up with all his teeth broken. It's a good story, but the last illustration is what I remember. The landscape of the desert that has surrounded all the story's characters is painted inside Coyote. I love that. It's as if he swallowed the mountain and the grassland

and wears them deeply inside, close to his heart. He doesn't wear them like decorations; rather, like blood and bones, they're part of Coyote.

When I tell my teacher-friend about Coyote's landscape, he tells me about his grade nine drama class. My students, he says, even the native ones whose clan is bear or wolf, do not identify with these animals. *Much Music* and Marilyn Manson are more charismatic than their totems. While my friend realizes that it's not so much Manson-the-idol, but belonging, with one's peers, to the cult of the *adoration of Manson* that is the underlying impulse. None of the students has broken an arm falling out of a tree, says my friend, none of them walks in the woods or knows where in the sky the sun goes down. *Where does the sun go down? What is its trajectory across the April sky? Do I know? Or the recently-arrived birds – what are their names? When and from where did they arrive?*

Lack of connectedness with the natural world is not just a local or age-related problem, but a universal one applicable to different cultural contexts. No wonder we have become disconnected – under our own hands the natural world has become poisonous. Recently I heard a mother scolding her rash-covered daughter: 'Don't you know better than to sit on grass?' This happened last May, the month when every second lawn in my neighbourhood is doused with herbicides and insecticides.

Consider Ontario's Lake Huron as a metaphor for current human relationships with the environment. The 'No Swimming' signs on the lake change according to the dangers inflicted by high coliform counts. People comprehend the words and obey, but their imaginations stop at the acrylic letters on the metal sign. Lake Huron has become something that people enjoy when the authorities allow. What's happened? When did things change? It seems we've lost our ability to see and read or notice the natural world in which we live. Once upon a time, deciding to swim was a matter of human desire and testing natural conditions. The big-toe-into-the-water test, for instance. When did our relationship with the living, breathing, speaking Lake Huron become mediated by authoritative words on a sign? When did we lose our friend the lake?

Academic Alienation from Place

Academia also perpetuates estrangement from the very forms of life we take for granted. Recently, I conducted an informal interview with three students who were finishing their fourth year of a program on a particular campus. I asked them what they knew about 'this place' (I gestured toward the quad and dorms) that had been their home for the past four years. The women told a few humorous anecdotes about the quad as a place of lunch-time gatherings (near the daffodils), and mentioned community events such as barbecues and summer balls. When I asked about other significant places on campus, one woman answered that in her third year she'd discovered the fish pond. 'It's because I became friends with people in science,' she explained. 'They showed it to me and we sometimes eat lunch there now. Before that I didn't know it existed.' The woman explained that she hadn't known about the pond before because it 'belongs to science.'

The student's answer is revealing. 'The pond belongs to science' parallels the notion that certain knowledge belongs in certain disciplines. Only when people admit other forms of knowing – such as experiential knowledge – into their defining paradigm will the pond extend beyond scientific experiment (however valuable that may be) into the more inclusive realm of lunch-time refreshment.

Coyote doesn't separate knowledge into the disciplines. He puts things into a holistic context. When Coyote has some thinking to do, he goes down to the creek, into the water, then into the mud. He sinks down, down, until he has an idea. For Coyote, thinking means immersing himself in the earth, quietly sitting and listening until something occurs to him. Coyote contextualizes his problem in the earth, which for him is the proper context.

The Educational Uses of Story

Most classroom teachers promote earth-friendly environmental practices such as recycling, composting, and energy conservation. An understanding of these practices and of their benefits for the earth is demonstrated by many children as they come to the end of their elementary school education. Still, a more meaningful change in values is needed.

Bowers (1993) argues that personal changes in behaviour are inadequate responses to the environmental crisis. Even such seemingly laudable activities such as recycling and tree planting contribute to a belief system that situates self separate from an external nature, that is, nature as something other and outside our well-being. Gough calls for a 'transformation from being the kind of people who are alienated from nature-as-other toward becoming people whose identity is inextricable from our environments' (1993, 13). He emphasizes that 'the pathologies we are addressing in environmental education are psychological, social, and cultural rather than ecological. Educators should see their work as being, in large part, a form of *cultural criticism*, paying particular attention to the narratives, myths, and rituals which have sustained and reproduced human society's alienation from the earth' (ibid.).

Carolyn Merchant places her hope in 'social movements that intervene at the points of greatest ecological and social stress to reverse ecological damage and fulfill people's basic needs' (1992, 13). My research project intended to "intervene at the points of greatest ecological and social' – not stress, but suitability. As children, my siblings and I had many opportunities to play with relative freedom in our neighbourhood, and to investigate many aspects of the natural world. Many of our stories hearken back to adventures in natural settings. Perhaps this project can be seen as adults giving back to children the right to enjoy and explore the natural world.

Storytelling is a practice that holds much promise for creating such cultural change and is perhaps the most overlooked facilitator of environmental education. Stories conjoin emotions and intellect. Facts are presented in the context of feelings. The act of organizing stories necessitates reflection; students need to consider *what happens* and *how they feel* about events. To tell a story is to create connections. Embodied connections. Stories embody lived experience – they are meant to move us. Stories are not just so much talk, they are talk in action. They are what head-talk becomes when it is joined to the body, or what ideas become when they are fused to lived experience. If we want students to care about the environment, we need to ensure that our curriculum is designed to elicit such responses. Descriptive language – facts and information – can achieve certain educational goals. Facts can move people emotionally, but often they do not. However, when facts are presented in the context of feelings – as stories – they engage people aesthetically. They appeal to people's emotions and imaginations as well as to their intellect. Facts alone (disembodied knowledge) separate students from the educational goal of creating a caring relationship between people and nature. Stories (embodied facts) can help to achieve such a relationship.

Drama enables participants to conjoin the energy of story conventions such as character, plot, and language with physical action. Students explore quality of movement and character suggested by the story. By exploring gaps in the story and alternative points of view, or through repetition, participants extend and embellish the original story. Stories delineate the patterns, power structures, and the struggles that inform them. The social nature of drama necessitates consideration of audience (be that one of peers or a formal audience), which in turn provides boundaries, group consideration, and motivation for work. Also, others' stories remind students of their own, and suggest new ones. Stories enable them to see the story form and content of their lives within their environments, and offer ways to transform both real and fictional experience into new and original structures. As Kathleen Gallagher says, '[D]rama is a way of looking, not at what something is, but what it might be' (1998, 141).

Vivian Gussin Paley's practice of storytelling and story-acting was the original model for this research project. As a senior educator in the Chicago lab school, Paley conducted pioneering work in the area of transcribing the stories her kindergarten children told and helping them act them out. She describes her activities as helping the many 'child selves' in the classroom begin the lifelong and essential process of making human connections. She believes that, 'in the matter of self, we are not connected to one another by the accumulation of skills and facts, but rather by inner fears and fantasies, impulsive urges and pleasure' (Paley 1990, 62). My research acknowledged the critical importance of self/self connections, but I wanted to extend that to include the self/ earth connection. If we provided the children with many experiences in the meadow, forest, and wetlands that lie adjacent to the school ground, what would happen to their stories? Is there room and desire in the child's work of connecting self to other selves for connecting self to earth?

Research Project

It seems there is. During the course of two years of research (1995–7) with senior kindergarten students and their teacher, Julie Berry, in St Thomas, Ontario, the children ventured further and further into the woods beyond the backyard of their school. Their teacher, a keen observer of her students, wrote:

> Walked for the first time with the kids looking for red things. 'Listen' says Amit 'and the world talks to you.' We do and we hear crickets and blue jays and Laura says fiercely 'I saw a cardinal yesterday.' (Teacher's journal, 3 Oct. 1995)

> Richi looks around, quite put out, as if nature has conspired to fill his path with lush green, growing things. We're walking the meadow through

goldenrod and milkweed. 'How did all that stuff get here?' Josh asks as he backs away from the milkweed silk as if he's afraid. Laura's a little afraid too. She holds my hand. Moses loves it and tells me so. 'I love coming out here, Ms. Berry.' (ibid., 15 Oct. 1995)

Julie and I originally concentrated on the ways the dramatic conventions of storytelling and story-acting connected children with the *outdoor school* beyond their classroom walls, and on the ways in which storytelling and story-acting are the equivalents of lived experience. Later, however, I came to focus on the ways drama informs and shapes our perceptions of the world and, thus, how it shapes our experience. This is, to me, the interesting question.

There were approximately seventeen children in each year's program. The variety of home situations and cultural backgrounds emerged from time to time in the children's stories, and in their ability to fully participate in the walks. Julie and I worked together to create greater environmental awareness through various drama and literacy activities such as telling stories and acting them out. Material records of the research include journal entries and fieldnotes (mine, the kindergarten teacher's, and that of Lorna Rorke, my research assistant), route maps made during pre-hikes, letters to parents, and the students' observations and stories. Three questions informed my research with these kindergarten students. What is the effect of dramatic conventions on the experiences of young students in the outdoors? Do these conventions facilitate students' perceptual awareness of the natural world and their ability to articulate that awareness, and if so, how? Finally, How does my work as a practising artist and ecofeminist frame this discussion?

The Stories Inside, The Land That Brings Them Out

Our outdoor program centred on walking as often as possible in the wetlands behind the school. Underlying those experiences were the dramatic structures that transformed our walks into adventures. I use the word 'adventure' with its sense of journey and anticipation of the unknown, as well as a sense of being prepared for the adventure. We created this feeling of adventure through specific dramatic conventions such as plot, character, naming, and metaphor; also by reading and acting children's literature, by recording and interpreting the journey, and through challenging the children to experience the natural world sensually.

We made acts of literacy explicit by explaining to the children that what they saw with their eyes could be spoken as words that could be captured by the pencils and paper the researchers held. 'Talk with the adults about what you hear, see, touch. We will write down the words you say.' These connections between the sensual world and writing interested the children, who moved effortlessly from story dictating in the classroom to data collecting in the outdoors. They were conscious of what we recorded, and were specific in their instructions about what to include. In the classroom they took part in deciding what to do with the words the researchers read back to them. Sometimes the children wanted to take their words home, sometimes they wanted to glue or rewrite them onto their artwork. The words were often incorporated into their stories – both those written in their storybooks and those dramatized.

Story-acting took place in a carpeted room free of furniture. The children sat around the perimeter of the masking-taped area that formed our stage-in-the-round, as it were. Each playwright chose the fellow students who would be in his or her play. Inanimate objects such as doors and the wind were included as roles according to the artistic dictates of the playwright/director (who usually chose the leading role for him or herself). Julie or I read the story, pausing often while it was enacted. We performed a story two to four times, so that the director, with help, could work on the acting. The audience clapped at the end of each performance.

I am convinced that the chance to act out their own stories was a prime motivation for the students. There was nothing – not the outdoor walks, not dictating the stories – that equalled the students' enthusiasm for performing their own work. 'Who has a story to perform today?' would invariably elicit a chorus of 'me, me, me.' The student director stood centre stage as he or she selected the actors from among a dozen pairs of waving arms. Although there was the typical rehearsal chaos, there was also considerable attention paid by the children themselves to providing acting opportunities for each child. When this was not the case, the teacher intervened. At the end of each performance the teacher and I would help the children reflect on their stories. 'Remember when Chloe fell into the mud in the creek?' we asked after a particular drama about *soakers*. Over the course of the programs, we selectively retold and discussed past events, the words that the children had conveyed to the adult recorders, where those words reappeared in the story, and how they appeared in the recent drama. The students often told the entire story of the event from their particular point of view in response to the reflective questions. Children were given many opportunities to see how their words translated into characters, motivations, settings and actions, and how those actions could be fine-tuned to greater effect. To hear and see the children make writerly connections between experience and symbolic expression was rewarding. Their everyday experience was not just validated ('owned,' in contemporary jargon), but celebrated in dramatic and literary forms. Our (physical) walk in the woods was translated into one symbol system (oral language), then another (written words), then into the narrative forms of story, and finally, through drama, the walk experience was returned to its oral, physical, immediate impulses. I imagine that even the performances were again *trans-created* when students told them as stories to other students and perhaps to parents at home. This great experiment in linking perception and words enabled the children to create their own images of the world. As far as I can tell, they were worlds in which humans and the natural world were deeply, curiously, and inextricably linked together.

During both years of the study students related literacy and environmental education, to varying degrees. Information such as 'Ms. Hoogland, I saw Canada geese flying in the sky yesterday' counted as important in our transactions. As the students learned ways of symbolically expressing their relationships, the richer became their experience of the environment. Telling others what we experience is a way of bearing witness to it, and suggests an approach to education far removed from more mundane forms of environmental education.

Over the course of each year that we ran the program, children gained a more intimate and knowledgeable relationship with nature. They anticipated changes, recognized plants, and asked the questions that they had learned were possible. They shifted in their perspectives from distance to intimacy, from viewing the natural world as *fearful other* to assuming the perspective of creatures and even plants. By mid-year it was difficult to remember that some of these children had earlier resisted leaving the path for a creek-side adventure, while others had been afraid of mud and crawly things on the ground.

Educating the Senses

Maxine Greene (1995) says that children cannot be taught to feel deeply; but they can be taught to look and listen in such a way that the imaginative emotion follows. We encouraged sensual exploration through reading and discussing many books, including one titled *To Rabbittown* (Wayland 1989). In this story a young girl travels beyond the rolling hills to 'the edge of it all.' Through engaging her senses the character grows rabbit legs and paws (and eyes and fur) and sings rabbit songs. We talked about using five senses with the children: 'The girl in the story grows rabbit ears. Imagine what it would be like if you could grow rabbit ears. What kind of things would you be able to hear?' (Research assistant's notes, 11 March 1997). The children took up the challenge; in fact, they embellished the rabbit theme so that once we were outdoors, rabbit paws and hopping like a rabbit were all the rage. When I asked the children how rabbit goes up a hill, I received a dozen demonstrations. And as happens in all the stories the children tell, the natural world coexists effortlessly with literary characters and with superheroes. Amanda, aged five, posed dramatically and said:

> I hear something
> Crystals and diamonds
> Somebody's robbing them
> I'm super bunny. All the way! [*Amanda runs off.*]
> I'm coming with my bunny ears.

Although I have many other examples of stories that included sensory awareness, it's clear that *action* rather than grand vistas or the smell of wild mint drives the literary adventures of this age group.

Plot and Character

> Beyond the chain link fence out across the wide green lawn to the big old maple. Through the meadow to the forest, to the top of the steep hill where we have stood countless times this year and looked down into the wetlands. 'Someday we'll go down there' we have said again and again. Today we do. Cross the log bridge. Follow the path through green to the stream and the green island. Cross the stream to the island, cross the stream to the hill. Climb the hill and follow the path through purple violets to the *One-Armed King*. Here is the place where we enter the *Forest of No Path*. Look for *Wake-Robin* and *Deep Green Sea of Mandrake*, for *Froth of Trilliums* the colour of green waves crashing into snow on a green beach. In all these places we stop and listen. In the first green tongues of humans on earth it is said the word for ear and wisdom was the very same word. We listen in all our budding wisdom. And unfurl. (Teacher's journal, 16 May 1996)

The above passage illustrates what drama offers to environmental education in terms of plot and character. The walk has been scripted, play-like, so that different geographies form its sections. As we named the places on our walk we created characters, but also plot. Just as the maple in the centre of the field began to take on various roles in the children's stories, so did the wildflowers, the insects, the hills, the streams and gullies themselves. Occasionally we stopped to ask ourselves, 'Let's pretend the One Armed King can tell stories. What stories would this tree tell?' These were the stories of the world in front of their eyes. There are also grand narratives – the seasons, weather, natural disasters such as earthquakes. Seasons emerge within cycles and rhythms, and we experience one season in contrast to the one that preceded it. There are stories of our own experiences in nature that have to do with capturing an animal, building a nest for it, hoping to raise it to reproductive age and then raise its babies. We wanted the children to find the stories contained in nature: *in front of, around, inside*; the narrative structure contained in the natural environment, in cycles, in people, and language:

> The bird flies from the tree. The squirrel climbs up the leaf. The sun flashes at the bird and it makes the bird fly and there are the birds sitting. The squirrel scares them. They have to have their own tree to their selves. That's all. The flowers just sets there. (Dara, November 1996)

Although the children did not often take up the idea of place names in their written stories, they were happy to join in the oral naming-game. Many of their suggestions were nonsensical and fun:

> Zoli Zoli Zoli
> Zoli Zoli Zoli
> House is my home. House is my home.
> Zoli Zoli Zoli
> Zoli Zoli Zoli. (Ben, December 1996)

The place names Julie and I instilled were the geographical terms of the wetlands conjoined with those of myth and mystery. We tried to create the sense that this was a mysterious, uncharted territory whose *props* and *setting* children are invited to interpret. How is this old tree like a one-armed king? How do you cross the forest without a path? How do you invent your own?

Suspense, Danger, and Joy

Like every good plot, ours created suspense. It's clear, for instance, that a particular walk has been anticipated. ' "Someday we'll go down there," we have said again and again.' Judging from the twisting, hovering, bodies peering over the edge of the ravine, this is all the suspense a drama could want. It also created danger.

The role of danger as a dramatic and pedagogical structure was one of our seemingly simple but surprising discoveries. Danger and safety from danger, along with loneliness and friendship, form the major themes of the children's play at this age level. But to use danger pedagogically is a radical concept. At the beginning of the year children expressed genuine fear of the outdoors. Walking through the tall grass, for instance, was impossible for some. And so before learning what to observe in nature, the children had to learn how to be comfortable in nature, and how to take risks. Our dry runs in the classroom included discussing and acting Rosen's *We're Going on a Bear Hunt* many times. In this story the characters enjoy scaring themselves as they learn to walk through (also over, under, or around) their adventures before dashing for the cover of bed at the end. They square off against tall grass, rivers, and snowstorms. This sense of walking through danger is delicious. There is danger and excitement in crossing a stream! There is wildness in mud! The research assistant wrote:

> Next we see a dragon's foot in the shape of a big hole. The girls are convinced that the woods are the home of dragons, dinosaurs, and other exotic animals. Half- way through the walk Rachel insisted on pretending she's in danger of slipping or falling and would scream until I help her to safety. Perhaps this is an extension of the idea of big exotic animals in the woods – mystery and the unknown. I reach out my arm in an exaggerated motion while Rachel grabs onto it and breathes a sigh of relief. Monique too soon joins in the fun. (20 May 1997)

In this material record there is also the pedagogy of love. It's important for the children to have love of the outdoors modelled and affirmed by an adult. Julie writes:

> Walking along with Jordan and I point out something – wood anemones or something – and Jordan asks, 'How come you know all this?' And I tell him that I love the woods and everything that grows in it and he says, 'You tell us too much' and I know it's true. (Journal, 30 May 1997)

> I take the students into the woods because I love ... how skunk cabbage looks as it pokes its purple beak out of the thawing earth. I love the fluorescence of green moss, the way sunlight glimmers off the topmost

twigs of the bare March branches, the sound of a dozen birds, the smell of
mud. I am a role model for joy. (Teacher's letter to parents, 11 March 1996;
never sent)

Teachers as role models for joy is a grand idea, but for all teachers'
sakes it's important that the emphasis be on the curriculum to *support
such an approach*, rather than on the teacher to be or to assume a certain
kind of persona. If our society values the natural world as being inti-
mately connected with humans, then the curriculum must support learning about the environment in ways conducive to that belief.

Yet the curriculum doesn't support arts-based education except in
peripheral ways. Julie never sent that letter. The current curriculum's
stress on academic skills and goals is antithetical to a pedagogy of
exploration and investigation that contains structured opportunities
for learning.

With the current literacy education that focuses on word and sound
recognition, as in the skills-based, achievement-oriented, kindergarten
curriculum (with programs such as 'Jolly Phonics' in Ontario), students
are able to recognize the discrete letters and read the text in front of
them, but they don't have a story about it. These children are literate in
a functional rather than a *storied* way. They don't know what the words
mean at the level of the *experiences* that drama and the arts provide.

Point of View

We were aware of the pressure on students to conform to the social and
cultural expectations of the classroom. It was suddenly cool to be envi-
ronmentally aware. For instance, saving worms from rainy sidewalks
became a regular pastime, as did bringing in bugs for identification.
Despite the sudden popularity of such activities and despite the pressures to conform, many of the children seemed to identify closely with
small creatures. Ladybugs, for instance, were a main focus of the walks
during one week in May. After the walk, back in the classroom, Kahil told
the following story, which was subsequently acted out:

Once upon a time there were 7 ladybugs. And they all lived in a hole and
everyday they gotted to see people walking by them. And one day people
didn't come by anymore but then the next day they came back again. And
then all the people got to see them everyday on trees and grass. The End.
Bye-Bye. (Kahil's story, 23 May 1997)

Telling his story from the point of view of the ladybugs was a shift in viewpoint, further confirmed when the story was dramatized. The children's stories during the *To Rabbittown* week assumed the perspectives of rabbits. Drama facilitates a multiplicity of perspectives, which often means that students can choose many new perspectives in the course of a year. The ability to assume different perspectives is a key element not only in drama, but in education generally, and in the process of becoming human.

I spent part of the ladybug week with Amanda, mentioned above. After hearing *To Rabbittown*, Amanda charged for the lost and found box and pulled out a pink acrylic hat with long scarf-like appendages. She called these her rabbit ears and throughout the walk she made much of holding up these ears to listen like a rabbit.

Cornelia. What do your rabbit ears tell you?
Amanda. I hear the ladybugs.
Cornelia. What noise do they make?
Amanda. Bee bee bee.
Cornelia. What's he (pointing to ladybug) looking for?
Amanda. Me.
Cornelia. What is he going to find?
Amanda. (*ignoring the question and speaking to the ladybug in her hand*) Cutey.
Cornelia. He doesn't want to leave you.
Amanda. (*absorbed in ladybug*) Cutey.
Cornelia. He's staying with you.
Amanda. She.
Cornelia. She?
Amanda. She's staying with *me.*
Cornelia. She's staying with you.

Nearing the end of our walk Amanda made an imaginative leap. I marvelled.

Amanda. I don't need these ears any more. (*She pulls off her hat.*)
I got my own rabbit ears. (*She draws imaginary, protruding rabbit ears with a finger, then stops.*)
Cornelia. Hmm.
Amanda. (*She points to her own ears.*) My ears are here.
Cornelia. You mean those ears (*pointing at her ears*) are rabbit ears?
Amanda. Yes.   (Field notes, 20 May 1997)

These childhood experiences are the way to intimate knowing. As a conscious, behaving agent Amanda negotiates a conscious, behaving world that is alive and vital. The result is a world embodied with voices that speak to children's sensibilities with a sensuous power of their own. The collapse of boundaries between herself and the ladybug created a reciprocity through which Amanda absorbs, and is absorbed. She is as much part of the natural world as it is of her. This sense of reciprocity is a major feature of children's relationships with the natural world.

Reciprocity

The world is a multi-vocal place, and the human is but one voice. The expressiveness of the land as well as of other species creates a link among them and human speech. This is evident in the ease with which young children move between this and other-worldly planes. From my work with preschool children I have come to believe that they have access to a multitude of languages. For example, Sage, aged five, is now a dog on all fours whose only pleasure is to bark and fetch bones. She tells me that her name is Cosmos, that she sleeps in her dog basket, that she is afraid of the wind. Well-meaning caregivers buy her a stuffed dog, thinking that she wants what they cannot give – a real dog. I believe what she really wants is her own dogness, her own bark and four-legged prowl.

The land is not passive, but is an active setting for the theatre of our walks. How easily the children orchestrate themselves into a bear family, all of us becoming members of the clan who seek out forest dens, cedar-bough beds, makeshift tables, and mud-pie food, who run from enemies and leave mysterious signs for those who follow. What appears to be a casual arrangement of logs is really an ideal seating arrangement, with just enough space in the centre for a fire. We are forever on the lookout for those places in the forest that speak directly to our needs of eating and sleeping, that suggest themselves as lookouts and secret glens. A multitude of attitudes and voices – human, animal, vegetable, topo-graphical – constitute our adventures along the river.

My research with the kindergarten classes involved many excursions to the ridge and wetlands just beyond the school. However, the day came when the children had to say goodbye to the maple tree that was the meeting point on our regular excursions. We suggested that the children say goodbye to the tree in any way they liked. Some waved. Some yelled 'Goodbye.' Others wrapped their arms around the big trunk and hugged. Jessica came up beside her teacher and said, 'Ms. Berry, when I kissed the tree it kissed me back.' 'Does it have lips?' Julie asked. 'Yes,' she said, 'big bumpy wooden lips.' And Soren, standing next to the tree, found a small interruption in its bark. 'Here's its mouth!' he pointed excitedly. 'And there are its eyes,' said Tobias, looking up into the branches. 'I think,' announced Lisa, as we walked back to the school, 'that our tree looks greener now.' Touching the tree is to be touched by the tree, just as listening to the tree means being listened to by the tree, and seeing the tree means to be seen by the tree. Children are witness to a world of voices that both speak and listen, a world where kisses are returned.

Children, Poets, and the Drama Curriculum

The children and their teacher have taught me a great deal about teaching and about the natural world. Julie Berry, a professional poet (*Worn Thresholds*, 1995), is a gifted writer. But her poetic use of language shouldn't obscure the fact that most of the educational experiences described here (educating the senses, storytelling, hiking with students) are similar to those used by any good teacher with a measure of curricular freedom. The difference lies in the setting and the intention of this research program, and in the risks involved in taking children outdoors. As with all exploratory pedagogy, the teacher often has to make the story up as she goes along, naming each place by what is in the moment. This is true for each year that a teacher spends with a class, but it is also true for each hike that we took. There must be a balance between what is known and unknown at the beginning of every journey the teacher begins with her students. For reasons beyond the obvious – practical ones related to planning, timing, and safety – the pre-hike experience was very important. On one such pre-hike, Julie wrote:

> As I emerge from the woods into a ploughed and harrowed field, three crows take flight. Their noisy protests give me the name for this place: *Crow Field* (*Field of Crows*)? If there are no crows tomorrow, I see by the soil, sprinkled with many small stones, that this place could also be named *Field of Stones*. I realize that I can't name this place until I come to it fresh; who knows, tomorrow there may be geese or a groundhog or some deer. (Journal, 19 June 1997)

As teachers and researchers we have already named the world for ourselves and the pleasure we get from this experience is huge. We can't wait to see how the students will name the world for themselves. The places that we have named are inside us now. Is it by naming that we possess something – love it? I can feel the hills, the pathways, the maple tree, the *One-Armed King*, in my gut the way the coyote in *Quail Song* contains the desert, the cacti, and the great orange sun inside his body. I have swallowed the meadow, the stream, the island, the *Forest of No Path*, the field, everything.

What viewpoints, approaches, and strategies does the above dramatically-based outdoor program suggest for environmental education? Will telling and acting stories extend students' perceptual boundaries? Will classroom instruction ever be adequate for students to make contact with meanings, feelings, and power in their backyards? How is the school/park/city a matrix for the complexity of meanings? Can students be taught to be sensually aware? Can they be taught to expect that their actions toward the natural world be reciprocated?

In storytelling and in drama generally, it's possible to consider the local environment, including that of the school, in ways that develop a consciousness of reciprocity. The same tree speaks in different voices in winter, spring, summer, and fall. Stories can thus be part of a personal cosmology that can point students to greater observation of the natural world, and can create within students a greater sensual and ecological awareness of that world. If we, as a society, are willing, the arrogance that underlies the current separation of culture and nature can be repaired in the younger generations. We would do well to look to children – the lucky ones who still play in mud and in tall grass – to remember the thrill of finding bugs underneath rocks and rushing home to tell the story.

VI. CREATIVE PROCESSES, AUDIENCE, AND FORM

The Significance of Theatre: A Commencement Address

RICHARD ROSE

Theatre: the origin of the word is the Greek verb 'to behold,' the simplest definition of which, in the *Oxford English Dictionary*, is 'to hold or keep in view, to watch; to regard or contemplate with the eyes; to look upon, look at.' But this definition also includes more complex and meaningful human experiences: 'to hold or contain by way of purport or signification, to signify, mean' and 'to regard (with the mind), have regard to, attend to, consider.' When I was asked to speak at this convocation, Dr Thompson suggested I might address the significance of theatre in contemporary society. I learned that we are gathered to celebrate not only the graduates but also the opening of a new theatre – the culmination of many years of hard work. Next month will truly see the birth of this theatre, with the premiere production of *A Midsummer Night's Dream*, one of the world's greatest plays. As we sit in this theatre on the cusp of its life, the question 'why' does gather importance.

My first theatrical experience surprised me. It happened in the winter of grade one.

I am beating up Joey, the class bully. I am sitting on Joey's back, having wrestled him into this position and I am pushing his face into the snow. We are fighting on the front lawn of a house a few doors up from my public school. I am pushing his face so hard I can see the grass. The fight is going well. I am feeling triumphant. I am feeling superior since I am punishing the class bully. In the audience are twins, Joey's younger brothers, crying. Their big brother hero is being humiliated. Standing beside them is Karen Horner, cheering me on: 'Hit him, hit him, hit him!' She hates Joey. She is screaming like a banshee. Joey and I are Grade One Gladiators.

We are coming to the climax of the play. Joey is about to give in. I turn to the audience triumphantly. But watching them watch me, I suddenly feel discombobulated. Something about the twins crying or Karen screaming disconcerts me. I find I am no longer able to push down on the back of Joey's head. I can no longer hit Joey with my fists covered in string mittens. Watching them watch me, I experience a feeling of having stepped outside of myself. Suddenly everything about the play, the audience, and the heroic role I am playing seems ridiculous or absurd. I don't even understand the experience – I am only six – but watching them watch me, I stop fighting. Karen Horner screams at me, calling me a coward. The twins are quiet. Joey is recovering more from shame than injury. I get up and walk away, very confused, frightened and feeling guilty.

I remember this for the rest of my life: me watching them watch me. I could no longer find the will or the reason to hit somebody or to fight. When I was challenged, the same feeling of guilt, confusion, and absurdity would well up in me and paralyse me. I couldn't raise my fists. I would step out of myself. For this reason, I suffered a number of humiliations during the course of my public-school years. Schoolboy fights were mythic events, frequent, topical, and sure to gather a big crowd. Our school days always seemed to be building up to a fight or relishing the highlights of battle in the aftermath. But I could no longer participate. A real-life event had become a theatrical experience. In the same instant, I was both a player in a life event and a spectator. This sudden and surprising change in my point of view and in my place in reality caused me to pause and then to decide not to fight or to hit anyone ever again. I had made my first moral decision – at six years of age, and more out of confusion and fear than thought – but a decision that I have held to throughout my life.

I wonder whether this experience was also at the root of my passion for and choice of a career in the theatre. The last time I was formally asked 'Why?' by an educational institution was at my interview for York University's Theatre Programme. When I was asked why I wanted to direct, I said that I wanted a better world and that the plays I would direct were intended to change people's lives. I believed it, whole-heartedly. I now dismiss that statement as being naive, but I am equally disturbed by the thought that it may not be so naive. I couldn't identify the feeling any better at eighteen than I had at six, but I may subconsciously have known the power of beholding.

Most of my work in the theatre has been in the genre of tragedy – the dark stories of the human experience, the plays with no hope that are about dread and the inevitable end of life. Mortality has always been a professional and personal passion. Two of my favourite lines from plays I have directed are 'We are born dying' and 'Death is just one breath away.' The content of tragedy alone could make you ask 'Why' – why would anybody want to attend a tragedy? One would think this would be a most unappealing theatrical experience.

In the opening scene of *King Lear*, the King, in front of his court, asks his daughters how much they love him. At the end of his life, this king is subconsciously afraid of not being loved. He knows he is going to die. He wants to 'unburdened crawl toward death.' He has decided to abdicate and divide up his kingdom among his daughters, and he will decide their inheritance according to how well they express love. King Lear already knows exactly who loves him most. He has divided the kingdom in advance and knows which daughter he will live with in retirement. Yet Lear tries to turn the expression of their love into a commodity. He asks for a public declaration from his daughters after a lifetime of cruelty, rashness, and creating a kingdom of 'haves' and 'have-nots,' 'legitimates' and 'illegitimates' with seemingly no other value systems, spiritual or moral. When the public declarations don't go according to plan, he rashly decides to divide the kingdom between the two daughters who don't love him. Whether Lear can admit his mistake or not, he knows the consequences of his rash change of heart. He has hastened his own death and it seems he will die alone. He spends the rest of the play consciously and subconsciously wrestling with his decision, why his daughters do not love him, and what kind of kingdom, court, and family he has fathered. His anxiety eventually leads him to madness, in the form of an emotional breakdown. *King Lear* is the bleakest of plays. It asks the audience to behold the story of a dying old man experiencing the destruction of his family, his country, and his legacy.

Tragedy creates feeling, and the feeling is fear, one of our most profound emotional and instructive experiences – whether we like it or not. It is about death – the time, the moment when we are most serious, when we weigh the future, weigh our past, weigh our choices, decide and act with varying degrees of awareness of the consequences. Tragedy is theatre's manifestation of an inevitable life experience. Why do we go to a tragedy? Usually we say for catharsis – the audience member has a cathartic experience that involves some kind of purification of emotion by a vicarious experience. Often this is referred to as a release.

That may be true, but watching a tragedy is also like a pre-scarring before you get cut, without the actual injury. When you've cut yourself once, you are that much more cautious about getting cut again. In a tragedy, we get an impression of what real fear might be like when we are eventually faced with the consequences of our actions or the end of our lives. The drama gives a warning that is at once visceral and at a distance. That distance permits one 'to regard with the mind.' Attending a tragedy is an opportunity to behold the consequences of a fatal choice. We go to a tragedy to experience and contemplate fear – fear in the mirror of the theatre. In hindsight, I think at six years old I became afraid of what I had become and therefore lost my capacity for violence. I wonder if a full, rich, and happy life doesn't include a number of necessary, fear-filled decisions.

The art of the theatre itself is, in a fundamental sense, a tragic art. The perishable performance is part of the theatre artist's everyday experience. In the rehearsal hall, we say that we are working a scene moment by moment – a scene is a sum of moments. The first part of rehearsal is spent creating the moments. The means vary, but essentially this is a process of discovery. Often the actor has no idea how a moment has been given birth. Once discovered, the moments, the scenes, will never be the same again. They cannot be repeated. Time and circumstances have changed. Rehearsal then becomes a labour to find some means to recreate the moment that was, and the actors and the director are filled with the fear that they will not recapture the brilliance, the truthfulness of the original spontaneous moment. The actor's desire to recreate a spontaneous moment resists fate and fights against the death and loss of the discovered moment. In the end, each performance will also perish, like the tragic hero. The rehearsal hall and the performance parallel the play. The play parallels the act of living. Mortality is a daily working condition in the theatre.

Yet laughter is also critical in the theatre. Comedy is not just more obviously appealing; it, too, gives the audience a mirror. There are many current theories – medical, psychological, and spiritual – about the healing powers of laughter. The laugh is a release of pressure – the body shakes, purging a little tension or loosening its limbs – it is a catharsis of a kind. But the laugh is the response of the body to the brain's recognition, and the moment after the laugh comes the provocation of thought – reflection on what we have just recognized. The preparation for the first laugh in a play must be carefully thought out and set up. I have often said to actors, 'This is the first laugh of the play, which you *must* get.' The first laugh from the audience means they are understanding the story or the situation or the world the characters live in. The subsequent laughter is their growing recognition of the story's progression and complications. Laughter is an act of the intellect.

In life, we, like the performer, are in the process of doing, of acting, in the present. We lack hindsight. We rarely see ourselves. In a way, we shouldn't, I suppose: too much self-consciousness might impede the process of living life to the fullest. We are in the stream of life and time moves forward. Occasionally, however, we see ourselves, or we observe others' behaviour, and we laugh. A moment of hindsight is a moment of recognition, and we chortle. Watching a comedy in the theatre is like taking a pause from participating in the stream. We get to sit outside our lives. We get to watch other people make the mistakes. We get to witness the compulsive behaviour of the ambitious businessperson, the old man who has fallen in love with the young maiden, the cowardly soldier quivering when his bravado is challenged, or the clown who never sees the banana skin. We laugh. In the moment before we laugh, our brain says, 'Oh, I did that once' or 'That's just like my boss' or 'My best friend is always making the same stupid mistakes.' Sometimes the laugh is a larger form of recognition – a macro point of view – wherein we see the blinding nature of desire, the injustices of society, the recurring patterns of human folly. I suppose a laugh is like a flag run up to signal the conscience that we should think about this before we find ourselves in the same situation, running down the road of life towards our own unseen banana skins. As with tragedy, the great power of comedy is the ability to give the beholder perspective, significance, and meaning.

Human experience is said to be ruled by two great forces: thanotos – death and destruction – and eros – life and creation. The theatre represents these two great forces through the genres of tragedy and comedy. The perspective of tragedy is that of a world of death, feeling, and fear. Comedy's perspective inhabits a world of eros, thought, and laughter. However, the two aspects of human experience and the qualities and effects of these theatrical genres are not mutually exclusive. King Lear's contradictory behaviour makes the destruction of his family believable, recognizable, and fearful. Yet the Fool in *Lear* tells acerbic jokes about the King's nonsensical and tragic actions. It is the Fool's comic point of view, in contrast to the tragic action, that gives us perspective on Lear's behaviour. No one point of view can tell the whole story. One summer at Stratford, I was rehearsing *The Taming of the Shrew* and *Coriolanus* (an even bleaker play than *Lear*) on alternate days. The rehearsal hall of the tragedy was often filled with laughter. But to create laughter in the comedy, the actors had to be deadly serious. If, in the third week of rehearsal, the director is still laughing at what is on stage, the actors are actually not creating a comic moment. A tragedy demands a sense of humour to survive it. Comedy is often about the pain of loving and living. The qualities of the two genres are intertwined in the play as well as in the rehearsal hall, as they are in life. You can sense that life in theatre is often about contradictions. The contradictions are necessary to the theatrical experience. They parallel life. If we are to pursue truth in presenting a play, we must grasp these contradictions.

Through my time in the theatre, I have come to recognize that there can be no homogeneous point of view to the act of beholding. Once, after a performance of Michael Ondaatje's *Coming Through Slaughter*, a stranger came up to me and said how grateful she was for the theatre that my company produced. She said: 'You do plays that allow us to forgive ourselves.' I have never received a greater compliment. I was also disconcerted. I joked that I wasn't a priest, just a theatre director. The next night, a friend told me the play was boring. I was stung. Since my university entrance interview, I have increasingly learned that I have no advice to give, and when I have tried to give advice, the contradictory position was all too apparent. I have learned that theatre is not a very good vehicle for changing lives and that my eighteen-year-old idealism was naive. I no longer make changing lives my goal. I do not set out to direct prescriptive plays or productions. What I want to do on the stage is to tell the story and represent life without offering advice; to sift out my opinion, prejudices, and commentary in the pursuit of the life-like. My artistic intent is to stay true to a story's inherent principles. Contradictorily, I have witnessed lives change. As you have heard, my own life was changed by a theatrical means – that act of beholding – me watching them watch me. And, of course, every story does have inherent principles, usually prescriptive ones, whether in the fearful warning of a tragedy or in the laughing recognition of a comedy. Should the audience member behold – in its richest definition, 'regard with the mind' – a moment, experience fear or laughter, have that moment of recognition, then the play – the story we are telling – has significance.

Possibly this speaks to Dr Thompson's question, 'Why theatre today?' It is, I suspect, not dissimilar to why theatre yesterday. Shakespeare had Hamlet instruct his hired performers to 'hold the mirror up to nature.' Three hundred years later, Antonin Artaud wrote one of the most significant modern texts about theatre and called it *Theatre and Its Double*. The word 'double' refers to life. The stories, the context, the styles may change, but the essential elements of actor and audience haven't changed: theatre is still the act of beholding.

This convocation celebrates the art of beholding. In Thorneloe College's new theatre, a place for beholding, we begin a journey: a new journey of a very old art form. I must admit that when I direct a play, I much prefer to work in an old theatre. In a new theatre, there never seem to be enough ghosts in the room: the ghosts of past productions or players or the residue from moments of creative brilliance, the fights, the tears, the smells of people who have trod the boards, the silent presence of an audience. Only time and many plays will give this freshly painted theatre the history I crave. I may feel this way because the art form itself is perishable – it resembles life: a sum of moments – and I would argue that the perishable factor is at the heart of the theatre. It forces the artist to keep renewing. It demands constant striving for a goal that, if one happens to achieve it, is lost instantly. It demands that we live every second on the stage to its fullest. We know it will die. As a lesson for living, I have found the theatre to be a great source of inspiration.

And now, contradictorily, some advice on how to make theatre:

- Follow the story. Make each artistic choice based on the action of the story. Try not to get in the story's way.
- Don't show off! The reviews may be gratifying, but the meaning will get lost. Create art, not artfulness.
- Get as many people as possible to see the play. But remember, in today's world the theatre is a rarefied art form. Not everyone will go. Theatre is not necessarily – and this is important – a mass social event.
- Pursue the audience member who wants to be there for himself or herself and not because it is the thing to do.
- Never expect unanimity among the audience. Never pursue unanimity; it is the fastest road to the lowest common denominator.

You will know you have succeeded if an audience member tells you, 'I saw your play a week ago and I can't stop thinking about it,' or better yet, 'Three nights later I had this dream about the play.' One goes to a play and, I think, forgets most of it almost immediately. It is like life: a stream of events, and you can't really remember what you saw in the middle of the first act. But what can be remembered is the thought, the personal thought the play provoked – the moment of recognition. Should you achieve this in the plays that you will work so hard to create in this new space, then you will have given worth to, and honoured in the most important way, all the time and effort that went into building this new theatre at Thorneloe College.

Education through Empathy: Using Laughter as a Way In

DIANE FLACKS

There are many historical examples that illustrate the essential connection between theatre and education. This chapter is about the experiences that led me to become a passionate believer in art that can't help but illuminate.

When I was in theatre school, I wanted to be an actor because I loved being on stage. It was simple. I loved surfing a real live moment in time with the audience, uniting in a communal experience. It was a non-intellectual, visceral passion. I had no intention of becoming a writer or someone who was motivated to (God forbid) 'teach' an audience anything.

When I pulled my bleeding and battered carcass out of the shredding grip of theatre school's humiliating maw, I entered the world of auditions. To my surprise, the material that I was suited for in the minds of agents and casting people was not the material that I was interested in or able to pull off. I couldn't give a hoot about drinking Coca-Cola at a pool party (even for $5000 in commercial residuals). I discovered, to my horror, that unless I cared about the material on even a superficial level, I was going to fail. I would be as mediocre as the material and then some. I needed to do work that I believed in, which meant that I would have to create it myself.

I co-founded a theatre company with two other women who had more or less survived theatre school with me: Wendy White and Victoria Ward. We cheekily called it Empress Productions. Our mission was to create theatre by women that inspired us and our audience with humour and humanity. We wanted to expose the ugly and tackle the things that frustrated us as young women. We wanted to debunk the myths that were limiting to us. We were shaky but proud feminists. We started to write.

I understand now that my impulse to write is based on my desire to make sense of events and people in the world that I don't understand. My passion to perform is based in the desire to express that new understanding in a clear and accessible way. In other words, my desire to write comes from my need to educate myself, and my desire to perform is inspired by my need to deliver that message to others. The underlying motivation for both is to affirm the interconnectedness of all of us and encourage empathy for each other. This has become a guiding mission statement.

In my first solo show, *Myth Me*, I entered the stage and said to the audience that 'we are all one big me ... in different moods.' Since we are all connected, we should be able to understand each other. In my third and latest solo show, *Random Acts*, the main character is Antonella Bergman, a motivational speaker who becomes a paraplegic after being pushed in front of a bus in a random act of violence. Before her accident, she would tell people that rage and revenge are absurd, since they come back to us in the end. In her opening speech Antonella explains that we are all connected, even the people we could live without:

> But the guy in the oversized Lexus who, in your 'road rage,' you gave the finger to, because he deserved it – he'll probably pass that finger on to the Danish woman in the Volvo who doesn't know you can turn right on a red in Toronto. And she'll give a big 'up yers' to the couple on the tandem bike who are trying just a bit too hard to salvage something a little bit too late. And they'll bang on the hood of the kid in his father's new jeep because it is *their* right of way they own it, and they're doing good things for the environment, and this kid will be so afraid of his dad seeing the dent on the jeep he will cruise right through the 4-way stop, almost hitting an off duty police officer, walking her rottweiler/sharpe cross after another frustrating day of inability to make a difference and Sunshine girls slipped into her 'to do' box by her brothers in blue, and she will throw a finger up in the air that will remarkably wind its way back to *you!* Stop the pay back! Court the Calm! Do it yourself first! We are all part of one body. You are the man in the Lexus! ...

The point I was proposing was that in investigating the mysterious details in ourselves, each other, and our worlds, we can bridge gaps between us, and hopefully connect in more meaningful, active ways – thus staving off the forces of ignorance that push us apart. (OK, it's a lofty goal. But in order for me to put my butt out there hanging for all to see, alone, on a stage, for an hour and twenty minutes, I had better have something significant that I need to communicate. I better have a point.)

Ostensibly, my initial reason for writing my second solo show, *By a Thread* was similar to that for my first: someone asked me to. Still, there were two educational goals for that show. One was that a friend was going through some tough times dealing with recent revelations of childhood sexual abuse in her family. I wanted to create and present a character that was struggling with memories of abuse, who was not a 'victim,' who was creative and funny and odd; whom an audience would be fascinated by, sympathize with, and love. My goal was for an audience to gain an understanding of what victims of child sexual abuse go through. Education through empathy, using laughter as a way in.

The other reason was a personal one for me. One night, when I was living in Toronto's Annex neighbourhood, I was arriving home late and was in the process of locking my bike up to my front porch, when I heard a sound coming from somewhere behind me. It sounded like a low guttural growl of breath 'hhhh,' and I had no idea where it was coming from. At that moment, I felt like the life force was leaving my body and it was paralysed, as my mind raced. I was terrified to look behind me, and I struggled to force my body up the stairs, as my numb hands fumbled with keys. I heard the sound again, behind me, closer, 'hhh.' I decided to turn and get a glimpse at how close he, my attacker, was. I looked back, and what did I see? My elderly neighbour horking on the sidewalk.

The urban terror that paralysed me, that stalks so many women in big cities, that shamed me with its power to reduce me to a passive stereotype was something that I needed to explore. I hoped to confront it by presenting it in the full light of the stage.

Living with suffering was a theme in *Random Acts*. My challenge arose in how to explore that without being maudlin or presumptuous. At the time, I was obsessed with some of the biblical stories I had studied in Hebrew school. I used the biblical character of Sarah, the original Jewish mother, to grapple with the meaning behind why some people suffer, and what it might be possible for a 'motivational speaker' (Antonella Bergman) to tell them:

So there she was, Sarah the biblical matriarch, the original Jewish mother, the person who coined the phrase, 'you could call,' there she was 90 years old, shaped like a question mark, and still waiting for a miracle. According to the old testament, Sarah was promised by god that she and her husband Abraham's offspring would be as numerous as the stars in the sky and the sand on the beach, yet here she was, 90 years old, and barren as a bucket.

And one day, some handsome angels came to her tent, and as she washed their butter soft feet, they revealed to her that she was now pregnant. What?! At 90?! Hysterical! Her breasts were two figs, her womb curled in unto itself in loneliness, her nether lips pursed together like a baby's fist! 'Get out of here god!'

So what did she do? Run? Beg? Scream? Tear her hair and rend her garments in true biblical fashion? No. It is recorded in biblical history: Sarah laughed. Screaming howling gut-wrenching gales of laughter spreading across the desert like a midnight wind. Because God's timing ... is a little funny.

Moving into television, I co-wrote a six-part series called *The Broad Side* with executive producer Jane Ford. We researched a different historical period in each episode and used broad humour to examine the tragic way women's lives were often controlled or dismissed. We hoped to have fun and to redress a lack of focus on women's history.

To follow, is an excerpt from our first episode, 'Chopin's Sister.' In this monologue, a character named Lady Bradley inspects Charlotte Beavertowntin, a potential bride for her son. (We used actual standards of beauty and intelligence for women from the Victorian era, and tweaked them a bit.)

Come let us have a look at you. Give us a spin. Yes, well, the posture's quite satisfactory. It has a good back, I see. Ah yes, fine wide hips for childbearing. Breasts a tad small, but not for long. Smile for me, dear. Yes. Do you have all your own teeth? Oh my goodness. Oh, I see you have a low forehead. A sign of dullness and stupidity. Well, we'll fix that. We'll simply remove some hair to approximately mid skull ...

An episode entitled 'Medieval Women' took place in the castle of Queen Gwynetheth of Lochlich, in the time of King Arthur. This was also the time when the goddess-worshipping religions were being decimated by the Christians. A favourite method of the Church was to co-opt pagan rituals, and rename them as Christian holidays. We had Lady Marycarry proclaim the following to a 'pagan' woman:

No! No! No! I will have none of your pagan rituals! Like your spring solstice with painted eggs and bunnies and sweets in a basket! Or that winter solstice with its gifts for children and winter solstice trees covered in candles and baubles and fat old men dressed in red suits, sliding down chimneys! It's Unchristian!!

Prior to *The Broad Side*, I co-wrote a series for the comedy channel called *Behind the Scenes*, also executive produced by Jane Ford. In mockumentary style, we went 'behind the scenes' of a different milieu in each episode. We explored characters and environments from a Men's Group to Hockey Moms to the Toronto Film Festival. The research was surprising, and I got to play fifteen characters, many of whom were involved in fields that I had no connection to, like playing in a girl band or being a bike courier. We were able to use the medium of television to explore people and events. It was great fun and offered the audience a twisted glimpse into both the exotic and the familiar.

My most recent television experience was with a more traditional sitcom, and because its content did not offer that much that enlightened, I am not surprised that it was short-lived. I truly believe audiences want more than what they already can easily access. Canadians, especially, seem thirsty to absorb something new from their art and entertainment. People have said that art that educates is bad art, but my experience has taught me that art that doesn't attempt to say very much at all can elicit an ambivalent response.

That said, there can be an educational element to almost any project in which you have been asked to create a character. People are endlessly fascinating. The challenge of creating a character who is not easy to understand, someone whose views or motives are repulsive to you, and endowing him or her with humanity, is a humbling experience. The lead character in the above-mentioned sitcom was one such study. She was ruthless, anxious, misanthropic, and amoral. But she was also a child and a social misfit. A character from *Myth Me*, Uncle Bill, was a racist misogynist and homophobic patriarch, but he was also living alone with no one but his old dog for company. The old bastard cracked me up.

Much of the art that I love is not only educational, but political. Working with Alisa Palmer and Richard Greenblatt (together on *Sibs* at the Tarragon Theatre) has assured me that political art can be funny and full of heart. Again, it was proven to me that the more specific the details that one offers the audience, the more universal the appeal of the material. Before I did *Sibs*, I wouldn't have truly appreciated the complex issues and emotions facing many younger siblings – I am a middle child – especially young men. Thanks to Richard's generosity in bringing his perspective to the piece, I approach sibling relationships very differently today.

The following 'He said She said' account of the siblings' mother's death illustrates our perspectives. (// indicates when they overlap each other's dialogue):

He. When my mother ... our mother died – after a person dies you sit Shiva, which lasts seven or eight days, I can't remember ...

She. There are seven days of mourning. Shiva, from the Hebrew word Shevah, meaning seven. A group of men, traditionally, ten men, form a minyan, minyan meaning ten // and they say this prayer.

He. It's like the Jewish version of a wake. It's a party really. The family all sits on these low stools, and you cover the mirrors // and you're encouraged to talk about the person who's died. It's really very beautiful.

She. So it was totally silent except for the sound of the men saying this prayer. Now traditionally, it is the men who say it. This *is* Judaism, the religion that gave us the prayer 'thank god I was not born a woman' and the 'you have to marry your rapist' laws, so anyway, well, // I happen to be the only one of the two of us who actually knows Hebrew and who excuse me, gives a shit, about prayer. So I joined in. Discreetly.

He. She has a way, my sister, of making everything about her. And this is my mother ... our mother, who died. A woman who didn't like to make waves; who knew there was a time // and a place for everything. And a funeral or a *wedding* is not exactly the time to make a strong feminist statement!

She. If God cares about what gender you are when you mourn I will be seriously disappointed. My mother rai-, our mother raised us to be equals, and was quite feminist in her own way, and she would have *wanted* me to say Kadish for her. And for my brother –

He. I didn't say anything –

She. – out of everyone –

He. – I didn't want to make a scene –

She. – to be the one to give me dirty looks

He. – I'm not going to change her now –

She. – at the funeral for my mother –

He. – we're both too old to change.

She. – like he was the head of the family.

Pause.

They look at each other, then look out to the Unseen Judge again and speak the last speeches simultaneously.

She. I mean, he doesn't even know the words, but he started to pray louder, like he wanted to be the big man, so he chose this funeral to try and become the older sibling. So I prayed louder to drown out the mumbo jumbo pathetic attempt at Hebrew, which was totally inappropriate, especially in front of Uncle Joey and all the men!
He. There are some traditions in Judaism that have survived for thousands of years for a reason, and yes it's a patriarchal religion, but it doesn't matter how hard she tries, she will never be a man. I mean, she was almost shouting to drown us out. It was ridiculous, and embarrassing and totally inappropriate especially in front of the whole family!

Beat.

She. What he did ...
He. I don't think she knows how // unfair it was.
She. ... was not fair.

Another of my personal mission statements, and a political imperative, is to explore the untold lives of women, as we did in *The Broad Side.* With Empress, we explored icons like the Greek goddesses and great literary and political figures from Cleopatra to Ophelia. We researched and revealed them through our own – as reform Rabbi, author, and educator Elyse Goldstein has called it – 'feminist lens.' The following edited monologue was originally from an Empress show, *Slow Thunder.*

Ophelia speaks. ... I am here to clear the air. I didn't jump. I was under a great deal of stress, and, I fell ... The stress was ... I am blessed with the knowledge of things unspoken ... Could I not have interrupted Hamlet's stupid little play and warned everyone? Could I not have taken the queen aside and simply said, 'HEY!' Could I not have watched where in hell I was walking?! No. I did nothing. That's what haunts me more than my father's or brother's or lover's chain-rattling, rank, and worm-infested ghostly apparitions in the mist. I am tormented by my own inability to act. My paralysis was ten-fold Hamlet's! 'To be or not to be?' THAT is a question?! 'Neither a borrower nor a lender be' – Oh please! Thank you so very much for the advice, now what about the bloodshed?! ...

Currently, I am working on revisioning bible stories from a modern perspective. I examine the text in the original Hebrew and reconceive it. Imagine, for instance, what Lot's Wife might have said or done to prevent her husband from offering their two pre-pubescent daughters to the frenzied mob of Sodom and Gomorrah had she only been given a name.

So often, it's easy to be discouraged, frustrated, demented, suicidal, jealous, and self-indulgent in the uncertain and cynical Canadian entertainment world. But having a point of view, being devoted to and passionate about the material and the characters that one creates, and knowing that what you are doing is in pursuit of learning and imparting knowledge, makes it worthwhile to dig deep and get back out there.

Those are my personal stories, but I have been inspired by so many generous, brainy, Canadian artists. Ann-Marie MacDonald's *Goodnight Desdemona (Good Morning Juliet)* was one of the first new Canadian plays that I saw as a graduate. Her exploration of language, feminism, and history was literally eye-opening for me. Equally inspiring was watching Sandra Shamas tell her modern, personal story using the ancient art of storytelling. Judith Thompson's heart-filled glimpses into the life of a quirky girl from Kirkland Lake, Brad Fraser's seedy Edmonton, George F. Walker's lunatic humanity, the worlds of Sky Gilbert, Daniel McIvor, the Smith Gilmour Theatre, and the Columbus Theatre, and so many others ignited a passion to reveal truths that set so many of us on our paths.

And recently, having seen *Wit* by Margaret Edison, *Harlem Duet* by Djanet Sears, *I, Claudia* by Kristin Thompson, *The Drawer Boy* by Michael Healey, and Tony Kushner's *Angels in America*, I have had startling experiences in the theatre that taught me facts, but also connected me with the universal human condition.

Most recently, I worked on *Smudge* by Alex Bulmer. It's a play by and about a woman who is losing her sight. Alex's experience in her world is so different from that of much of the audience, but her struggle with loss resonates in places many of us have chosen to avoid. The play served the purpose of art that educates, enlightens, and entertains, with generosity and without sentimentality. I felt privileged to contribute to it.

Grappling with things we don't understand is a great challenge to actors and writers. But theatre is truly relevant when the audience can leave having experienced a new perspective for thinking about our world.

Intellectual Passions, Feminist Commitments, and Divine Comedies: A Dialogue with Ann-Marie MacDonald

ANN-MARIE MACDONALD AND

KATHLEEN GALLAGHER

Kathleen. What did you think about contributing to a book called *How Theatre Educates?*

Ann-Marie. I wondered *what* is theatre, and how *does* it educate?

Kathleen. The reason I ask this question, Ann-Marie, is because in conceiving this book, I was acutely aware of how theatre artists, and perhaps artists more generally, don't necessarily consider what they do as educational, or even as having much to do with educating people.

Ann-Marie. That's true. I guess, my question to you is, What is the difference between theatre in education, versus drama and education? I am interested in knowing, from your point of view, what that is.

Kathleen. I have never believed in these polarities, for one thing, and I have never been particularly convinced by theatre in education as a genre, divorced from the larger tradition of theatre in general. I think the terminology tells us something; the language is revealing and the differences important. We are seeming to say that what we are doing in classrooms is different from what is going on in theatres, and, of course, it is different. But it is rooted strongly in theatre conventions.

I wanted there to be a book that spoke to those kinds of cross-border relationships wherein I think education ultimately rests, or unrests. And I wanted teachers to feel that this was a world that one could access without forgoing the classroom curriculum and also to consider – for those working in what I am imagining is often a very insular kind of theatre world and community – the notion that the audience is not some generic group, but people whose lives sometimes turn on a dime because of something that they've seen. Writers often don't know that. I wanted this to be a book that made people wonder what the term 'education' really means. My question back to you then is, What do you imagine yourself to be doing with or for a group of people? Maybe you have a heightened sense because you have had some connections with schools and young people.

Ann-Marie. First of all, I have never, ever, ever imagined that I was just doing it for myself. Now, I know that this is a romantic notion, the idea that an artist is someone who doesn't care if anybody pays attention or if they get it, or preferably hopes that people don't get it, that you're misunderstood and you do it for yourself, because you are a genius. And that became a given; something that everybody took for granted. Well, not everybody. These are gross generalizations. With pop culture and even the kind of education that I received, there was that sense that of course an artist is an isolated, misunderstood person who doesn't care if anybody notices. That was often applied to visual artists but also to poets, writers, and theatre artists. I think that is only one among many world views. When I was much younger I did not understand that, and I found myself a little out of step with what was current, what was cool, because what was cool for artists is that twentieth-century romanticism was like an extended adolescence. 'Fuck off, you don't get it.'

It is a very important place to start out – for nurturing a certain defiance – but the idea that that would define an entire adult career is absurd to me. I have always thought of myself as an entertainer and a communicator, and as I grew older and realized I had a point of view in politics and a different identity, I wasn't just interested in perpetuating some kind of crap fluff. I remember being disappointed in my early twenties, emerging from theatre school, to realize that I felt that things were really polarized. There was art and there was entertainment. There were politics and there was entertainment. And the idea of putting the two together (I guess a lot of people wanted to do that, and I was certainly far from alone) was always my passion. I didn't understand how they ever became separated. When did that happen, when did they diverge? There were, I guess, a lot of reasons for that divergence, but for me, it was always about trying to get these things working together, to make them indivisible, because that is how theatre occurs to me. The first thing I wanted to be, when I was a little kid, was a stand-up comedian. I never had the nerve to do it. But today, I do it for the audience. And for me that was always really self-evident. People say: 'Whom do you mean by audience?' Well, anyone who wants to hear a story or is interested in taking a trip. I guess I am not very articulate when it comes down to that, but I have always – even in my early days when I was working in really small theatres – told people to come. I didn't care who they were.

Get anyone here and I will make them stay. It was that kind of bravado. I don't fool myself that everything I am going to do will please everyone all the time; that's ridiculous. But I always, always had the conviction that I could play a hand of cards and there would be something, one card in that hand, that would make someone in that room stay. Maybe they wouldn't relate to the whole thing, but there would be one part that would keep them, and maybe, for that other person over there, two parts. Maybe someone would get the whole thing. That was always my aim.

Kathleen. Sounds like a classroom.

Ann-Marie. Yes, I guess so. That's an interesting analogy, because I have always had a huge respect for teachers who made a difference to me. I always had a passion for teaching, too. I consider myself a closet academic/teacher. I never understood the sort of cynical cliché 'Those who can, do; those who can't, teach.' I never literally understood that because I always thought: 'No, actually teaching is a passionate vocation, and if you're good at it, you're great.' And I guess, as in any profession, you could also say that of actors: 'Oh, they're a failed this or that, because everyone thinks they can act.' Very few people are going to commit to it as a career, but everyone thinks they can act, and probably everyone thinks they can teach.

Kathleen. That's absolutely the comparison. Even kids in school who have to do an arts credit and think they can't do anything else, choose drama.

Ann-Marie. Yes exactly. It is the catchall, a fall back.

Kathleen. You don't have to have any particular talent.

Ann-Marie. It is interesting because both those areas – theatre and education – are very, very forgiving at one level, but they are the most rigorous at another. Yet there is also something very humane about both pursuits. The fact that they can tolerate a multitude of ineptitude doesn't take away from the fact that they are driven by excellence, like anything else. It is human activity with a very, very wide embrace. There are probably not that many charlatans in the acting world or the teaching world, but it is interesting that actors are often dismissed as people who are not intellectual giants, and it is alright to make fun of actors intellectually. You know, that's when I actually cancelled my subscription to *Harper's* magazine years ago – I got so sick of reading that among Ronald Reagan's poor qualities was the fact that he had been an actor. I say: 'Don't blame the actors.' People like to blame, like to think of actors as kind of ditzy. In fact it is very, very important for an actor to remain intellectually hungry, open and changeable, qualities that have been encouraged traditionally in women, who are also supposedly ditzy. Because you, as a human, are supposed to be available to a lot of points of view, you are supposed to be able to facilitate a lot of different points of view and create liaisons between people and among ideas and make everyone in your home feel relaxed, as though they have something to talk about at the dinner table. Good actors get passionately interested in whatever they are working on at the time. It is the only thing that exists. A good actor finds a reason to love the show, to love the play, to love what they are doing and it doesn't mean that you abandon all critical perspective, because obviously, you have to maintain a critical perspective. But a poor actor, or an actor who isn't thoroughly an actor, is the one who allows their bitterness and their critical perspective to overwhelm this sort of clown-like openness to whatever it is. That's why you sort of think: 'Geez, how can an actor be so dumb as to think that they are in a good show!' Part of their job is to believe that they are in a good show! That's not because they are stupid and they don't know any better. It's called imagination. And it is a failure of imagination to cease to believe in what you are doing; and it's a tension to keep your critical faculties alive, but also it's the ability to give of yourself. That's part of the art.

Kathleen. Because something will be worth giving to?

Ann-Marie. Well, it has to be. If you said you would do it, and at a certain point you know it's crap, you also have to subordinate that to a degree. It doesn't mean pretending that it wasn't crap; it just means knowing the difference between generalized negativity and genuine critical perspective. And I suppose we are talking about bitterness. That can creep in anywhere. But there is a common ground between teaching and acting, I think.

I never feel like I give an adequate answer to the question 'Who do you do this for?' I say, 'the audience,' and for me it has always been. I have never had to question who or what that is. I have always, always wanted a very, very big audience regardless of where I am. To me, it is not a frustration, whether I was in a 60-seat house or an 800-seat house. 'That's the show and let's fill it.' And maybe this particular show won't go beyond 60 seats, but let's get everybody in here we can possibly cram in and from every different walk of life.

I have heard theatre artists say, 'Well, you know, people get into theatre because we are all misfits and are looking for family,' or 'We really do this for each other or for people who are in the know.' I actually heard a colleague of mine say, 'I wish someone would question me, take me to task for my moral position.' And I thought, you mean you wish you'd get a bad review? Talk to me, I've had a million of them. I am being continually assailed for my moral position, which is 'Come watch the show.' But I'm a comedian too, and this other person was definitely not a comedian. There is a very different point of view between the two. What I try to do as a comedian is as much edgy stuff as I possibly can, get it under the radar, and make people laugh and go home, saying, 'Holy shit! I identified with a fag' or 'What if that person at work has something they need to tell me and maybe I'm ready to hear it now.' Not that I'm doing social work. It's just that I know that comedy can be very, very radical without seeming to be, and deadly serious without getting – but this is my little bitterness – without getting the credit for being so. For me, I'm always just trying to get direct access to an audience, without having to go through the media hoops, or even the 'produceorial' hoops. I make sure I get a good producer and I don't do theatre for other artists. I love working with other artists; the other artists are my friends, they are my colleagues, and if they are in the audience, I hope they can feel like civilians. (I rarely feel like a civilian, so I don't necessarily expect it of other colleagues, but if they can feel that way, that's great.) I have always wanted, actually very badly, to be understood without talking down. Basically saying all kinds of unpalatable things: 'Now eat it and ask for more.' It's like Humphry Bogart: 'You'll eat it and you'll like it. You'll watch it and you'll like it.' 'You'll watch it and you'll like it and you'll tell your friends.' I guess it's subversion, combined with real, absolute love of the audience and love of performing. When you try to put all those things together, it's not always an easy fit, it doesn't always work.

Kathleen. So you felt these inclinations from a very early age.

Ann-Marie. It was called 'show off.'

Kathleen. And after 'show off' came theatre school?

Ann-Marie. No, just a lot of intellectual passions and the sense that showing off is a very shallow way to spend your life. I found a great intellectual hunger and curiosity, combined with a love of stories and a love of the fabulous. Your teaching analogy was really good. I think I feel a lot like a teacher, without the pedagogical aspects. Pedagogical, that's not a dirty word is it? I want to give the audience a reason to stay, give them a reason to want to find out more and to want to identify with different points of view, different experiences. For me, that's my hard-core passion: put yourself in someone else's shoes.

Kathleen. Let's face it, when you have a lot of curiosity you learn a lot more about yourself and about what it is that you're passionate about. And you are talking now about sharing that.

Ann-Marie. I also had to go into a smaller world in order to forge. It's sort of like reducing the sauce. For several years I worked (I wouldn't say exclusively, because I still did television), but I did focus a lot on collective creation, on non-traditional collaborations and major feminist issue-oriented shows, which nonetheless always had an aesthetic imperative that was indivisible from the politics. That was my education. And doing that on the fringe or in the alternative theatre scene, as we called it then, that was really my cauldron, that was my crucible. It was extremely important to enter into that and not give a shit about who thought what. It was extremely important to work in a feminist context and to be out of a context where I would be apologizing for anything or deferring to anybody. It's just like going to a girls' school and being able to assume any role in the hierarchy of the group dynamic: none of them is reserved on the basis of gender. I remember Banuta Rubess, who ran this workshop before I even knew her. I didn't take the workshop, but I remember the title: 'Acting without Charm.' Some of the principles were that when you come to do an improvisation you don't apologize, you don't say 'um'; you don't explain, you begin. And you never, ever say the words 'I'm sorry.' And coming out of the National Theatre School, it was extremely important for me to jump into something like that. Over the years, I've come out of that feminist hotbed, and that is just a natural part of getting older and continuing to do my work, continuing to do my art. But it's also knowing that there is a broader audience for my art, now, because of the social changes that have taken place in the meantime. It is satisfying to know that I have been part of that. Then *Goodnight Desdemona* gets on the Bluma Apel stage and no one bats an eye. It was a fringe show; it was a piece of alternative theatre.

Kathleen. I want to talk about *Goodnight Desdemona* because one of my interests is the way in which it has been taken up in academia. It made really critical lists, fairly quickly. I think it came to represent an alternative voice even in some academic dramatic literature programs, and it obviously challenged on several fronts. What effect did that have on you? Had you anticipated something like that?

Ann-Marie. No, I didn't anticipate that. I knew that I had a show that a lot of different people could come and enjoy, whether they ever read the play or not. That was important to me. In those days I didn't imagine that my work would be studied or not studied; that wasn't even on my radar. I just thought: 'I'll finish it and put it up and hopefully it will get produced again.' I didn't think beyond that. And now when I look back on it, I guess it makes sense. It is a perfect case study for a script. It's good for a lot of different purposes, and especially since that play grew up at the same time that Women's Studies grew up, and at the same time as a lot of feminists started getting their tenure or tenure-track positions, and so the timing was really, really apt.

Kathleen. And with your early feminist collective stuff, there was something about the revisioning that was happening on several fronts – in theatre contexts and in classroom contexts – where feminists were challenging the canon. There was an interesting integration across several planes, a reconstructive looking, particularly in post-structural times.

Ann-Marie. That's right, people were doing it in completely non-feminist contexts, too.

Kathleen. Yes, there was this discourse analysis, a deconstruction that was happening in a much broader way. Then there was this appreciation of gender in new ways, as in Shakespeare, as you were doing. And obviously a large part of that had to do, as well, with the political imperatives. You've had this long-standing parallel existence with academia. And then, you create Constance Ledbelly. Then, these years later, you've also now just played Constance. What was that like?

Ann-Marie. That was fun. It was a very physical Constance, a very clown thing, but that's my take. That's what I do. I have seen it done very differently, but my Constance was just magically able to trip and fall. I guess I never really progressed much beyond the 'show-off.' What surprised me about the play, coming back to it, was just how passionate it was, how very, very emotional. I didn't realize that Constance cared so deeply about all these things; it was very moving for me. I thought she could have been weeping for an entire essay. The ideas were incredibly moving. Also meeting the Shakespearean characters, particularly Desdemona and Juliet, but all of them, really. It was extraordinarily moving, the idea that these fabulous powerful creatures were real and also so terribly vulnerable, because when you are that big and that magnificent, you are extremely vulnerable. It's like a rare, rare beast that, once it falls down, will never get up again. But they are all unicorns. Also there is that misfit quality, a classic comedic thing (well, also a classic tragic thing depending on whether you're Dostoyevski or Woody Allen), but the idea that 'I am an outcast'; 'I have a crazy point of view'; 'I am a laughing stock.' But I've finally found where I belong: the world of imagination. I suppose that is a very youthful perspective, too. And that is maybe why students relate to this play, in spite of all its educational value.

Kathleen. Yes. In spite of it. I want to pick up on something you said earlier. 'Improvising without charm,' the particular challenges of women working in the theatre. In academia, one of the struggles for me is that we're now moving into a so-called 'post-feminism phase,' and this is a serious movement even within feminist circles. Now, clearly I am standing outside of the theatre world, but noticing that problems of inequity are not all gone. You obviously have different sets of challenges now from when you were beginning, but what's your sense about women in the theatre?

Ann-Marie. My sense is still that women do not have a lot of power in theatre. There are still not many artistic directors, very few directors (very, very few directors) who are women. And sometimes they have a narrow band of operation. There are few who can cross over in terms of theatre size and genre. Women have always been 'allowed' to write (not always, but for a couple of hundred years) and then, in the last century, more and more women began to write plays. Women have been more acceptable as writers than directors, and the director is still a position of authority. There are no two ways around it: directors are still mostly men. There is still a lot of really unquestioned sexism that has just sort of relaxed back into itself: 'Ah, we can forget about that now; no one is upset about that anymore.' And I also find it really odd when there is now a sort of received, polite collection of what is considered to be misogynist. Half the time I disagree. I sort of say: 'It's not misogynist at all. That over there, disguised as something else, that is misogynist.' For example, the play by Jonathan Wilson, *Kilt*, which I really, really liked. It was the opinion of the *Globe* reviewer (and I find the *Globe*, for the past twenty years, has sort of made it their business to present a very skewed point of view when it comes to women, or anything the slightest bit alternative) that it was misogynist, because there were these wacky aunts, these two Scottish aunts who were hilarious and strong and funny. She was offended by that, but then the *Globe* has often been offended by comedy per se, and I think that's probably not even worth talking about. But there is now a kind of a standard polite list of what's nasty and what's nice. Yet I don't always find myself agreeing with what's nasty or what's nice. A lot of what is considered good family entertainment is hideously violent. I'd sit down and watch Clint for days. I'll just take my vigilanteism straight, thank you! Let's not have it dressed up as any kind of liberal nonsense. I just watched *A Time to Kill* the other night. It is all dressed up with nice little liberal values disguising an extremely right-wing point of view, which is why I prefer Clint. If I need the vigilante catharsis, I know where to go. It is clear, it's honest, and then I can forget about it and return to my old moral tensions of consensus, knowing that everything has to be messy and that's the nature of democracy, and I don't believe in capital punishment. Let's keep muddling along one inch at a time.

Kathleen. *Anything That Moves.* I would like to jump into that because – not that there is any surprise about you moving into all kinds of different directions, I certainly wasn't surprised by that – it was a different kind of revisioning. At least that's my view. You were revisioning again, moving past the hotbed of feminist concerns and moving into (certainly one way of looking at it) the classic heterosexual love story, and spinning it on its head a little bit. And so I was thinking about it, thinking about what more possibilities there are in our midst, in our imagined scenarios, in our collectively appreciated 'boy meets girl' and other disproved 'universals.' When you created that, I was wondering whether you were consciously troubling the conventions of musicals that people love them for or hate them for, and whether again this is an example of your preoccupation with structure and form as the way to turn things inside out.

Ann-Marie. I have been a bit out of step, in a way, this whole last half of the century. I tend to leave the forms intact or use the forms and not simply deconstruct them, not simply chop them up and not put them back together again. I love the integrity of forms that work. Left to my own devices, I don't do groovy things with form. I do groovy things with content and I let the form work for me. I love the fact that there is a structure for a love song, and how you can fool around and make it work even better. I love form. I suppose it's a love of craft really. A sonnet works; it just does. I feel a song coming on. Everybody knows what that means and for many people, myself included, it is delightful at the core. What is not delightful is if there is no content. That was what, for me, was very disappointing about the mega-musicals. There is no story. There is nothing really going on. It's easy to be dismissive of the plots and scripts of the 1950s musicals, but when I actually started investigating them, I was surprised by how hard-hitting *South Pacific* was in terms of taking on interracial relationships and things like that. They're actually saying something that they would have had to have done a hard-hitting drama to get across in any other way. But they did it with songs.

Kathleen. You collaborated with your musical?

Ann-Marie. I collaborated with the composer and with the director Alisa Palmer, who also had a major hand in the script. I have always taken forms that work, that delight me – once upon a time, beginning, middle, end, surprise, climax, twist – all those things which are, for me, fundamentally delightful because I love stories. And I guess that's the kind of creature that I am. I felt a song coming on, and I wrote it. First of all, I began with an image; that is usually how it begins for me. I saw an image of this older person, and they'd get up from this old armchair, walk across the stage in order to get a glass of brandy; and in the time it takes for you to pour that drink and drink it, and return to the chair, an entire show has gone by, and somehow they are reminiscences. Of course, that has nothing to do with what you saw on stage, but then I realized (because that is where I began) there has been this image of the hermaphrodite that has obsessed me. A duality, some sort of reconciliation of opposites. Somehow, there is this twinning idea; we want to get back together. It is not a prescriptive, schematic union to kind of take on the world necessarily, because I don't believe that just because I am a woman, I therefore have an anima. Nothing is that simple, but there is a reason why twinning has been magical for people. There's a reason why there is such a thing as a unicorn, in your imagination, or a hermaphrodite. And then I actually realized that I was afforded a glimpse of the manifestation of what my muse looks like – my muse is an old person who loves stories, who doesn't get out much anymore. The muse drinks. I can't tell if it's a man or a woman, and quite literally it doesn't matter. Or what matters is that I can't tell, and that matters profoundly. It's that the muse is both. And also that's a dangerous thing to be, a social outcast. But there is something sacred about it, which is another way of saying endangered.

But the musical has the spirit of that in it, because I'm exploring a range of sexuality. In the first version there was a queen, and we are not supposed to tell whether it was a man or a woman. I cut that character because it was like putting the subtext on stage. And when I cut the character, all his/her energy went into all the other characters and freed something up, liberated everybody to be more fully themselves. But there is the blessing of pansexuality on the play, which is not just a romantic idea of a 'Oh, aren't we all a little bit that way?' No. Some of us are, and some of us aren't. And some of us are everything. But I wanted to show a continuum. And make no bones about it: the old-fashioned way is to have the gay characters be witty and interesting and even likeable now; they don't have to be alcoholics or self-destructive. We've moved beyond that. But they could also end up, as in Shakespeare, partnered off at the end, which is why I wanted the two men there. There is the implication that there will be a relationship there. At the end of a good Shakespeare comedy, you know, everyone finds a partner, almost everyone. So in the case of the lesbian and Fleur, the mom, there is a sense that there is a flirtation, there's a friendship. They're probably not going to become lovers, but who knows what might happen after one evening in P-town! What I imagine is that they don't develop a lover relationship, but that they become great friends. Not in spite of the sexuality difference, but somewhere the sexuality is part of that friendship; it is part of what has brought it to life and what makes it lively and fun. Not that it doesn't matter. It always fucking matters what you are, so let us put it front and centre and come together through it, not in spite of it. It's the difference between those old movies and plays around race in the fifties and forties based on religion, where it was like: 'But it doesn't matter!' Well it does. It matters that I'm a Jew, that I'm black or that I'm gay. It matters that I'm part of this society. I am not supposed to now de-race myself, de-sexualize myself so that I can reassure everyone that I can work beside you in this office and that it's OK. In fact, the world has to get a little more textured.

Kathleen. What struck me about your musical was the fluidity of sexuality, and that didn't mean fickle. It didn't mean uncertainty; it was absolutely certain, in all its uncertainty.

Ann-Marie. That's a nice way of putting it.

Kathleen. That's what really struck me and resonated with me: the sense that the categories are inadequate. As soon as you let go of the categories, it's not that they disappear. In fact, it's the opposite. They no longer have a hold on you.

Ann-Marie. That's right. You get to be a person. I guess the idea is to have people come to the theatre and laugh, and to not even notice, maybe until they get home, where they have just been. That's my subversion, I suppose.

Kathleen. Yes I like that. I appreciate that. I do that in my classrooms.

Kathleen. OK, Ann-Marie, another question about your writing: writing a novel like *Fall on Your Knees*, as opposed to writing theatre that will communicate in the flesh. The communication in your novel is going to happen between imaginations, through imaginations, in worlds that you can't anticipate and will never know, so I was thinking about your voice, getting back to the solitary artist. In moving from theatre to prose, were you consciously putting a certain kind of voice to rest and bringing out another? Or was there something more organic for you where, at a certain point (and I don't mean to mystify this) was there a need to speak differently from how you had been speaking? Possibly that's true for each project.

Ann-Marie. Well I think it's true with the book. It became much more private and intimate. And I said before that I never do anything just for myself, and that is true, because I always imagine that it has to be for someone else, in the end. But in writing the book especially, I have to believe when I'm writing, that it is completely private. No, I have to fool myself into believing that no one is going to read this, not that no one is ever going to read it, but fool myself into believing that it is a completely private thing. Because to create it is a completely private thing. That's been much harder working on the book that I am working on now. But I think it's just that I forgot how hard it was. I know different things now, but I actually don't believe that it can be harder than the first book. I think there is a mysterious thing that happens (I never think of myself as writing anyway); I somehow am accumulating something that eventually will integrate itself into what is called a book. But I did not write a book. The thing, the book, is what results from a lot of wandering around, saving this and throwing that away, distilling that and moving this around. The idea of sitting down and writing a book is foreign, and I wish someday I could do that. There is a novel, which I look at, and it's a book. I seem to have a book. And then it comes to actually writing a new one. That's the process of remembering that actually I didn't write for the book. There is a book, and eventually there will be another book. But don't kid yourself, it's probably no harder than it was the first time around. Every now and then I get a glimmer of that: 'Oh, well actually maybe I am on to something.' Now there is the sense that, well, people actually expect to read another book. And that is a very different thing. That doesn't do me any good at all.

Kathleen. I would like to pick up on something, specifically, that you said. When recently I was speaking in Seattle to graduate students who were on the verge of completing dissertations, or defending dissertations, they asked: 'Do you know things now that you wish you'd known, that would have caused you to do things differently?' The first thing I thought was, 'I know so many things now that, thank god, I didn't know then.' Because they would have caused me to do things differently and it would have been a different experience entirely.

Ann-Marie. Yes, yes.

Kathleen. Yes, it would be a different experience. I am truly glad that I didn't know a lot of things.

Ann-Marie. It's hard, yes. You cannot unknow things once you know them.

Kathleen. That's right.

Ann-Marie. You can't ever go back. It's hard to keep it mysterious, to keep it unpredictable, to keep faith in the fact that there is a story that wants to be told, and it will reveal itself given enough patience. The weight of all that other exterior knowledge of how a book is built and sold and marketed, and who is the agent, and which publisher next time, in which country, and should I tolerate that kind of translation or book cover, and all of these things, which I'm now privileged to ... that's the tension. So I understand why people retreat in order to write, but I refuse to do that. Retreat from where? Somewhere the challenge is always to access the unpredictable, beautiful, strange, scary place where one has to be extremely patient. It's like waiting for the animals to come out of the woods and into the clearing. You don't startle anything. Meanwhile, you know that there is this huge constructed solid world, like whole buildings built on publishing, and it is actually kind of disorienting. It's just this odd, odd sense that these insubstantial thoughts and workings of the imagination get translated into those bricks and mortar. I suppose I could have a big romantic crisis over it.

You asked about the difference between writing a book and writing a play. It is true that the voice for fiction is far more intimate. This is where Alisa was extremely helpful with *Anything That Moves* because she virtually badgered me about it, and said, 'How come you hide when you are writing theatre? Why are you willing to be so much more exposed in fiction?'

Well part of it, too, is that when it comes to theatre I'm definitely a comedian, so far. I want to make them laugh. But she really hounded me, and asked me the most embarrassingly basic dramatic and character questions for the play, because she was convinced that I was resisting the emotional truths of these characters, and she was absolutely right. I was basically kind of dragged (kicking and screaming) to really exposing everything through these characters: what it means to fall in love or to worry about it. She really insisted on my taking it seriously. What it really boils down to – there is no other way of saying it – is taking the process of writing for theatre seriously and not simply wanting to resolve everything with a laugh and make everything easy for the audience. I think that is a mid-life thing that I was heading for, of wanting to make everything okay all the time because we are all in the same room together and god knows I want to go home happy. Yet when I sit down to write a piece of fiction, I will disturb, excoriate, and eviscerate you emotionally. I'm not sure what that's about, but there are two very, very different faces. I suppose that it's the old comedy/tragedy face. They seem to be divided by genre, divided by medium, for me. And I think, possibly, it is the comedian or the performer somewhere within myself that, if it is theatre and if it's live, then I am up there and you are looking at me, so who knows, I may give a couple of glancing looks, but you will not find out anything about me I don't really want you to know. But I want you to look at me.

Kathleen. It is that whole public-private thing. Whereas if someone can't read another word and places the novel on her bedside table, you'll never know that. And they're not subject to any public humiliation ...

Ann-Marie. That's right.

Kathleen. ... about not being ready for what's there. But that is very different in a theatre, because it is the collective experience. It's not an individual experience.

Ann-Marie. That's right. You can't be putting it down, then coming back to it.

Kathleen. You can leave. But sometimes under great duress.

Ann-Marie. That's right.

Kathleen. And exposure. With the book, no one knows that you couldn't finish it.

Ann-Marie. I think it was my tendency to hide. Alisa wanted to encourage me not to hide, in a public form, and that was really very important because, I think, that bore fruit, as it were. It really did. I think it made the show richer than it would have been had it been left to me only.

Kathleen. So there is something qualitatively different in these different forms of writing.

Ann-Marie. I am much more ready to be more exposed right off the bat in fiction than I am with theatre. It's more organic or more exposed. And I think I would much rather be up there cracking jokes. I could tell you about my terrible childhood as long as we are all laughing, you know, and I'll even have to make it more fabulous. There will be many, many costumes; there will be many, many masks through which to convey whatever it is that is at the heart of it. It probably has to do with exposure and with feeling that fiction is a much more private place. Also I feel that fiction makes the jump into belonging to the reader. I can be more invisible in fiction, and probably, as I get closer to feeling that I could be that way in theatre too, maybe my work will evolve somewhere. It will change somewhat.

Kathleen. And what about your voice? Because you have had such acclaim. There have been a great many moments for you in a variety of ways over the last several years, and I sometimes think about how far away (it sounds like a good problem to have), how far away you can get from your voice, when your voice has been displayed and then recreated by so many other people, not to mention the expectations that your audiences have. And what kind of balancing act do you do between moving to say something that is the 'new something,' and other people's determinations of you based on the 'old something'?

Ann-Marie. I always have a great deal of faith in audience and readers, because I think that people who are just hungry for the story and for the art intuitively, or maybe consciously, accept the fact that both are coming from the same place. That's sort of really a journalist's question and it's a good one, so no wonder they ask it: 'How do you do all these different things?' And I say: 'I don't.' They are all different forms because I love the tools and all the forms and I love craft. But it's all narrative. Northrop Frye boiled it all down to one story. And I think he was right! But I see it all as being part of the same thing.

Kathleen. But to have facility with all those forms; and to venture into new forms ...

Ann-Marie. Someone is waiting for the next musical or the next play or the next book, and they are saying, 'How come you didn't give me that? How come you went off in a different direction?'

Kathleen. 'How come it's not a book like the first one?'

Ann-Marie. Well, I can't tell you the number of people who ask me if I'm working on a sequel.

Kathleen. It's the culture.

Ann-Marie. Yes. Then I think well, actually, that just means that they wanted more, and that's good. They wanted to revisit those characters to see what happened next. There is a beautiful readerly naivety there: More story please! I look at other authors of books that I have loved and see what they do next, and I look at all kinds of cautionary tales for myself and I wonder: 'How come that author went off the rails, or did they? Or are they just doing something that is interesting to them, which is disappointing to me as a reader because I wanted more of the same?' 'Or did that author get flipped out by the fact that they knew that the next book was going to be published?' Often I find what happens to a really great literary writer, who is also very good with narrative, is sometimes the next book will have intellectual pretentions, which don't necessarily ring true, or that stultify the narrative. You know, scar tissue. Things aren't as fluid narratively, because, obviously, they are trying to show that they are smart too. Or that they have thought about some large questions. I am also aware of that.

Kathleen. I make another analogy to being a 'beginning academic,' or to the clichés of publish or perish. Academia often favours a certain kind of 'productivity,' that sometimes encourages artistic and intellectual short cuts. That is one of the things I am really glad I didn't know or didn't believe, or didn't have enough experience about when I began writing. So my task now is not knowing it when I do. It's a real challenge.

Ann-Marie. It's very hard. You can't un-know what you know now. You can't pretend you don't have that information, and you can't also romantically go back and toil in the darkness of your blissful ignorance. That's called regression, and you'll just kind of write this semi-delirious ...

Kathleen. Yes, those are the binaries in terms of creating ... creating something new.

Ann-Marie. It's hard also, because we live in a world that also rewards, especially in Canada, the first new thing. That is why there is so much play development but very little beyond that. There is still more play development than there is 'Okay, it works, let's produce it again; let's produce it now; let's run it for another six months; let's make a connection to a larger theatre if that is where it wants to go.' That next level of letting something live out its whole full life is still missing here and there are reasons for that: it's a smaller country, a smaller industry (and it becomes industry at that level). The combination of art and industry, in terms of theatre, is still very, very thin here. And for me, I keep coming up against that and thinking: 'Now I want this show to run for a year (and I know it can't). This is a huge city. There are tons of people who'll come to the show.' And how many producers are there who are doing anything but importing the mega-musicals – and that is also a part of the economy of the city; I have no problem with that – but there is a whole level that is missing still, and that is the great divide between the 'commercial' over here and our play development programs, and don't we have a lot of geniuses. So come and see it because it's running for two weeks and it will disappear, and it will never get polished or produced again. There is that gap, all these ghosts falling into it. It's very hard in

Canada, culturally, to let things grow up. Part of it, too, is that you've got to take your lumps. I always think of Margaret Atwood as a very good example. She has been in everything. She has been a favourite cultural scapegoat, villain, goddess, queen, you name it, and the thing is she just keeps on doing her work, which is a very simple and Zen-like prescription, but it's true: just keep doing your art, keep doing your work whatever it is. But it is extremely difficult when you are rewarded for being new. And people tend to drop off culturally in Canada. You are brilliant, thirty-two, and then, well ...

Kathleen. Yes I see. Has it ever made you want to leave?

Ann-Marie. Oh, I never wanted to leave Canada. I'm Canadian. The thing is the Canadian perspective, as far as I am concerned, is extremely international and you don't further that perspective by leaving necessarily, or by saying, finally I have been hired by the *New Yorker* or whatever. Which is fine, if that is what you want. But I've always been passionate about this place and seeing the whole world from here. I think it is a pretty humane place in which to be positioned.

Kathleen. These are clearly some of the major challenges for Canadian theatre, for forging connections between education and theatre, both of which seem to be experiencing considerable hostility at the moment, particularly in Ontario. It always makes me think about what this does to one's resolve to create, or resolve to be educated, to see education more broadly, despite the mandated curriculum; or resolve to have an extended run of a play, despite the limitations of production even in a city as great as Toronto. So the flip side then is, what is it here that supports your work, besides your own fascination with being here?

Ann-Marie. Well, there was a very robust public arts funding organization, called the Ontario Arts Council [OAC], and there is still the Canada Council. The OAC has just been hacked away, as has the Toronto Arts Council, which had been very, very strong and well funded and the reason why I could do my art here. Otherwise, I would have left. It's not just my own integrity; if there hadn't been an OAC, I would have gone to London. I remember knowing, when I was a lot younger, that I'd probably go to Britain if Toronto wasn't rich, if I weren't supported. And that wasn't necessarily about dreams of fame and wealth; it was just, 'Where can I do this?' In Toronto, when I first came here in 1980 from Montreal, from the National Theatre School, it was a very rich and exciting time. With lots of money available (not that you always got money when you applied for it). Even though it never seemed like there was tons of money, in retrospect, there was. And new work was supported either independently or via theatres – it was a very rich time – and that is why I did my art here. It fostered an extraordinarily rich community that is still thriving, but beleaguered somewhat in terms of funding. I think it would be really great to see the commercial-industrial side start to make more connections with the independent and not-for-profit sector, to see more and more crossover. That's beginning to happen, and that's rich, because that is where more and more Canadians will see more and more Canadian theatre on stage. And it will not be just a select audience who dares to venture to a small place downtown.

Kathleen. Is anything lost in those joint ventures?

Ann-Marie. Well, the stuff that ends up being a product of that will have probably a broader appeal and, yes, sometimes stuff is lost. Some edge is lost, but not necessarily, not all the time. I would just like to see the range rather than a gap or a moat, with it being really rich over here, with *The Lion King*, then there is this really groovy thing that's happening over there, and in the middle there is a no-man's land. I would like to see that get filled in with stuff, and there is no reason why ultimately it cannot. It's a really, really big city with a lot of people who are ready to go out.

I remember the relief when my book came out and I realised: 'I don't have to invent Canadian literature. It was invented, man!' And I am reaping the benefit. When I go to a different country they say, 'Oh, a Canadian author.' Working in theatre in the early eighties, inventing the idea, although I wasn't in the first generation of pioneers, but perhaps in the second generation of original pioneering, collective creations – all of that was exciting and radical. When I was in my twenties and you said the words 'Canadian film' to most people in Canada, they would just yawn. But they don't do that anymore. The same with Canadian theatre. But it still is not as robust as it could be, and it is not taken for granted, as much as it could be, as something Canadians are proud to own, as much as Canadian literature is.

Kathleen. Right. If we can use the term Canadian Theatre, which obviously homogenizes more than we would ever intend, do you think there are any typically 'Canadian,' I hate to use the word, 'concerns,' or rather thematics at the moment?

Ann-Marie. Probably identity is a big one, eh!

Kathleen: When hasn't it been?

Ann-Marie. Yes, regardless of how, stylistically, it is presented. And making connections with others. I am going to see *Lonely Nights* next week. And then there are *The British* and *The Epic Period*, which I haven't seen yet. It is so disparate, it really is. I can't sum it up.

Kathleen. I couldn't even articulate the question, so you don't have to answer it! It's too broad and eclectic, which is what you would want. And yet you can make the decision to say, 'No, this is really Canadian material. I am writing a Canadian book and it's going to be different from everything else.' But try to put the finger on what that is ...

Ann-Marie. I wonder if there is more of an emphasis on an ensemble feeling. I would not be surprised if that came up somewhere, that Canadian theatre is not driven by the 'hero' so much, with the magnificent, long monologue at the end. You can think of exceptions, but usually the plays where there are few magnificent monologues, and there is a competition around who really is the protagonist or the hero, maybe these are Canadian. That sense of 'Wait a second, I have got something to say about that,' and the points of view are multifarious.

Kathleen. I'd just like to finish with a reflection on that invitation of long ago to come and work with my students. When was that? Maybe 1990. That's my greatest sense of you: teaching the art of playwriting, in that stolen few hours, with those amazing young women. I guess I want to get back to my preoccupations with theatre that educates. The teaching that you did that day, the disseminating of all that you've learned, the communicating with others so that they might create with their own voices ... What would you say about all of that? What was it like for you? What struck you about that experience?

Ann-Marie. That experience with your girls? I was completely spent and exhausted after it. And exhilarated. I loved it. Well, I think, when we began this conversation, you said, 'Well that's a classroom.' I think that really struck me because I don't think I've thought about it like that for years, but it's so completely true. Now, I know that there is a connection between the vocation to teach and communicate, between that and what I do, which is to write stories, or to act in them. I have always had a passion combined with compassion around trying to make it possible for everybody to understand. I don't know why that has been so important; it's always been so important to me because from the time I was very, very small, I remember knowing when other kids didn't 'get it.' So it's probably because I didn't get it half the time. I had problems in school, early on, and so when I snapped out of that, I realized how easy it was for people to get left out. In fact, I had very, very bad early report cards. But always there was that sense of knowing that the concept had not been expressed in a way that everybody could understand and feeling like I could explain it. And I never attached that to the idea that a kid was too stupid to get it. It didn't seem to be connected for me to intelligence.

Kathleen. Somehow, even in something like teaching, it is considered popularizing; that there is some reduction in making it accessible. This has somehow always been central to me, as well, this question of access. Nothing else follows, if it isn't utterly clear.

Ann-Marie. That's right. It has nothing to do with dumbing down; it has to do with opening up, so that there will be a portal for lots of different ways of accessing the information. Or of making it interesting, which is sometimes synonymous with understanding. Because if you are bored, you are not going to get any of it. If something interesting was being presented as boring, most of us were not going to listen. But it is passion and compassion in the sense that everybody has the right to be included. And maybe that is profoundly Canadian. I don't know, but that's a major drive.

Kathleen. That's a gender thing for me.

Ann-Marie. Ah, because often the girls are left out.

Kathleen. Well, it's always preoccupying for me the way 'access' and 'understanding' get played out in terms of gender.

Ann-Marie. Yes. You think that you are one of 'us' until a gendered pronoun is used: 'Oh, you weren't talking about me, after all. I'm not part of this world; I am not a subject here. I am not implied in the subjectivity here.' I remember that *I Am Canadian* ad in the Irishman's pub. This big Irishman (and I have good friends in Dublin who would be appalled by it, because it's got nothing to do with being Irish), he keeps saying, 'I love your hockey and I love your beer, and I love your women.' And I thought: 'Oh, up until then I was with you, and I was buying the beer.' It came as a short, sharp shock in this supposedly happily post-feminist world to realize that I was not a person. I am not a Canadian because they're talking about 'your women,' and I guess I am someone's woman. That was supposed to be charmingly Old World sexism, which, of course, would not fly in Dublin these days either. As young women, we grew up with that as little girls, reading stories and suddenly realizing that we are identifying with the protagonist but we're not supposed to be. This is actually not my world. But it should be and why can't it be? For me, it is getting broader all the time. It has gone beyond gender too; disability, race, lots of things, and at the risk of sounding 'out there,' species too. Which isn't to say that everything gets flattened out or that everything is the same, because everything is definitely not the same. And as with *Anything That Moves*, it's not about mulching into each other, into sameness, because if we've got to be the same as someone, what is the dominant identity that we are all supposed to be like?

Kathleen. What difference does difference make?

Ann-Marie. Peter Singer, the animal ethicist, wrote a book called *Animal Liberation*. He makes the point that it is about equal consideration; it's not about sameness. It boils down to: think about it and see the world through this pair of eyes. Where are the priorities now? How do they shift? Can these things coexist, and can we or can't we hammer out something?

Kathleen. That is why when people talk about theatre over here, and drama in schools over there, and 'Aren't you teaching them to act?' I have always had this feeling that what we are doing through role playing, in imaginary play, in improvised work, is getting rid of the things that prevent people from acting. It's not about teaching acting; it is about getting past those things that prevent us from doing it.

Ann-Marie. That's interesting.

Kathleen. And that happens in schools all the time. How do we create? One of those ways is by knowing that we have a story, and that our story is different from others'.

Ann-Marie. It was like spending the afternoon with those girls and getting them to create stories. There are often many excuses that have got to be brought to bear to justify such an afternoon: 'Oh, it's therapeutic, or it's this or it's that, or what have they, therefore, learned?' Still, it's very important for people to learn how to create narrative because we're surrounded by it. It's called history, it's called the way our society is organized, and it's called patterns. I guess we can look at it from a management-consultant point of view and ask, What are the dynamics? What are the human systems at work? What is the fucking narrative, you know? Who is the bully? Who is facilitating it? Who is passively watching? Who is trying to make a difference? And there are narratives absolutely everywhere; that's just how I see the world. Yet it must be very, very empowering for students to create their own narratives and thereby see through a different pair of eyes for a minute. It can be destabilizing, but it ultimately can make you much more humane, which I think is the purpose of education ultimately.

Kathleen. Like giving a play to a group of actors so that they give it to an audience. This constant handing over or entrusting.

Ann-Marie. It keeps it fluid, keeps it alive; it keeps culture from becoming dead, because as soon as it stops moving, that's it.

Toronto 2001

Contributors

Maja Ardal was born in the north of Iceland. She learned English in Scotland, where she attended school in the winter. She immigrated to Canada as a young actress, and was mentored by the late George Luscombe at Toronto Workshop Productions. From 1990 to 1998 she spearheaded initiatives at Young People's Theatre, Toronto, in racial diversity and new play development. Maja has directed for National Theatre School and the University of Toronto and is the 2002 recipient of the George Luscombe Award for Mentorship in the Theatre. Maja's work is now mainly in playwriting.

David Booth is professor emeritus at the Ontario Institute for Studies in Education (OISE), University of Toronto. He teaches graduate courses in literacy and the arts in education, and speaks at international education conferences on these issues. He is the author of many books for educators and parents, and has won several awards for his picture books for children.

Patricia Cano is a Canadian/Peruvian singer-actor-student who was born and raised in Sudbury, Ontario. She is currently finishing a double major in Spanish literature and theatre in the drama program at University College, University of Toronto, where she also performed in the world premiere of Tomson Highway's musical *Rose*. Patricia and Tomson continue to collaborate. They recently performed Tomson's new children's musical for the Stratford summer music festival, and in Sudbury and Berlin, Germany.

Diane Flacks is an actor/writer known for her three solo shows *Myth Me*, *By a Thread*, and *Random Acts*. They have all been critically acclaimed internationally, with tours to Los Angeles, New York, and across Canada. Diane co-wrote the hit play *Sibs* with Richard Greenblatt, and recently performed in *Smudge* by Alex Bulmer and an all-female *Midsummer Night's Dream* directed by Kate Lynch. She has collaborated on films with Bruce McCulloch and Jeremy Podeswa, and she co-wrote and performed in the CBC series *The Broad Side* and *PR*. Upcoming is a television co-production in the United Kingdom, and a new CBC series. Diane is also developing a new work of fiction.

Kathleen Gallagher is assistant professor in the department of Curriculum, Teaching and Learning at OISE/UT. Her recent book *Drama Education in the Lives of Girls: Imagining Possibilities* (University of Toronto Press, 2001) won the American Education Research Association's most outstanding scholarly book award for curriculum studies. Kathleen's research, teaching, and writing continue to address questions of equity, diversity, and pedagogy in drama/theatre education practices.

John Gilbert has juggled two careers. With an Oxford MA and a Harvard PhD he taught French, film, and drama at the University of Toronto. He was for years a member of the Shaw and Stratford festival companies, and of Necessary Angel Theatre, and has made many TV and film appearances.

Sky Gilbert, a writer, filmmaker, director, and drag queen extraordinaire, is one of North America's most controversial artistic forces. Born in Norwich, Connecticut, he made Toronto his home in 1965. He was co-founder and artistic director of Buddies in Bad Times Theatre (North America's largest gay and lesbian theatre) for eighteen years. At present, Sky is working on a PhD in drama at the University of Toronto.

Jim Giles is an elementary educator with the Toronto District School Board. He has been an instructional leader at the Haliburton School of the Arts and has taught on numerous additional qualification courses for the University of Toronto and York University. Jim has published several articles on the importance of arts education, equity issues, multi-age teaching, and strategies for assessment and evaluation in education.

Linda Griffiths is a playwright and actor. Her plays include *Alien Creature: A Visitation from Gwendolyn MacEwen*, *The Darling Family*, *The Duchess*, and *Maggie & Pierre*. She is the winner of five Dora Mavor Moore awards, a

Gemini award, two Chalmers awards, the Quizanne International Festival Award, and Los Angeles's A.G.A. Award (for her performance in John Sayles's *Lianna*), as well as receiving numerous nominations for both acting and writing. Linda has twice been nominated for the Governor General's Award. An anthology of her work, *Sheer Nerve: Seven Plays by Linda Griffiths*, was published by Blizzard Press in 1999. A new play, *Chronic*, is in development.

Janice Hladki is assistant professor in film and performance in Theatre and Film Studies, School of the Arts, McMaster University. As an artist, she has worked in theatre, film, video, and performance art. Her publications focus on interdisciplinary theories and the investigation of issues in art and culture.

Tomson Highway is a Cree from the Manitoba/Nunavut/Saskatchewan border area who writes plays, novels, and music. His first training was as a classical pianist at the universities of Manitoba and Western Ontario, as well as in London, England. Perhaps the best known of his many works are the plays *The Rez Sisters* and *Dry Lips Oughta Move to Kapuskasing* and the novel *Kiss of the Fur Queen*. Tomson divides his time between northern Ontario, the south of France, and Tokyo, Japan. His languages are Cree, Music, English, and French.

Cornelia Hoogland is associate professor at the University of Western Ontario. Her latest publications are *You Are Home* (Black Moss Press, 2001), *Salmonberry: A West Coast Fairy Tale* (International Plays for Young Audiences, Meriwether, 2000), *Marrying the Animals* (Brick Books, 1995), and *Wire-Thin Bride* (Turnstone, 1990). Hoogland has performed, lectured, and worked internationally in the areas of poetry and drama.

Ann-Marie MacDonald is a writer and actor. She is author of the internationally best-selling novel *Fall on Your Knees*. Translated into seventeen languages, it has received the Commonwealth Prize, the Canadian Authors Association Award, and two Canadian Booksellers Association Libris Awards. Her first play, *Goodnight Desdemona (Good Morning Juliet)*, was premiered in 1988 by Toronto's Nightwood Theatre, and has since had over 100 productions internationally. The play has been honoured with the Governor General's Award, the Chalmers Award, and the Canadian Author's Association Award. MacDonald's new musical comedy *Anything That Moves* won the Dora for outstanding new musical.

Lori McDougall was the project manager of BBC World Service Trust's leprosy media campaign in India, 1999–2001. Educated at the University of Toronto and the London School of Economics, she has worked as an editor at *Quill & Quire* and *Chatelaine*. She has worked as a communications volunteer for World Literacy of Canada and co-edited the anthology *Women Travel* (Rough Guides, 1999). She is currently the project manager for the BBC's HIV-AIDS media campaign in India.

John Murrell's plays have been translated into more than fifteen languages and performed in more than thirty-five countries around the world. He has worked as playwright-in-residence at Theatre Calgary and Alberta Theatre Projects, as an associate director of the Stratford Festival, and as head of the theatre section of the Canada Council (1988–92). In November 1999 he became Artistic Director / Executive Producer of Theatre Arts at the Banff Centre. His plays *Waiting for the Parade, Farther West,* and *The Faraway Nearby* were all honoured with Chalmers Best Canadian Play awards; and *Democracy* received the Canadian Authors Association's and the Writers Guild of Alberta's best play awards in 1992. A production of Murrell's new translation of *A Doll's House* by Henrik Ibsen recently won seven Dora Mavor Moore awards in Toronto.

Domenico Pietropaolo is a professor of drama at the University of Toronto and former director of the Graduate Centre for Study of Drama. Currently he holds the Emilio Goggio Chair of Italian Studies. Writing in English and Italian, he has authored many books and articles, with a focus on Mediterranean theatre and culture and on dramaturgy, and is an authority on the theory and history of *commedia dell'Arte*.

Walter Pitman has been a member of both Canada's House of Commons and the Ontario Legislature, and he has held the positions of dean of Arts and Sciences at Trent University, president of Ryerson University, and director of OISE and of the Ontario Arts Council. An Officer of the Order of Canada and a Member of the Order of Ontario, he has been the recipient of honorary degrees from McGill, York, Brock, and Trent universities.

Richard Rose is the founding artistic director of Necessary Angel Theatre and has directed most of the company's productions since 1978. At the Stratford Festival, for nine years, he directed many productions and was director of the Young Company (1994–6). He was an associate director for the Canadian Stage Company, where his credits include *Arcadia* and *Transit of Venus*. Richard was awarded an honorary Doctorate of Sacred Letters (juri dignitatus) from Thorneloe University, Sudbury, Ontario. Recently, he was appointed artistic director of the Tarragon Theatre, Toronto.

Jason Sherman's plays include *An Acre of Time, It's All True, Patience, None Is Too Many, Reading Hebron, The Retreat, Three in the Back, Two in the Head,* and *The League of Nathans*, many of which premiered at the Tarragon Theatre, Toronto. His plays have received the Governor General's Award for Drama (and been nominated three other times) and the Chalmers Canadian Best Play Award (twice, along with three other nominations). A collection of six of his plays has been published by Playwrights Canada Press.

Lynn Slotkin's first professional theatre review was published in 1972, and since then she has been published in the *Toronto Star*, the *Globe and Mail, Performance Magazine, American Theatre Magazine*, and others. She has been writing her theatre newsletter *The Slotkin Letter*, in one form or another, for twenty-five years. Lynn also does theatre reviews for the CBC on *Here and Now*, and sees on average 235 productions per year.

Larry Swartz is an instructor in the preservice program at OISE/UT, as well as principal of the Dramatic Arts Additional Qualification courses. He has been a classroom teacher and consultant for the Peel District Board of Education for the past twenty-five years. Larry is author of the books *Dramathemes* and *Classroom Events through Poetry*, as well as co-author of the language arts series *Impressions, Meadowbooks*, and *Out Loud*.

Judith Thompson is the author of *The Crackwalker, White Biting Dog, I Am Yours, Lion in the Street, Sled, Perfect Pie*, and *Habitat*, as well as two feature films, *Lost and Delirious* and *Perfect Pie*. She has won two Chalmers Best Canadian play awards, the B'nai B'rith Media Human Rights Award (Radio Category), Nellie Radio award, Toronto Arts Award, Prix Italia, and two Governor General Literary Awards for Drama. She is a professor of drama at the University of Guelph.

Guillermo Verdecchia is the author (or co-author) of *Fronteras Americanas,*

The Noam Chomsky Lectures, Insomnia, A Line in the Sand, and *Citizen Suàrez.* He is the recipient of the Governor General's Award, several Chalmers awards and Dora Mavor Moore awards, as well as film festival awards. He is currently artistic director of Cahoots Theatre Projects.

Belarie Zatzman is an associate professor of theatre, Faculty of Fine Arts, at York University, Toronto. She teaches courses in drama and education, theatre for young audiences, and arts education. Her research focuses on history, memory, and identity. She has both written about and worked internationally in fine arts and Holocaust education.

References

Abella, I., and H. Troper. 1982. *None Is Too Many: Canada and the Jews of Europe 1933–1948*. Toronto: Lester and Orpen Dennys.

Acoose, J., / Misko-Kìsikàwihkwè. 1995. *Iskwewak-kah' ki yaw ni wahkomakanak: Neither Indian Princesses nor Easy Squaws*. Toronto: Women's Press.

Anderson, K. 1996. 'Engendering Race Research: Unsettling the Self–Other Dichotomy.' In N. Duncan, ed., *Bodyspace: Destabilizing Geographies of Gender and Sexuality* (197–211). London: Routledge.

Ang, I. 1997. 'Comment on Felski's "The Doxa of Difference": The Uses of Incommensurability.' *Signs: Journal of Women in Culture and Society* 23(1): 57–64.

Anzaldua, G. 1987. *Borderlands/La frontera: The New Mestiza*. San Francisco: Aunt Lute Books.

Apple, M.W. 1993. Series Editor's Introduction to C. McCarthy and W. Crichlow, eds, *Race, Identity, and Representation in Education*, vii–ix. New York: Routledge.

Artaud, A. 1958. *The Theatre and Its Double*. Trans. M.C. Richards. New York: Grove Press.

Bennett, S. 1990. *Theatre Audiences: A Theory of Production and Reception*. London: Routledge.

Berry, J. 1995. *Worn Thresholds*. London, ON: Brick Books.

Bhabha, H.K., and J. Hassan. 1995. 'Identity and Cultural Displacement.' A dialogue presented at the Art Gallery of Ontario, Toronto.

Bischoping, K., and N. Fingerhut. 1996. 'Border Lines: Indigenous Peoples in Genocide Studies.' *Canadian Review of Sociology and Anthropology* 33(4): 481–506.

Bissoondath, N. 1994. *Selling Illusions: The Cult of Multiculturalism in Canada*. Toronto: Penguin.

Black, M., G. Marsolais, G. Peacock, C. Porteous, and J.-P. Ronfard. 1978. *Report on Theatre Training in Canada*. Ottawa: The Canada Council.

Bohm-Duchen, M. 1995. *After Auschwitz: Responses to the Holocaust in Contemporary Art.* London: Northern Centre for Contemporary Art.

Boler, M. 1997. 'The Risks of Empathy: Interrogating Multiculturalism's Gaze.' *Cultural Studies* 11(2): 253–73.

Bolton, G.M. 1984. *Drama as Education: An Argument for Placing Drama at the Centre of the Curriculum.* Harlow, Eng.: Longman.

Booth, D. 1994. *Drama and the Making of Meanings.* Newcastle upon Tyne, UK: National Drama Publications.

Bowers, C.A. 1993. *Critical Essays on Education, Modernity, and the Recovery of the Ecological Imperative.* New York: Teachers College Press.

Brant, B. 1993. This Is History. In C. Fife, ed., *The Colour of Resistance: A Contemporary Collection of Writing by Aboriginal Women,* 162–72. Toronto: Sister Vision.

Britzman, D. 1991. *Practice Makes Practice: A Critical Study of Learning to Teach.* Albany: State University of New York Press.

– 2001. The Arts of Inquiry. *Journal of Curriculum Theorizing* 17(2): 9–26.

Brodkey, L. 1996. *Writing Permitted in Designated Areas Only.* Minneapolis: University of Minnesota Press.

Brook, P. [1973] 1995. 'From the World as a Can Opener.' In R. Drain, ed., *Twentieth-century Theatre: A Sourcebook,* 320–2. London: Routledge.

Buell, L. 1995. *The Environmental Imagination: Thoreau, Nature Writing, and the Formation of American Culture.* Cambridge, MA: Belknap Press of Harvard University Press.

Carey, V.S. 1990. *Quail Song: A Pueblo Indian Tale.* Illustrated by I. Barnett. New York: G.P. Putnam's.

Chow, R. 1992. 'Postmodern Automatons.' In J. Butler and J.W. Scott, eds, *Feminists Theorize the Political,* 101–17. New York: Routledge.

Clark, J., W. Dobson, T. Goode, and J. Neelands. 1997. 'Drama Structure 2: Black Spruce Narrows.' In *Lessons for the Living: Drama and the Integrated Curriculum,* 52–67. Newmarket, ON: Mayfair Cornerstone Ltd.

Courtney, R. 1991. *Play, Drama and Thought: The Intellectual Background to Dramatic Education.* Toronto: Simon and Pierre.

Cowley, M., ed. 1959. *Walt Whitman's Leaves of Grass.* New York: Viking Press.

Davis, D. 1981. *Theatre for Young People.* Don Mills, ON: General Publishing.

Deshpande, S. 1997. 'Of Consumers and Kings.' *Seminar* 38(7): 23–6.

Eisenstein, S. 1945. 'A Close-up View.' In *How to Read Film.* New York: Oxford University Press.

Eisner, E.W. 1985. 'Why Art in Education and Why Art Education.' In *Beyond Creating: The Place for Art in America's Schools,* 64–9. Los Angeles: J. Paul Getty Trust.

Ellsworth, E. 1997. 'A Third Paradox: Teaching as a Performance Suspended in the Space Between Self and Other.' In E. Ellsworth, ed., *Teaching Positions: Difference, Pedagogy, and the Power of Address*, 158–64. New York: Teachers College Press.

Esslin, M. 1987. *The Field of Drama: How the Signs of Drama Create Meaning on Stage and Screen.* London: Methuen.

Farnsworth-Alvear, A. 1997. 'Orthodox Virginity/Heterodox Memories: Understanding Women's Stories of Mill Discipline in Medellin, Columbia.' *Signs: Journal of Women in Culture and Society* 23(1): 71–101.

Felski, R. 1997. 'Reply to Braidotti, Cornell, and Ang.' *Signs: Journal of Women in Culture and Society* 23(1): 64–9.

Fine, M., L. Weis, and L.C. Powell. 1997. 'Communities of Difference: A Critical Look at Desegregated Spaces Created for and by Youth.' *Harvard Educational Review* 67(2): 247–84.

Fisher, B.M. 2001. *No Angel in the Classroom: Teaching Through Feminist Discourse.* Lanham, MD: Rowman & Littlefield Publishers.

Flax, J. 1993. *Disputed Subjects: Essays on Psychoanalysis, Politics and Philosophy.* New York: Routledge.

Forbes, J.D. 1988. *Black Africans and Native Americans: Colour, Race, and Caste in the Evolution of Red-Black Peoples.* Oxford: Basil Blackwell.

Foucault, M. 1980. *Power/Knowledge: Selected Interviews and Other Writings 1972–1977.* Ed. C. Gordon. Trans. C. Gordon et al. New York: Pantheon Books.

– 1982. 'The Subject and Power.' *Critical Inquiry* 8(4): 777–95.

Freire, P., and D. Macedo. 1987. *Literacy: Reading the Word & the World.* South Hadley, MA: Bergin & Garvey Publishers.

Gallagher, K. 1998. 'Girls, Experience, and Voice.' In D. Booth and J. Neelands, eds, *Writing in Role: Classroom Projects Connecting Writing and Drama*, 141–54. Hamilton, ON: Caliburn Enterprises Inc.

– 2000. *Drama Education in the Lives of Girls: Imagining Possibilities.* Toronto: University of Toronto Press.

Gilbert, S. 2000a. 'Drag Queens on Trial.' In J. Wasserman, ed., *Modern Canadian Plays*, vol. 1. 4th ed. Vancouver: Talonbooks.

– 2000b. *Ejaculations from the Charm Factory.* Toronto: ECW Press.

Giles, J. 2001. 'The Importance of Children's Theatre in Elementary Schools.' *Voice* 3(2): 10–15.

Gilman, S. 1997. 'Making Face: Aesthetic Surgery and Its Origins in the Science of Race.' Paper presented at the University of Toronto, July.

Giroux, H.A., and P. Shannon. 1997. 'Cultural Studies and Pedagogy as Performative Practice: Toward an Introduction.' In Giroux and Shannon, eds.,

Education and Cultural Studies: Toward a Performative Practice, 1–9. New York: Routledge.

Gomez-Peña, G. 1989. 'The Multicultural Paradigm.' *High Performance* 12(3): 18–27.

– 2000. *Dangerous Border Crossers: The Artist Talks Back*. London: Routledge.

Gough, N. 1993. 'Neuromancing the Stones: Experience, Intertextuality, and Cyberpunk Science Fiction.' *Journal of Experiential Education* 16(3): 9–17.

Greene, M. 1995. *Releasing the Imagination: Essays on Education, the Arts, and Social Change*. San Francisco: Jossey-Bass Inc.

Griffiths, L., and M. Campbell. 1989. *The Book of Jessica: A Theatrical Transformation*. Toronto: Coach House Press.

Gumucio Dagron, A. 2001. *Making Waves: Stories of Participatory Communication for Social Change*. New York: Rockefeller Foundation.

Gunn Allen, P. 1990. 'Some Like Indians Endure.' In G. Anzaldua, ed., *Making Face, Making Soul = Haciendo Caras: Creative and Critical Perspectives by Women of Color*, 298–301. San Francisco: Aunt Lute Foundation Books.

Hall, S. 1990. 'Cultural Identity and Diaspora.' In J. Rutherford, ed., *Identity, Community, Culture, Difference*, 222–37. London: Lawrence & Wishart.

– 1992. 'New Ethnicities.' In J. Donald and A. Rattansi, eds, *Race, Culture and Difference*, 252–9. London: Sage Publications.

Hobgood, B.M., ed. 1988. *Master Teachers of Theatre: Observation on Teaching Theatre by Nine American Masters*. Carbondale: Southern Illinois University Press.

Hoogland, C. 2000a. 'Bodies of Knowledge: Making Sense and Sense-Making.' *Taboo* 4(1): 109–22.

– 2000b. *Salmonberry: A West Coast Fairy Tale*. In R. Ellis, ed., *International Plays for Young Sudiences: Contemporary Works from Leading Playwrights*, 11–43. Colorado Springs, CO: Meriwether Publishing Ltd.

– 2001. *You Are Home*. Windsor, ON: Black Moss Press.

hooks, b. 1994. *Teaching to Transgress: Education as the Practice of Freedom*. New York: Routledge.

Horowitz, S.R. 1998. 'Auto/biography and Fiction after Auschwitz: Probing the Boundaries of Second-Generation Aesthetics.' In E. Sicher, ed., *Breaking Crystal: Writing and Memory after Auschwitz*, 276–94. Urbana and Chicago: University of Illinois Press.

Jennings, E., ed. 1970. *The Sonnets of Michelangelo*. Garden City, NY: Doubleday & Company.

Jipson, J., P. Munro, S. Victor, K.F. Jones, and G. Freed-Rowland. 1995. *Repositioning Feminism and Education: Perspectives on Educating for Social Change*. Westport, CT: Bergin & Garvey.

Johnson, K. 2000. *Television and Social Change in Rural India.* New Delhi: Sage Publications.

Johnson, T.H., ed. 1960. *The Complete Poems of Emily Dickinson.* Boston: Little, Brown and Co.

Kanneh, K. 1995. 'Feminism and the Colonial Body.' In B. Ashcroft, G. Griffiths, and H. Tiffin, eds, *The Post-colonial Studies Reader*, 346–8. London: Routledge.

Knight, W.G. 1949. *Principles of Shakespearean Production, with Special Reference to the Tragedies.* Harmondsworth: Penguin.

Knowles, C., and S. Mercer. 1992. 'Feminism and Antiracism: An Exploration of the Political Possibilities.' In J. Donald and A. Rattansi, eds, *Race, Culture and Difference*, 104–25. London: Sage Publications.

Knowles, R.P. 1995. 'This Discipline Which Is Not One.' *Theatre Research in Canada* 16(1/2): 82–91.

Kulchyski, P. 1992. 'Primitive Subversions: Totalization and Resistance in Native Canadian Politics.' *Cultural Critique* 21: 171–95.

Lather, P. 1991. *Getting Smart: Feminist Research and Pedagogy with/in the Postmodern.* New York: Routledge.

Linscott, R.N., ed. 1959. *Selected Poems and Letters of Emily Dickinson.* Garden City, NY: Doubleday Anchor Books.

Lushington, K., M. Mojica, and D. Sears. 1993. 'Onions, Strawberries, and Corn.' Unpublished manuscript.

MacDonald, A.M. 1990. *Goodnight Desdemona (Good Morning Juliet).* Toronto, ON: Playwrights Canada.

Mamet, D. 1997. *True and False: Heresy and Common Sense for the Actor.* New York: Pantheon Books.

McCarthy, C. 1997. 'The Problem with Origins: Race and Contrapuntal Nature of the Education Experience.' In H.A. Giroux and P. Shannon, eds, *Education and Cultural Studies: Toward a Performative Practice*, 119–38. New York: Routledge.

McClintock, A. 1995. *Imperial Leather: Race, Gender and Sexuality in the Colonial Contest.* New York: Routledge.

McLaren, P. 1997. 'The Ethnographer as Postmodern *flâneur*: Critical Reflexivity and Posthybridity as Narrative Engagement.' In W.G. Tierney and Y.S. Lincoln, eds, *Representation and the Text: Re-framing the Narrative Voice*, 143–77. Albany: State University of New York Press.

McMichael Canadian Art Collection. 1999. *Down From the Shimmering Sky: Masks of the Northwest Coast.* Kleinberg, ON: McMichael Canadian Art Collection.

Merchant, C. 1992. *Radical Ecology: The Search for a Livable World.* New York: Routledge.

Mohanty, C.T. 1992. 'Feminist Encounters: Locating the Politics of Experience.' In M. Barrett and A. Phillips, eds, *Destabilizing Theory: Contemporary Feminist Debates*, 74–92. Stanford, CA: Stanford University Press.

Mojica, M. 1991. *Princess Pocahontas and the Blue Spots: Two Plays.* Toronto: Women's Press.

Moraga, C., and G. Anzaldúa, eds. 2000. *This Bridge Called My Back: Writings by Radical Women of Color*, 27–34. New York: Kitchen Table – Women of Color Press.

Norquay, N. 1998. 'Family Immigration (Hi)stories and the Construction of Identity.' *Curriculum Studies* 6(2): 177–90.

– 2000. 'Where Is Here?' *Pedagogy, Culture and Society* 8(1): 7–21.

– 2001. 'Talkin' About the "S" Words: The Myth of the Rugged Individual.' Presented at CSSE, Learned Societies of Canada annual national conference, Laval University, Quebec City, May.

Oakeshott, M.J. 1989. *The Voice of Liberal Learning: Michael Oakeshott on Education.* Ed. T. Fuller. New Haven: Yale University Press.

O'Neill, C. 1995. *Drama Worlds: A Framework for Process Drama.* Portsmouth, NH: Heinemann.

Onwurah, N. (Director). 1990. *The Body Beautiful* [Motion picture]. Great Britain. 23 min.

ORG Centre for Social Research. 2001. *Impact Evaluation of Song and Drama Interventions in the Modified Leprosy Elimination Campaign.* Delhi: ORG Centre for Social Research.

Paley, V.G. 1990. *The Boy Who Would Be a Helicopter.* Cambridge, MA: Harvard University Press.

Rich, F. 2000. *Ghost Light.* New York: Random House.

Richards, S.L. 1993. 'Caught in the Act of Social Definition: On the Road with Anna Deavere Smith.' In L. Hart and P. Phelan, eds, *Acting Out: Feminist Performances*, 35–53. Ann Arbor: University of Michigan Press.

Rokem, F. 1990. 'On the Fantastic in Holocaust Performances.' In C. Schumacher, ed., *Staging the Holocaust: The Shoah in Drama and Performance*, 40–52. Cambridge: Cambridge University Press.

Rushin, D.K. 1983. 'The Bridge Poem.' In C. Moraga and G. Anzaldua, eds, *This Bridge Called My Back: Writings by Radical Women of Color*, xxi–xxii. New York: Kitchen Table – Women of Color Press.

Salverson, J. 2000. 'Anxiety and Contact in Attending to a Play about Land Mines.' In R.I. Simon, S. Rosenberg, and C. Eppert, eds, *Between Hope and Despair: Pedagogy and the Remembrance of Historical Trauma*, 59–74. Lanham, MD: Rowman & Littlefield Publishers.

Sicher, E., ed. 1998. *Breaking Crystal: Writing and Memory after Auschwitz.* Chicago: University of Illinois Press.

Simon, R. 2000. 'The Touch of the Past: The Pedagogical Significance of a Transactional Sphere of Public Memory.' In P. Trifonas, ed., *Revolutionary Pedagogies: Cultural Politics, Instituting Education, and the Discourse of Theory,* 61–80. New York: Routledgefalmer.

Simon, R.I., S. Rosenberg, and C. Eppert, eds. 2000. *Between Hope and Despair: Pedagogy and the Remembrance of Historical Trauma.* Lanham, MD: Rowman & Littlefield Publishers.

Singhal, A., and E.M. Rogers. 2001. *India's Communication Revolution: From Bullock Carts to Cyber Marts.* New Delhi: Sage Publications.

Smith, L.T. 1999. *Decolonizing Methodologies: Research and Indigenous Peoples.* London and New York: Zed Books; Dunedin, NZ: University of Otago Press.

Smith, S. 1993. *Subjectivity, Identity, and the Body: Women's Autobiographical Practices in the Twentieth Century.* Bloomington: Indiana University Press.

Spiegelman, A. 1997. *The Complete Maus: A Supervisor's Tale.* New York: Pantheon.

Spivak, G.C. 1993. *Outside in the Teaching Machine.* New York: Routledge.

Stoler, A.L. 1995. *Race and the Education of Desire: Foucault's History of Sexuality and the Colonial Order of Things.* Durham and London: Duke University Press.

Strindberg, A. 1964. In M. Meyers, trans., *Strindberg Plays: One.* London: Methuen.

Swartz, L. 1996. 'Behind the Scenes.' In D. Booth, ed., *Meadowbooks: Arts Alive,* 28–31. Toronto: Harcourt, Canada.

Swortzell, L., ed. 1997. *Theater for Young Audiences: Around the World in 21 Plays.* New York: Applause Theater Book Pub.

Tabori, G. 1979. *My Mother's Courage.* Berlin: Gustav Kiepenheuer Puhnen-vertruebs-GMBH.

Taylor, C. 1993. *Reconciling the Solitudes: Essays on Canadian Federalism and Nationalism.* Montreal: McGill-Queen's University Press.

Threadgold, T. 1997. *Feminist Poetics: Poiesis, Performance, Histories.* London: Routledge.

Tippet, M. 1994. *Emily Carr: A Biography.* Don Mills, ON: Stoddart.

Tova, T. 1998. *Still the Night.* Toronto: Scirocco Drama.

Trifonas, P.P. 2000. *Revolutionary Pedagogies: Cultural Politics, Instituting Education, and the Discourse of Theory.* New York: Routledge.

Trinh, M.T. 1991. *When the Moon Waxes Red: Representation, Gender and Cultural Politics.* New York: Routledge.

Tsing, A.L. 1993. *In the Realm of the Diamond Queen: Marginality in an Out-of-the-Way Place.* Princeton, NJ: Princeton University Press.

Verdecchia, G. 2001. 'Seven Things About Cahoots Theatre Projects.' Presented at Learned Societies of Canada annual national conference, Laval University, Quebec City.

Visweswaran, K. 1994. *Fictions of Feminist Ethnography*. Minneapolis: University of Minnesota Press.

Wayland, A.H. 1989. *To Rabbittown*. Illustrated by R. Spowart. New York: Scholastic.

Weedon, C. 1987. *Feminist Practice and Poststructuralist Theory*. Oxford: Basil Blackwell.

Welsh, C. (Director). 1994. *Keepers of the Fire* [motion picture]. Vancouver: Omni Film Productions. 55 min.

Willett, J., ed. and trans. 1964. *Brecht on Theatre: The Development of an Aesthetic*. London: Methuen and Co. (original work published 1957).

Wood, D., and J. Grant. 1997. *Theatre for Children*. London: Faber and Faber.

Young, J.E. 2000. *At Memory's Edge: After-images of the Holocaust in Contemporary Art and Architecture*. New Haven: Yale University Press.

Young, R.J.C. 1995. *Colonial Desire: Hybridity in Theory, Culture and Race*. London: Routledge.

Zatzman, B. 1998. 'Holocaust Stories.' In D. Booth and J. Neelands, eds, *Writing in Role*, 125–40. Hamilton, ON: Caliburn Enterprises Inc.

– 1999. 'Traces of the Past: Practice and Research as Shifting Structures in Drama and Holocaust Education.' In C. Miller and J. Saxton, eds, *Drama and Theatre in Education: International Conversations*, 142–54. Victoria: International Drama in Education Research Institute in Association with the American Educational Research Association: Arts and Learning Special Interest Group.

– 2001. 'Drama Activities and the Study of the Holocaust.' In S. Totten and S. Feinberg, eds, *Teaching and Studying the Holocaust*, 263–79. Boston: Allyn and Bacon.